ORNAMENTAL CONIFERS

ORNAMENTAL

CONIFERS

HAFNER PRESS

A Division of Macmillan Publishing Co. Inc., New York

First published 1975
A.H. & A.W. REED LIMITED
Wellington, New Zealand

This edition 1975
Published in the United States of America by
HAFNER PRESS
A Division of Macmillan Publishing Co. Inc.
866 Third Avenue, New York, N.Y. 10022
Collier-Macmillan Canada Ltd

Library of Congress Cataloging in Publication Data

Harrison, Charles Richmond.
Ornamental conifers.

Bibliography: p.
1. Coniferae. 2. Ornamental evergreens. I. Title.
SB437.5.C6H37 635.9'775'2 74-11229
ISBN: 0-02-845760-X

Typesetting by Consolidated Press Ltd, Wellington.
Printed and bound by Kyodo Printing Company Ltd, Tokyo, Japan

CONTENTS

ACKNOWLEDGMENTS

While most of the photographs in this book were taken by either the author or members of the family, we wish to acknowledge the assistance of the following in supplying photographs for Plates — 3, 4, 8, 11, 15, 40, 231, 321, 336, 339, 416, 418, 424, 431, 500, 512, 515, D. Woodland; Plates 262, 288, 301, 487, Monrovia Nursery Co; Plate 428, US Department of Agriculture; Plate 398, D. Alfieri. Plate 306, Clarence, E. Lewis.

We are also much indebted to the following firms, persons or institutions for particular assistance in various ways (such as allowing us to photograph on their premises), for advice in nomenclature, or for the supply of botanical specimens:— *Britain* — Mr H. G. Hillier of Hillier's Nurseries, Winchester; Mr H. J. Welch of Wansdyke Nurseries, Wilts; Mr G. Pilkington, Surrey; Lord Aberconway, Bodnant Gardens, Denbighshire; Mr F. Knight of RHS Gardens, Wisley. *USA* — The Monrovia Nursery Co., California; Golden Gate Park, San Francisco; The D. Hill Nursery Co., Illinois; Dr Skinner of the US National Arboretum, Washington, DC; The Brooklyn Botanic Gardens, New York. *Netherlands* — Dr B. K. Boom, Wagenhingen; Mr G. Bootsman of Pinetum Blijdenstein, Hilversum; The Old Farm Nursery, Boskoop. *France* — Pepiniére Croux, Châtenay. *New Zealand* — Mr W. Sykes of Botany Division, DSIR, Christchurch; Mr B. Blackman, Te Kuiti; Messrs Duncan and Davies, New Plymouth; Mr H. Redgrove, Auckland; Mr J. Clark, Auckland; Mr L. Metcalf, Christchurch; Mr C. Cox, Wanganui; Mr S. Preston Dunedin.

Many others assisted in various ways, sometimes unwittingly, but without whom it would have been a lot more difficult if not impossible to have produced this book at all.

INTRODUCTION

THE AIMS OF THIS BOOK

THIS BOOK was designed to fill the long-felt need for a popular all-colour guide to garden conifers, written and compiled in such a way as to be easily used and understood by the average home gardener. It was never intended to resolve all the questions and arguments on conifer nomenclature that many enthusiasts seem to find so interesting, yet it will I feel, through the medium of colour reproduction coupled with verbal description, help to resolve many questions on similarity of varieties that are often cause for dispute among growers.

The main aim is simply to bring together about 500 or so of the world's most attractive ornamental conifers in colour in one book, so that choices and comparisons may be made by those who are interested in conifers but are not well enough acquainted with the usually very complex botanical names that many of these plants labour under. The question of common names will no doubt arise in the minds of some. This method of naming has been used in other books on the subject and is still employed in the nursery industry in the United States today, but the problem often arises where for example the name 'White Pine' can mean *Pinus parviflora* in Japan, *Pinus ayacahuite* in Mexico or *Podocarpus dacrydioides* in New Zealand, and yet other names in other countries. Clearly such a system is of some local value but of little use world-wide. Vernacular names where known are therefore included below the botanical names in this book and are useful in identifying or helping to recognise a species or cultivar.

The author has made every attempt to keep conifer names in line with the latest available literature. The following three major works have been a constant source of reference, and are recommended to anyone wishing to delve deeper into the subject of conifer identification — though the subject is so vast that none of the three has covered everything. Firstly there is *A Handbook of Coniferae and Gingkoaceae* by Dallimore and Jackson, for many years the standard work on conifers and recently revised by S. G. Harrison and reprinted in 1966. This book covers the wide field of conifers in its fullest extent, with over 700 pages packed with vital information including the uses of timber types and interesting historical notes, but does not always include as full a detail of cultivars and varieties as one may desire; neverthless it is an enormous and valuable work.

Secondly, there is the *Manual of Cultivated Conifers* by den Ouden and Boom. This contains a lifetime of records and practical experience with conifers by the Boskoop (Netherlands) nurseryman P. den Ouden, and completed after his death by Dr B. K. Boom, horticultural taxonomist at Wagenhingen. Published in 1965, it covers in more than 500 pages the field of cultivars and the subtle distinctions between names and types in a most reliable and authoritative manner, complete with references to information on all listings, so that, if desired, one may conduct one's own private research. This work must surely be the standard in this field for many years to come. It does, however, have one shortcoming, in that only those conifers hardy in the cold and warm-temperate zones are included. To the vast majority of plant lovers this is no problem, but occasionally one draws a "blank" when looking up certain items, for example a semi-tropical species of pine, native to Mexico. Such items are of course well covered in the first book mentioned.

The third volume is no less valuable, and although still more restricted in subject carries the fruits of the latest research on many varieties and is probably the book most likely to appeal to the keen gardener, especially if he has an interest in dwarf conifers. This is H. J. Welch's *Dwarf Conifers*, printed in 1966, nearly 350 pages of well-researched information set out in an interesting and easily-read manner and amply supported with photographs. Also worthy of mention are the works of H. G. Hillier, nurseryman of Winchester, England, who has given us the valuable booklet *Dwarf Conifers* (1966) as well as the more recent *Hillier's Manual of Trees and Shrubs*. The author appreciates Mr Hillier's personal assistance and advice on problems associated with the compiling of this book. There are many more authors of earlier works, such as Beissner, Hornibrook, Bailey and Kruessmann, to name a few, which I have preferred to leave alone, mainly because these more recent works have been either based on the findings of such pioneers or are the result of much research in disentangling the confusion that often existed between them.

There probably never will be the complete book on conifers containing all that anyone should desire on the subject; anyway, should such a book exist, its cost would no doubt be prohibitive. At least in the three main works mentioned one is able to see a greater consistency in names and descriptions than ever before. It is hoped that this volume will further reinforce and also serve as an illustrated supplement to those books, while adding a further dimension by way of colour photography.

HOW TO USE THIS BOOK

AS HAS BEEN SAID, the aim of this book is to provide the gardening public with as many colour illustrations of the most popular garden conifers as can economically be contained in one book, and also to provide him with information to help him decide what is best for his garden. Before he purchases a plant he is going to ask the salesman a lot of questions. How big will it grow? How long will it take to get to that size? What is its spread? Can it be pruned? Does it need full sun or semi-shade? Can it stand wet conditions? What kind of soil is best? Is it prone to any specific diseases? What sprays should be used, if any? How hardy is it? These are some of the questions usually asked by the prospective conifer buyer; we seek to answer them within the pages of this book.

GROWTH RATES

Foremost is the question of size and growth rate, which is not constant for all climates. It stands to reason that a conifer hardy enough for Zone 5 conditions is likely to be a faster grower in Zone 7 conditions, unless there are factors in the warmer climate that are detrimental to the growth of that particular plant. The mere fact of having a longer growing season in the warmer climate is in itself more likely to produce a larger plant within the same space of time. So that the growth rates quoted in this book and usually related to a ten-year period, while being an excellent guide, need to be related to the hardiness zone rating in which the plant is to be grown to give a true picture of what size that plant will be in your garden in five years' time. An example comes to mind — that of *Thuja orientalis* 'Meldensis'. At Palmerston North, New Zealand (Zone 8), with its high sunshine average, good rainfall and mild winters, a specimen of this dwarf conifer reached 70cm (27in) in two years. In a Zone 6 part of Europe, with less sun, overall cooler summers and cold winters, six years was needed to reach the same height. (Soil conditions are not taken into account in this comparison.) Thus it is clearly illustrated that growth rates are not by any means fixed for any plant, but can be up to three times faster under ideal conditions. Quoting an ultimate height can be a point of interest to a buyer, but if the tree is likely to take up to 500 years to reach its maximum of 20m (65ft) our gardener is not going to be too worried about having that plant in his rockery for the first fifty or so years of its life.

HARDINESS

It is obviously not enough to quote such vague expressions as "hardy" or "near hardy" as they have no international bearing whatever, and can be used only in a strictly local sense. For this reason we have used the United States system which is now fairly widely recognised and is set out below related to both Celsius and Fahrenheit temperature scales. It should be remembered that if a conifer is rated as hardy in, say Zone 4, it is not necessarily at its happiest in those conditions but nevertheless will survive and make growth in those conditions. On the other hand it is often possible to plant (for example) a Zone 6 plant in a Zone 5 area provided it is located in shelter and not fully exposed to the elements. One must always be prepared to lose such plants, however, during exceptional cold snaps, there being many examples on record of mature trees some thirty or so years of age thriving happily in such conditions until an extra period of cold puts an end to their gamble with the elements.

Given below is the relation of zones to actual minimum temperatures. One can use this system in two ways. Firstly, knowing your average coldest winter temperature, you can arrive at the zone number for your area. You will then be able to plant any conifer rated at that number or lower. For example, if you are Zone 5 you will be limited to growing only plants hardy in Zones 5 down to 1. It may be, however, that you know of Zone 6 plants growing happily in your particular area through your winters, in spite of the scale rating you as 5. This is sometimes the case where the factor of low humidity or dry winters interfere or even air currents on a sloping site, and in such cases you can safely assume, that you are able to plant Zone 6 plants as well. At best the zone system is a rough guide, and observation and trials for your area are in the end your best indicators.

HARDINESS CHART
Approximate Average Minimum Temperatures For Each Zone

Zones	Fahrenheit (°H)	Celsius (°C)
Zone 1	Below −50	Below −46
Zone 2	−50 to −40	−46 to −41
Zone 3	−40 to −30	−41 to −35
Zone 4	−30 to −20	−35 to −30
Zone 5	−20 to −10	−30 to −24
Zone 6	−10 to 0	−24 to −18
Zone 7	0 to 10	−18 to −13
Zone 8	10 to 20	−13 to −7
Zone 9	20 to 30	−7 to 0
Zone 10	30 to 40	0 to 5

THE LOCATING OF SPECIMENS

When it was decided some time in 1967 to produce a colour book on conifers we already had on hand a range of conifer photographs taken in Palmerston North, or elsewhere in New Zealand. But to give the book international appeal we needed world-wide coverage of popular ornamentals and so my wife and I set out in April 1968 with two camera bodies, three lenses, two flashguns and enough colour film for 3,000 photos, for a seven-week world circum-navigation.

We even found conifers on a short two-day break at Honolulu. There we noticed *Thuja orientalis, Juniperus, Cupressus, Podocarpus, Araucaria* and various species of pines used ornamentally in private gardens, oriental shrines, in parks and roadsides — ample proof that however tropical the climate, certain conifers can be used effectively in landscaping. From there we moved on to Los Angeles for a very busy three days' photographing in what is probably the most conifer-conscious residential area in the world. Landscapers in these parts have developed the use of conifers to a fine art, prompted no doubt by the natural resistance to heat and dry of the range of conifers grown. It is noteworthy that very little interest is shown there in large golden-foliaged conifers, presumably because the tree looks as though it could be dying of drought, and some of the most popular cultivars in that region possess bright-green foliage the year round. (Plates 517–524.) Some of the finest conifer plantings can be found in the course of a drive around the Beverly Hills and Bel Air areas, and it will be noticed that many of the photos in this book have been secured in this region. Another fruitful area was found in the San Marino district, where the beautiful Huntingdon Gardens are located and where I obtained several shots of pines, junipers and cypress in the Japanese garden and also in the greater park area. It was most gratifying to find the plants carefully and accurately labelled, something often lacking in parks and even some botanic gardens I have visited. Another day was spent in a visit to the Monrovia Nurseries, the largest container-plant nursery in the USA, growers of conifers in large quantities, with a particularly wide range of the very latest in ornamental junipers. I am indebted to them for help and advice in identification and in compiling this book and for the supply of colour slides of some cultivars that I missed. It was with reluctance that we finally headed north for San Francisco, the prime object there being the James Noble conifer collection which is now permanently on display to the public at the Strybing Arboretum, Golden Gate Park, and features 500 different conifers mainly in the dwarf and medium-sized ornamental range. Unfortunately our time there was limited to two hours of rather frantic photographing but nevertheless proved to be a happy hunting ground; most of the photos in this book located "San Francisco" were taken there. The plants are beautifully planted round a series of irregularly-shaped ponds, excellent mature specimens in good health and a credit to those in charge of their upkeep. A short distance away are the famous Japanese Tea Gardens

(Plate 552) where several examples of pruning and dwarfing techniques can be seen, including a *Pinus thunbergii* at least 15m (50ft) high and systematically pruned to the very top. A drive round the residential areas in San Francisco and Oakland yielded a different range of conifers than that seen in the drier, hotter Los Angeles, and it was noticed that greater use was made of *Chamaecyparis* and *Cedrus* and less of *Juniperus*.

Our next move was to Chicago, Illinois, and the well-known D. Hill Nursery Co., at Dundee, specialists in conifers and evergreens since 1855 and the publishers of that excellent conifer book with colour illustrations, *The Friendly Evergreens* by L. and L. Kumlien, written with the average keen gardener in mind. The range of conifers offered there is further changed, the hardiness zone rating being at the best 5, so that all those species rated higher cannot survive the cold of the winters there, and this includes all *Cedrus* and *Chamaecyparis* species. Added to the list, however, are *Abies*, *Picea* and *Taxus* species which are not happy in the warmer climates but thrive in these regions where fungus and insect attack is kept at a minimum by the rigorous winters. Conifers play an important part in these northern gardens, being one of the few plants that can maintain some kind of cheerfulness through snowbound winter months, and are widely used in landscaping and foundation plantings. Some of the erect conifers owe their existence in the garden scene mainly to their ability to resist snow damage, and such plants are usually in possession of a stout tapering leader with short horizontal side-branches that afford a minimum of area for snow to build up. All photos captioned "Dundee, Ill." were taken at the Hill garden centre or in the nursery itself.

From Chicago, still emerging from the grip of winter in late April and as yet showing no fresh growth in gardens, we flew to Washington DC, to find spring well under way with fresh green leaf already on the deciduous trees. Our object in this city was the United States National Arboretum where the Gotelli collection of dwarf and slow-growing conifers now resides. This must surely be the finest collection of its kind in the world, for there were 750 different conifers recorded on Mr Gotelli's list before presentation to the Arboretum, with more added since that time. The plants are attractively laid out in a spacious area, the dwarfs tastefully worked into a rock setting on a slope, while the larger specimens are given ample lawn space to develop, and each plant has its name clearly engraved on a tab in front of it. (Plates 527–528.) I might add that the names applied to the plants were in most cases those under which Mr Gotelli purchased them, and before they could be included in this book I sometimes had to search the books to bring an older once-used name into line with present-day nomenclature. As can be seen from the number of slides captioned "Washington DC", this area yielded a lot of material and even though we spent two days there we still missed a number of good cultivars that could well have been included.

Our next call was New York and the Brooklyn Botanic Garden which does have a fine collection of dwarfs but was rather an anti-climax after Washington, and yielded very little fresh material. The Japanese Garden here was the most impressive item, with its flowering cherries and maples in fresh leaf, miniature lake and the fine old Mugo Pine at the top of the waterfall. (Plate 529). There are some excellent bonsai specimens of conifers on display in one of the greenhouses, and Plates 406 and 415 were taken there.

Well aware that we had nothing like fully covered the field in the USA, we nevertheless yielded to our itinerary and took off for Britain in the hope that what we had missed in the United States we would find elsewhere. A day spent at the Royal Horticultural Society's gardens at Wisley fully realised our hopes: Eighty hectares (200 acres) of first-class gardens of all types, including the Nisbet collection (Plate 506) of dwarf conifers tastefully laid out in a series of beds, clearly (but not always accurately) labelled, with the plants well cared for and in good shape. You may wonder about the label "dwarf conifers", when some of the specimens are 2 or 3m (6 or 10ft) tall. I found in my travels that if I did not ask to be directed to the dwarf conifers (or failing that, the rock garden), I would generally be shown a pinetum of towering specimens hundreds of years old and be expected to be duly impressed. Not that I wasn't, but it was not altogether what I was looking for, and I have come to the conclusion that the bulk of garden ornamental conifers fall into the "dwarf" category by such standards. Once again we did not really have time to do the place justice but secured all that we could, both in the Nisbet collection and on the rock garden where we also took several good photographs. There was just enough daylight left to dash down to Haslemere, Surrey, to see one of the finest private collections of conifers, that of Mr Geoffrey Pilkington at Grayswood Hill, and we spent a most enjoyable afternoon viewing and photographing in the company of Mr Pilkington himself and the gardener. Slides captioned "Haslemere, Surrey" were taken in this garden. The trend in these parts was noticeably towards the *Chamaecyparis* cultivars and away from many of the *Juniperus* found in the United States.

Our direction was now south-east towards Sussex and some of the stately homes and gardens of England, including Leonardslee, Wakehurst, Nymans (Plate 534), and Borde Hill, finding one or two specimens to enlarge our range. By this time I was becoming a bit hard to please, having seen and photographed so much already and in many cases I would bypass a specimen unless it was superior to one already taken. I found young plants preferable to fully mature ones in most cases, as I could photograph the whole plant and still give some idea of foliage detail, and in any case the five-to-fifteen-year phase of life is the period that the home gardener is most likely to be interested in.

From Sussex we headed west for Winchester, and Hillier's Nursery and Arboretum at Ampfield, an outstanding combination of commercial plant nursery and thirty-two hectares (80 acres) of specimen plants of all kinds, including a very wide range of conifers. The planting also includes the residence of Mr H. G. Hillier, who conducted us around the arboretum, making our task very easy as well as most enjoyable. Mr Hillier's knowledge of plants in general and conifers in particular is well known in the nursery world, and his assistance in compiling this book is much valued. We then moved north-west towards Devizes, Wiltshire, the location of the Pygmy Pinetum and nursery of Mr H. J. Welch, who wrote *Dwarf Conifers*. This is probably one of the most comprehensive collections of dwarf conifers anywhere, there having been 400 plants on record at the time of publication of his book in 1966, and I should imagine that that number has been substantially added to since then. We are much indebted to Mr Welch for his unscrambling of so many conifer conundrums, having used *Dwarf Conifers* constantly as reference and guide during the writing of this book.

Our next call was at the Bodnant Gardens at Tal-y-Cafn, North Wales, residence of Lord Aberconway and one of the most beautiful gardens in the United Kingdom. Climatic conditions are kind in this part of the country, with ample rainfall but moderate winter cold, and no doubt this was one of the prime considerations when the gardens were first planned. Conifers tended to be on the grand scale, having been planted some sixty to 100 years ago, but all in perfect shape thanks to the shelter of hills on three sides, and one could not help but be amused at the size of a row of *Chamaecyparis lawsoniana* 'Erecta', a co-called "dwarf" conifer at the height of 15m (50ft) at least, and almost 100 years old.

A quick visit to the Edinburgh Botanic Gardens confirmed that it was rather too early in the season for good conifer pictures, and besides it was raining steadily. No doubt there are excellent conifer collections in Scotland, and of course Ireland where Mr Welch found much of interest, but it was not our privilege to visit them. In the process of moving ever eastward we flew back to London and spent the day in Kew Gardens and Syon Park. Kew of course is not by any means devoid of conifers both big and small, and although it does not have a specific area set aside for dwarf conifers they are effectively worked into the large rock garden (Plate 533). Syon Park gardens nearby, which had just been opened as a horticultural showplace, yielded a few new specimens, but should be better when the newly-placed plants have added a few years' growth. But I have always regretted not taking a photo of the curious cypress "knees" growing from the roots of the grand old *Taxodium* beside the water. I never came across them anywhere else.

The Netherlands proved to be a fruitful area, with the Pinetum Blijdenstein in Hilversum the main attraction. One could easily mistake it for a large private garden behind its tall hedge, but once through the gate and past the house you come upon conifers of all shapes and sizes (Plate 535), from cedars 20m (65ft) tall to the lowest of dwarfs, well spaced in a lawn setting and all clearly labelled with their Latin names (I was thankful they were not labelled in Dutch). We spent a busy afternoon photographing, and further extended our collection. An un-expected bonus was the Madurodam Model City at The Hague where we found dwarf conifers right in their element providing natural greenery in a city made for people 5cm (2in) high (Plates 536 and 538). Most of the planting I understand is the work of dwarf conifer specialists, Tempelhof Nurseries (Konijn & Co.) from near Boskoop, and is certainly well blended in with the small-scale architecture.

The Old Farm Nurseries owned by the den Ouden family (whose late father co-authored the *Manual of Cultivated Conifers*) was a further source of material and information, as was the whole nursery area of Boskoop where 700 nurseries live side by side in an area of only 600 hectares (1,500 acres) and have been doing so for 600 years. Also at Boskoop is the Horticultural Research Station which has plantings devoted to the standardisation of plant names, and the conifer area, with groups of the cultivars of all one species set together, is a great help in sorting out name differences, and also yielded more good photographs. I am aware that there are many more fine pineta and conifer plantings in the Netherlands but we were not able to visit them, although I did make a gallant attempt to drive to Utrecht and Wagenhingen, but wasted too much time with my own poor navigation to get there before dark. And so ended a very pleasant and profitable week in Holland, and apart from two specimens of cedar obtained later in France, our search for conifer photographs in Europe.

Back home with over 2,000 colour slides (but many of them duplications of the same cultivar) to classify and identify, the work was just beginning in earnest; in fact the photographic side of this work has definitely been the easier one.

Australia has yielded some photographs during our visits to that country, and is noted for its wider use of *Cupressus* cultivars, some of them mixed-up as to names, there being a number of golden *C. macrocarpa* cultivars in the trade under various names such as 'Lutea', 'Aurea' and so on, that have probably never been tried in other countries and could well equal or better some of the European cultivars. Being in parts a tropical country of Zones 9 or 10, Australia has many species of *Araucaria* and other subtropical genera that are little-known in colder climates, but most of these are large trees that are too big for the home garden, and in the main one sees there a similar range of conifers to that used in California.

It has been both an interesting and arduous task of photographing, sorting and writing about conifers and one that seems to never end with the continual discovery of fresh or better specimens to photograph, but we feel that we have now arrived at the point where our range is as representative as it will ever be, and any further improvements will have to be held for future editions.

C. R. HARRISON

1 *Abies balsamea* 'Hudsonia'. Spring. Surrey, England.

2 *Abies balsamea* 'Nana'. Summer. NSW, Australia.

Abies balsamea 'Hudsonia'

1 The Balsam Fir of Canada has given us several compact cultivars, the best known of which are 'Nana' and 'Hudsonia'. Both these cultivars are excellent compact rockery subjects and often have their names confused. They can be sorted out easily enough by examination of the foliage. as 'Nana' carries its leaves radially arranged on the branchlets, while 'Hudsonia' has them semi-radially, so that when viewed from above a parting can be usually seen running along the branchlet between the rows of leaves. Both are slow-growing dwarfs which in ten years would be doing well to reach 30cm (12in) in height and perhaps a little more in width.   Hardiness 3.

Abies balsamea 'Nana'   Dwarf Balsam Fir

2 As mentioned about the preceding cultivar, 'Hudsonia', 'Nana' has a radiate leaf arrangement with no parting among the leaves and can be easily distinguished by this feature. A deservedly popular dwarf conifer which presents a tidy and attractive appearance at all times of the year.   Hardiness 3.

3 *Abies borisii-regis.* Cones and foliage. Autumn.

Abies borisii-regis

3 A native of the Balkans including northern and central Greece, obtaining its unusual title when named after King Boris of Bulgaria. It is closely allied to its neighbouring Grecian Fir, but carries a longer (to 35mm/1¼in) blunter leaf with similar colouring and radiate placement on the stems, and carries more rounded-shaped cones which can measure up to 15cm (6in) in length. An erect, tapering conical fir which can eventually attain a height of 30m (100ft).   Hardiness 5.

4 *Abies cephalonica.* Cones and foliage. Autumn.

Abies cephalonica   Grecian Fir.

4 A native of the higher mountains of Greece, occurring at altitudes around 1,500m (5,000ft), which compared with other firs is most closely allied to *A. pinsapo*, the Spanish Fir. It has longer leaves however (to 25mm/1in), which are radially set on non-vertical growths deflecting towards the upper side, and are a lustrous bright green above with several stomatic lines below, giving the silvery effect that shows up dramatically in a flash-illuminated photo. It grows best as an ornamental in moist but not water-logged soil, with an ultimate height of 20–30m (65–100ft). The narrower-than-usual cones measure up to 18cm (7in) in length. Three cultivars worthy of mention are 'Aurea' a golden yellow form, 'Meyers Dwarf', a slow-growing compact with no leader, and 'Robusta' which has erect branches with a spirally-arranged disposition, rather slower-growing than the type.   Hardiness 5.

5 *Abies concolor.* Winter. Gore, New Zealand.

Abies concolor   Colorado Fir. White Fir.

5 A beautiful fir from the mountains of Southern Color-ado, California and Northern Mexico, and easily identi-fiable by its long (5–8cm/2–3in) blunt-ended leaves which can carry any colour from light grey-green to bright silvery-blue. In its native state it is known to reach heights of 60m (200ft) but for garden purposes one need not expect an annual growth in excess of 30cm (12in) once the tree is established. Among firs it is noted for its out-standing tolerance to hot and dry conditions, and can be recommended as one of the finest of conifers for orna-mental planting. There are twenty listed forms and culti-vars of this species, the most popular being the blue selections which are usually propagated by grafting, but among seed lots a few good blues occur and these are usually (but incorrectly) offered by nurserymen under the name of 'Glauca'.   Hardiness 4.

6 *Abies concolor* 'Candicans'. Autumn.
Gisborne, New Zealand.

Abies concolor 'Candicans'

6 In foliage colour 'Candicans' represents the brightest silvery blue obtainable among the many forms of *Abies* and probably the brightest blue of any conifer in existence. Unfortunately such beauty is never likely to be readily available as grafting is as yet the only reliable method of propagation, and it is not possible to take more than a few suitable strong terminal shoots from a tree without disfiguring it. Less-vigorous side shoots can be used for grafting but such scions are liable to produce a leaderless plant of spreading habit and lacking the symmetrical conical form that is so attractive in a tree of this type. In growth 'Candicans' is a little slower than the species, and can be expected to average a 15cm (6in) increase in height a year. This cultivar can also be found listed in some books under the name 'Argentea'.   Hardiness 4.

7 *Abies concolor* 'Compacta'. Spring.
Ampfield, Hants, England.

8 *Abies delavayii* var. *forrestii*. Cone and foliage. Autumn.

Abies concolor 'Compacta'

7. This, the only true dwarf among the Colorado firs has an ultimate height and width of little more than 1m (3ft). The leaves, which are usually a little smaller than the type, are a silvery blue and for this reason it is often classified under the names 'Glauca Compacta' or 'Nana Glauca'. The name under which we list it however has priority, with no need for 'Glauca' to help describe the leaf colour, and is the one which we must in future use if we are to abide by the rules of the naming game. A fine little blue conifer that would be used a lot more if it were more readily available. Hardiness 4.

Abies delavayii var. *forrestii*.

8 *Abies delavayii*, a native of Western China, can be found in a greater altitudinal and latitudinal range than any other Chinese species of fir, and shows a considerable degree of variation between areas, so much so that some botanists prefer to list the three varieties *faxoniana*, *forrestii* and *georgii* as separate species. They all, however, have in common the attractive 6–10cm (2½–4in) long cones, purplish-black when young, a dark glossy-green leaf marked beneath with two whitish stomatic bands. They grow to quite large trees, to 40m (130ft), have massive branches, and are capable of yielding large quantities of timber. This variety, *forrestii*, occurs in Yunnan, and on the Burmese border at altitudes around 3,500m (11,000ft). Hardiness 7.

Abies fargesi

9 The beauty of young purple fir cones and emerging leaf buds is well illustrated in this close-up of a branch of *Abies fargesi*. I imagine that this particular plant is some kind of a dwarf (although not labelled as such), being one of the specimens in the James Noble collection of dwarf conifers at Golden Gate Park, San Francisco, and this explains why the growth is more branching and twiggy than normal. In its native China it makes a wide conical tree to 40m (130ft), dark green in leaf but liberally coated on the undersides with a glaucous bloom. In growth it averages around 30cm (12in) a year.
Hardiness 4.

9 *Abies fargesi*. Spring. Young cones. San Francisco, USA.

10 *Abies grandis.* Spring. North Wales.

11 *Abies homolepis.* Branch and cones. Autumn.

12 *Abies koreana.* Spring. Hilversum, Netherlands.

Abies grandis

10 A species that identifies itself from other *Abies* by means of distinctly pectinate leaf arrangement, a feature that it shares only with the longer and lighter-leaved *A. concolor* described earlier. The glossy dark green leaves are arranged in tidy rows on opposite sides of the twig, in appearance not unlike the teeth of a two-sided comb, and in spring the tree becomes tipped on all extremities with lush light green of great beauty and freshness as the new season's growth is added. Younger plants make fine tub specimens for some years before permanent planting is necessary, and once established an average growth of 30cm (12in) can be expected, making best growth in conditions of medium humidity and ample soil moisture.   Hardiness 6.

Abies homolepis   Nikko Fir.

11 No prizes for guessing where this fir comes from. A native of the mountains of Japan, it has much to commend it in hardiness and resistance to air pollution, thriving under conditions fatal to many other firs. While optimum growth is obtained in rich moist soil it will also grow satisfactorily under drier conditions, and makes a broad pyramidal tree reaching in time to 40m (130ft), the smooth purplish cones up to 10cm (4in) in length taking on a brownish colour when mature. There is on record a greenish-coned variety, var. *umbellata*.   Hardiness 5.

Abies koreana   Korean Fir.

12, 13 The Korean Fir is found in abundance only in one or two isolated mountain areas in Korea, but since being introduced into the world of horticulture it has proved to be a popular and hardy garden ornamental. Foremost among its virtues is the symmetrical, uniformly-tapering growth habit at a speed that is more sedate than its giant brothers, making it usable even on a rockery for several years before one is obliged to move it on. It cones freely at an early age and they are an interesting violet-purple colour, cylindrical, 5–7cm (2–2¾in) in length and stand erect on the branches. The spring growth comes in a bright silvery-grey colour in contrast to the darkness of the dark green mature leaves, the backs of which are a shining glaucous blue. In all, an interesting and versatile fir tree that seldom exceeds 10m (33ft) or 3m (10ft) in the first ten years.   Hardiness 5.

14 *Abies koreana* 'Compact Dwarf'. Spring. Hilversum, Netherlands.

Abies koreana 'Compact Dwarf'

14 A very compact, slow-growing form of the preceding Korean Fir that does not bear cones and has no leader, remaining in a bun shape and increasing in size at about 5–8cm (2–3in) a year.   Hardiness 5.

Abies lasiocarpa 'Compacta'   Dwarf Arizona Fir.

15 *Abies lasiocarpa* var. *arizonica*, the Arizona Cork Bark Fir, is usually a tall, sparsely-furnished specimen of marginal ornamental value that seems ill-adapted to garden conditions away from its native alpine habitat. In this dwarf form, however, we have a garden gem that is at home among rock plants or dwarf conifers and an asset to any garden. It is the perfect little fir tree, silvery blue-green in colour, with a definite leader and broad pyramidal form, and foliage sufficiently densely-set to give it that "well-clothed" appearance. Needless to say it is not rapid in growth, requiring probably ten years to reach 70cm (28in) in height, and because of this and the fact that it is propagated by grafting, one is never likely to find this plant inexpensive or readily available. Many growers and pineta still list this one under its old name of *A.arizonica* 'Compacta'.   Hardiness 5.

15 *Abies lasiocarpa* 'Compacta'. Spring. Wisley, Surrey, England.

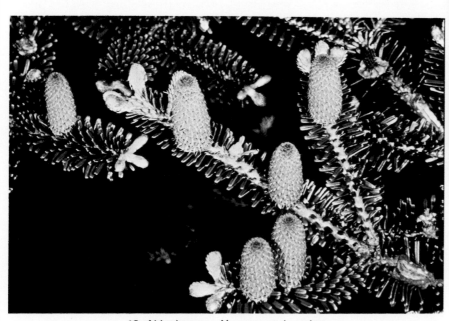

13 *Abies koreana*. Young cones in spring.

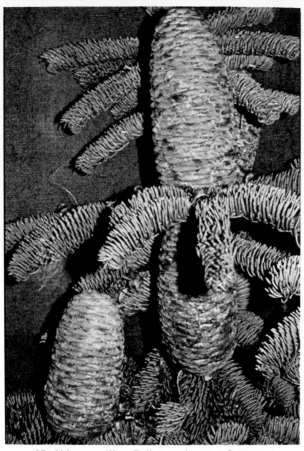

16 *Abies magnifica.* Foliage and cones. Autumn.

17 *Abies nordmanniana.* Winter. Christchurch, New Zealand.

18 *Abies pinsapo.* With cones. Autumn.

Abies magnifica   Californian Red Fir.

16 One of the larger firs from the mountains of Oregon and California with a definite preference for high altitudes, being most common at around 2,000m (6,500ft) in the north to as high as 3,500m (11,500ft) at the southern extent of its nativity. It is not happy in warm lowland or mild winter areas, but as its name suggests it is a magnificent tree when provided with the right conditions—cool and moist with cold winters. The name Red Fir refers to both the reddish-brown bark and the reddish timber which is one of the best fir woods, and due to the size of the tree (to 60m/200ft) is available in large dimensions for beam and construction uses. The large cones are violet-purple when young, maturing light brown, the leaves glaucous green and very similar to those of *A. procera*. The variety *shastensis*, native to Mt Shasta, is a more compact version with shorter cones, and there are three cultivars worthy of mention — 'Argentea' with bluish-white leaves, 'Glauca' with deep glaucous-green leaves, and 'Prostrata', a low-growing spreader.   Hardiness 5.

Abies nordmanniana   Caucasian Fir.

17 This native of the mountain regions of the West Caucasus occurs mainly at altitudes around 2,000m (6,000ft) and is known there to reach to heights of up to 60mm (200ft). It is the typical fir tree, attractive at any age or height with its straight trunk and narrow pyramidal form. The leaves are shining dark green, and serve to identify this species by giving off, when crushed, an odour similar to that of orange peel. Cool, moist conditions seem to produce the best growth on this species. In ten years one can expect to have a tree of 5m (16ft) in height.   Hardiness 4.

Abies pinsapo   Spanish Fir.

18 As indicated by its common name, this fir is native to the mountains of Spain, where it occurs at altitudes around 1,500m (5,000ft). It is easily distinguished from other abies by its stiff, short (1cm/$\frac{1}{4}$in) radially-arranged needles, more so than any other fir, its rigid, angular branching and its altogether solid habit of growth, the leaf colour being usually a greyish-green. It has enjoyed some popularity as a tub plant in sizes up to 2m (6ft) and seems tolerant to most soil conditions except bog areas. In ten years one can expect to have a tree 4m (12ft) high by 2m (6ft) wide at the base.   Hardiness 6.

19 *Abies pinsapo* 'Glauca'. Autumn. Blenheim, New Zealand.

20 *Abies procera*. Spring. Wanganui, New Zealand.

Abies pinsapo 'Glauca'   Blue Spanish Fir.

19 A beautiful conifer for the larger garden or park, with its soft powder-blue foliage colour and tapering pyramidal form—an attractive tree at any time of year. Apart from leaf colour it is similar in all respects to the preceding fir, having originated as a seedling selection. It is possible to raise bluish seedlings from seed of this form, but the best trees are grafted and can trace their lineage back to the original raised in France around 1860. The tree illustrated has three leaders, two of which should have been removed many years ago to maintain a more uniform shape.

Hardiness 6.

Abies procera   Noble Fir.

20 Better known as *A.nobilis*, this fine fir had to undergo a name-change when research proved that another species already had prior claim. It will always be known as the Noble Fir, however, a name that is well suited to this majestic tree which in good conditions is capable of reaching to 80m (260ft). The leaves are one of the heaviest in texture and most densely-set among firs, averaging 3cm (1in) long, are blunt-ended and rich green, sometimes glaucous, and clothe the tree thoroughly almost to the ground if grown in plenty of space. As well as being an important timber tree in its native North America, it is grown extensively from seed as an ornamental, thriving best in a cool, moist climate in well-drained soil.   Hardiness 4.

Abies procera 'Glauca'   Blue Noble Fir.

21, 22 This best-known form of Noble Fir is a much sought-after conifer for garden or park planting, rivalling even the best of the blue spruces with its lovely silver-blue foliage. It is unfortunate that supply of good specimens of this form will always be limited, as plants grafted from anything but leader scions are unlikely to ever grow into good specimens, but tend rather to be spreading and irregular in habit. Once it gets established it can be expected to add 30cm (12in) in height per year, and usually cones when past the 5m (15ft) mark.   Hardiness 4.

21 *Abies procera* 'Glauca'. With cones. Autumn.

22 *Abies procera* 'Glauca'. Leader growth emerging from lateral foliage.

23 *Abies procera* 'Glauca Prostrata'. Summer. San Francisco, USA.

Abies procera 'Glauca Prostrata'

23 It is debatable whether plants labelled as above are merely the product of grafts taken from weak side-growths of the breeding cultivar, or are in fact true dwarfs developed from seed; but whatever the genealogy it is still a desirable low-growing blue-green conifer with definite uses on the border or rockery. What often happens with such cultivariants (as they are called) is that they eventually develop a leader and proceed to grow into a normal specimen of *A. procera* 'Glauca', which it probably has been all along anyway, but in that stunted condition because of the type of grafting wood used for its propagation. Some authors prefer to leave the 'Glauca' off the name and call it 'Prostrata'.   Hardiness 4.

24 *Acmopyle* pancheri. Foliage.

Acmopyle pancheri

24 A little-known genus composed of three semi-hardy species—*A. alba* and *A. pancheri*, natives of New Caledonia, and *A. sahniana*, a native of Fiji. Of the three, *A. pancheri* is the tallest with a potential height of 15m (50ft) in its native tropical climate. It is an erect-branched evergreen clothed in yew-like leaves that vary in length from 1cm to 2.5cm ($\frac{1}{3}$-1in). The cones consist of a number of fleshy, warty bracts fused together to hold one globose seed, and the generic name derives from this feature in combining the two botanical terms *apical micropyle*.   Hardiness 9.

Actinostrobus pyramidalis

25 A genus of West Australian origin closely allied to *Callitris* but differing in cone detail. These are woody, rounded or oval in shape, about 2cm ($\frac{3}{4}$in) in length, are encircled at the base with a collar of closely pressed bracts, and split open into six sections to release one or two three-winged seeds. As a garden plant it fairly rapidly makes an erect pyramidal bush up to 2m (6ft) in height, composed of five cupressoid scale-like leaves set in threes around the stem. Male and female strobilii are carried on the same plant. The only other species, *A. acuminatus*, is smaller-growing and finer in foliage, but otherwise very similar to the above.   Hardiness 8.

25 *Actinostrobos pyramidalis.* Foliage with male strobilii.

26 *Agathis australis.* Summer. New Plymouth, New Zealand.

Agathis australis   Kauri.

26 Pride of place among the twenty recorded species of kauri pines must surely go to the New Zealand native, *A. australis*, undisputed king among New Zealand forest trees. Fine specimens still exist in North Auckland forests with a trunk diameter of up to 8m (26ft) and a height of 50m (165ft); such trees are protected to prevent further depletion through the demand for its high-quality timber. It does not, however, become embarrassingly large when grown as an ornamental away from its rain-forest habitat, and normally can be expected to make a tree of 5m (16ft) in ten years, growth rate becoming correspondingly slower in regions colder than its native climate. For a conifer it has large (5cm by 1cm/2in by $\frac{1}{3}$in) flat leaves, although among agathis it is one of the smallest. Kauri gum, the fossilised resin found in swamp areas previously covered in forest, was another lucrative by-product of this remarkable tree.   Hardiness 8.

Araucaria araucana   Monkey Puzzle.

27 This well-known South American conifer should need very little description, as most will be familiar with this stiff, prickly and formally-shaped specimen, eagerly planted as a street, park or garden specimen some years ago but losing some popularity now in favour of a less-formal outline. It is the only araucaria that is hardy in Britain, and is not difficult to establish once the young frost-tender stage is passed, thriving best in loamy soil with adequate moisture supply. The edible 3cm (1in) seeds are borne in large cones which take two to three years to mature, and fall to pieces when the seed is ripe. It begins life in a burst of growth that can bring it to 6m (20ft) in ten years, but this slows down as the tree fills out and takes on greater foliage density.   Hardiness 7.

27 *Araucaria araucana.* Winter. Rotorua, New Zealand.

29 *Araucaria bidwillii.* Foliage.

Araucaria bidwillii   Bunya-Bunya.

28, 29 This native of the coastal regions of Queensland, Australia, has found its way as an ornamental into many parts of the world where the climate is sufficiently mild to allow its establishment. It makes a broad, uniformly pyramidal tree of up to 50m (165ft) in favourable climates, and lower and more rounded in marginal areas, the rich glossy green, prickly foliage seemingly held in large bunches at the ends of the branches. The large, edible seeds are borne in cones weighing up to 4.5kg (10lb) each, and are much prized by the Aboriginals for food. In ten years' growing one may expect a tree of 4–5m (13–16ft) in height. It produces a good-quality softwood timber, and could well be forested more in areas unsuitable to other pines.   Hardiness 7.

28 *Araucaria bidwillii.* Winter. Toowoomba, Queensland.

30 *Araucaria heterophylla.* Spring. Queensland, Australia.

Araucaria heterophylla   Norfolk Island Pine.

30 A beautiful symmetrical tree, found originally only on Norfolk Island, which is now a popular ornamental in warm temperate zones throughout the world, as well as being an indoor pot-plant in less temperate countries. It has a height potential of 60m (200ft), grows incredibly straight, the branches originating in whorls from the trunk and spaced in almost perfect regularity up the trunk, giving a tapered many-tiered effect reminiscent of a Chinese pagoda. One is, however, able to change the character of this tree completely by removing its leader when young, and if this is done repeatedly it grows into a very dense, conical shrub not unlike some types of cryptomeria. Although not regarded as hardy, it is not a difficult tree to establish in marginal areas provided it has some frost protection until up to the 3 or 4m (10 or 13ft) level. Previously known as *A. excelsa.*   Hardiness 8.

31 *Athrotaxis laxifolia.* Foliage and cones.

33 *Austrocedrus chilensis.* Spring. Surrey, England.

34 *Callitris columellaris.* Spring. Queensland, Australia.

32 *Athrotaxis selaginoides.* Foliage with strobilii.

Austrocedrus chilensis   Chilean Cedar

33 The genus *Austrocedrus* contains this one-only species, native to Chile and the Argentine. It is an interesting, erect-growing small tree that should be grown more than it is. In the past it has been placed either among the genera *Libocedrus* or *Thuja*, which latter rather resembles it in leaf detail if nothing else, but our botanists now find sufficient differences to place it in a genus of its own. Close examination of the much flattened leaf sprays reveal its distinct leaf arrangement, with broad whitish stomatic bands displayed on the reverse side making an interesting and distinctive pattern that is dissimilar to any other conifer. It bears tiny cones no more than 2cm (¾in) long which are solitary and carried on the same tree as the male strobilii, which are often very prolific and give the whole tree a yellowish hue when the pollen is ripe.   Hardiness 7.

Callitris columellaris   Murray River Pine

34 The genus *Callitris* is divided into some thirteen separate species, all natives of Australia or Tasmania, and capable of tolerating the heat and drought encountered there. One of the more ornamental types is *C. columellaris*, seen here in the grounds of Brisbane University displaying the typical erect habit with the trunk divided into several tapering leaders. The foliage is fine, almost threadlike, and arranged densely on the branchlets so as to almost completely hide the inner structure of the tree, usually a rich green but sometimes glaucous. Although capable of reaching 25m (80ft), for garden use it can be regarded as a tall shrub, and can be expected to make not more than 3m (10ft) in ten years' growing. To maintain a tidy habit it should be grown in full sun.   Hardiness 8.

Athrotaxis laxifolia   Tasmanian Cedar.

31, 32 The genus *Athrotaxis* is represented by three species, easily distinguished from each other by differences in foliage, which ranges from the closely-pressed, thick and whipcord-like leaves of *A. cupressoides* through to the open and loosely-arranged cryptomeria-like 1cm (¼in) leaf on *A. selaginoides*, with *A. laxifolia* providing an intermediate between these two. All eventually grow to tree size in their native country, in some cases to 30m (100ft), rather irregular in habit when this size, but in colder climates are slow-growing enough to be used as dwarf conifers and maintain a more uniform habit under these conditions. Male and female strobilii are borne on the foliage tips on the same bush, the rounded spiny cryptomeria-like cones measuring up to 2cm (¾in) in diameter.   Hardiness 6.

36 *Callitris oblonga.* Foliage and cones.

35 *Callitris oblonga.* Summer. Palmerston North, New Zealand.

Callitris oblonga   Tasmanian Cypress Pine

35, 36 A half-hardy conifer that is easily raised from seed, and rapidly builds itself up into a tidy-looking bluish-green upright bush densely furnished in fine threadlike foliage. It is sometimes used as a tub plant, being tolerant of dryness, and should be used more as a quick-growing ornamental or hedge. Seeds are borne on relatively young bushes in shiny black 4cm (1¾in) almost-round cones. In ten years it can be expected to reach to 3m (10ft) by 2m (6ft) in width.   Hardiness 8.

Calocedrus decurrens   Incense Cedar

37 Formerly known as either *Heyderia decurrens* or *Libocedrus decurrens*, this conifer has been given a change of genus, along with its two related species, *C. formosana* and *C. macrolepis*. It is a handsome clean-growing tree that warrants more use than it seems to get, with its glossy rich-green, clean-looking fans of foliage and contrasting red-brown stems. It is one of those trees that begin in a rather fat rounded bush, but with maturity continue upwards to make a tall, narrow column of up to 50m (165ft) in their native North America. A ten-year-old specimen can be expected to reach 4–5m (13–16ft). The wood is often used for making pencils.   Hardiness 5.

Calocedrus decurrens 'Intricata'

38 Among the seven recorded cultivars of the Incense Cedar, 'Intricata' seems to be the best known. It is quite a dwarf, making less than 1m (3ft) in height in ten years, has a dense, intricate branching system with closely packed and twisted small sprays of foliage, tinged bronze during winter. Two other recorded dwarfs are the very similar 'Nana' and Compacta'.   Hardiness 5.

Cedrus atlantica   Atlas Cedar

39, 40 A native of the Atlas mountains of Algeria and Morocco, the Atlas Cedar is grown widely as an ornamental conifer throughout the world, and is also used successfully in France for timber production in areas with poor soil. A wide range of forms and colours is included in the classification of *C. atlantica*, and most of these are seed-grown trees which show variation even from batch to batch, along with further variations caused by climate and soil conditions. Our photograph, taken near Los Angeles, illustrates one such variant with decidedly weeping tips promoted by warm, fast-growth conditions in California. In its native state it is an erect straight-trunked tree to 40m (130ft) with near-horizontal branches, with some areas solely occupied by blue-foliaged forms as glaucous as the best cultivars. Seed from such stands usually produce a high percentage of good blue-foliaged trees.   Hardiness 6.

37 *Calocedrus decurrens.* Summer. Palmerston North, New Zealand.

38 *Calocedrus decurrens* 'Intricata'. Spring. Ampfield, Hants, England.

39 *Cedrus atlantica*. Spring. California, USA.

40 *Cedrus atlantica*. Cones.

Cedrus atlantica 'Aurea'   Golden Atlas Cedar

41 This cultivar is no problem to identify, with its tips liberally dusted a distinct golden yellow, fading to a normal glaucous green on the inner, less exposed parts of the tree. It carries itself in classic, erect pyramidal Atlas Cedar style, with none of the weeping pendulous habit of some forms, and can be expected to reach to 4m (13ft) in a ten-year growth period. It is reputed to have originated in Boskoop around 1900, and is normally propagated by grafting on to any other cedar stock.
Hardiness 6.

41 *Cedrus atlantica* 'Aurea'. Spring. Hastings, New Zealand.

42 *Cedrus atlantica* 'Fastigiata'. Winter. Christchurch, New Zealand.

43 *Cedrus atlantica* 'Glauca'. Summer. Palmerston North, New Zealand.

Cedrus atlantica 'Fastigiata'

42 Among the several forms of Blue Cedars, 'Fastigiata' stands out with reasonable distinction with its erect pyramidal form and predominantly upward-facing branch attitude, becoming near-horizontal only close to ground level. This tree never seems to develop that round-topped semi-spreading effect seen on other cedars when they become of age at around the 20m (65ft) height. The leaf colour is bluish-green, not unlike that of 'Glauca', and this is no doubt why it is more often seen labelled with that name. It is to be recommended for planting where a more formal shape is required. Hardiness 6.

Cedrus atlantica 'Glauca' Blue Atlas Cedar

43, 44 It is doubtful whether the many trees labelled with the above name can trace their lineage back to the original blue selection, there having been so many blue forms raised from seed over the years that show good colour yet exhibit different growth habits. The typical form has conspicuously bluish-white leaves, begins growth as a straight-trunked pyramidal tree for about the first ten years (4–5m/ 13–16ft high), but showing an increasing tendency to hang its lower branches and take on a more informal habit. This feature becomes more pronounced as the tree grows, and a mature specimen such as the one in Bodnant Garden, North Wales, with great sweeps of the foliage descending almost to grass level, is a most impressive sight. Climate and soils influence habit quite strongly, however, and the same clone grown under harder, drier conditions would no doubt display a more erect and stiffer growth habit, so that the uninitiated could well mistake it for a different cultivar. Hardiness 6.

Cedrus atlantica 'Glauca Pendula' Weeping Blue Cedar

45 A beautiful spreading, weeping tree and no doubt one of the original plants, photographed at Châtenay near Paris, where it was first raised, and reputed to be now 100 years old. This cultivar must be grafted on to a 2–3m (6–10ft) standard in order to give it its initial height, and from here the branches are trained horizontally to carry the long trailers of short-needled bluish foliage which in places sweeps right to ground level. Plants grafted at ground level never make much height unless trained, and normally do not develop into attractive plants. Hardiness 6.

44 *Cedrus atlantica* 'Glauca'. Cones.

Cedrus atlantica 'Pendula' Weeping Atlas Cedar

46 Not to be confused with the preceding cultivar, this green-leaved weeping form is more suited to a rockery, border, or for trailing over a bank, with its more modest growth rate and less pendulous habit. It seems to have enough rigidity to hold itself at least a little off the ground, and the plant illustrated would be about twenty years old, and had reached a height of 1m by 2m (3ft by 6ft) wide in that time. Hardiness 6.

45 *Cedrus atlantica* 'Glauca Pendula'. Winter. Châtenay, France.

48 *Cedrus deodara*. Cones.

46 *Cedrus atlantica* 'Pendula'. Spring. Washington, DC, USA.

Cedrus deodara
Himalayan Cedar. Indian Cedar.

47, 48 *Cedrus deodara* can usually be distinguished from other cedars by its longer (4cm/1½in) leaves and more graceful, flexible growth habit with pendulous leader, and makes a fine, well-furnished pyramidal ornamental that requires little or no attention once established. While specimens in their native state are known to reach 60m (200ft), the more modest height of 5m (16ft) can be considered average for a ten-year-old tree. The general colour is a glaucous green, but many seedling variants have occurred over the years, ranging from bluish to golden yellow, and twenty-six of such forms are at present named and on record. Warm, humid climates seem to induce a more pendulous, flexible type of growth to this normally erect conifer. It carries attractive barrel-shaped cones up to 10cm (4in) in length.   Hardiness 7.

47 *Cedrus deodara*. Spring. London, England.

50 *Cedrus deodara* 'Nana'. Spring. London, England.

Cedrus deodara 'Aurea'   Golden Deodar Cedar

49 'Aurea' is probably the best known colour form of the Himalayan Cedar and is easily recognised with its golden colour on all exposed leaf, the colour becoming weaker in the inner, more sheltered parts of the tree. It has the same pyramidal shape of the type but is slower in growth, making about 3m (10ft) in height in ten years. Some trees do not seem to possess particularly good leaf colour, and I suspect that such forms are an inferior seedling selection or possibly seed-grown plants from the above tree.   Hardiness 7.

Cedrus deodara 'Nana'   Dwarf Deodar Cedar

50 A very slow-growing low bush that seems to prefer to grow twice as wide as high, and put on no more annual increase in size than 1 to 2cm ($\frac{1}{3}$ to $\frac{3}{4}$in). Seen here in the flush of spring growth, the foliage makes a lighter-than-usual fresh green.
                                                                Hardiness 6.

49 *Cedrus deodara* 'Aurea'. Spring. Washington, DC, USA.

51 *Cedrus deodara* 'Pendula'. Summer. Netherlands.

Cedrus deodara 'Pendula'   Weeping Deodar Cedar

51 This form would be better suited to the name 'Prostrata' because when left to itself it merely spreads flat on the ground, with just the occasional branch-end feebly attempting to rise. In order to grow in a form that is more true to name it needs to be trained upwards or grafted on to a standard a metre or so from the ground to allow the foliage to fall in true weeping manner.   Hardiness 6.

52 *Cedrus libani*. Winter. Châtenay, France.

53 *Cedrus libani* 'Nana'. Spring. San Francisco, USA.

55 *Cephalotaxus fortunei*. Foliage.

54 *Cedrus libani* 'Sargentii'. Spring. San Francisco, USA.

Cedrus libani   Cedar of Lebanon

52 Although closely allied to the Atlas and Deodar cedars, *C. libani* can usually be identified by its shorter, darker green needles, with foliage densely arranged in horizontal planes, and the generally stiffer, more rigid appearance than that of the other two. It is maintained by some botanists that a positive identification of this species is possible only by detailed examination of the cones and seeds. Though well-known in Biblical times, this tree is now reputed to be rare in its native Lebanon mountains. In the meantime it has become a popular park and garden tree in temperate zones throughout the world, its first recorded introduction to Britain being in the mid-1600s. Although the tree illustrated is 300 years old, it is quite a rapid grower in its earlier years.
                                                                              Hardiness 5.

Cedrus libani 'Nana'   Dwarf Lebanon Cedar

53 It appears that more than one dwarf form of the Lebanon Cedar has found its way into the nursery trade under the name of 'Nana'. All are rather similar in bushy compact habit and shortened growth, and none is sufficiently distinct to warrant a name of its own. The plant illustrated actually carried the name 'Compte de Dijon' (which is a clone of 'Nana' but is a larger pyramidal bush, horizontally branched), and it may be safely assumed that having proved not true to name it belongs back in the 'Nana' group. It is slow-growing dwarf with needles of 2cm (¾in) and an annual increase of 2–4cm (¾–1½in), usually making a bush as wide as it is high.
                                                                              Hardiness 5.

Cedrus libani 'Sargentii'

54 A popular weeping form of Lebanon Cedar which, because of its longish needles and pendulous tips, looks as though it should more correctly be classified among the Deodar cedars. It is one of those weepers that needs to be stem-trained when young to make any trunk at all, unless required as illustrated to sprawl over a bank, which it does very admirably, covering the ground in blue-green needles. Growth is slow enough for it to be classified a dwarf conifer, with an estimated coverage of 1m (3ft) for ten years, plus any height that may have been built in through upward training. Sometimes confused with *C.l.* 'Pendula', a tree-like weeping form. Hardiness 6.

Cephalotaxus fortunei   Chinese Plumyew.

55 The *Cephalotaxus*, natives of China, Korea and Japan, are in external appearance closely allied to the taxus but it is generally agreed among most botanists that the former belongs in a genus of its own, while a few go further in maintaining that it really should be classified in a completely separate family, the *Cephalotaxaceae*. Our photo depicts the leaf similarity to taxus, which in the species *C.fortunei* has probably the longest of any in the genus—up to 8cm (3in) long, curved, arranged on the stems in opposite ranks and displaying a rich glossy green colour. It makes a spreading bush which in ten years should reach 3m (10ft) in each dimension, and has the peculiarity of conifers of bearing male or female flowers on separate trees. These are located on the undersides of the leaf sprays, and on the female this develops into an olive-green fruit up to 3cm (1in) in length.   Hardiness 7.

56 *Cephalotaxus harringtonia.* Spring. Sussex, England.

57 *Cephalotaxus harringtonia.* Foliage.

Cephalotaxus harringtonia   Japanese Plumyew, Cows-tail Pine

56, 57 Rather similar to *C. fortunei* is the Japanese Plumyew, growing in the same rounded bushy spreading shape, sometimes making a small tree and having the same dioecious feature with flowers of one sex only per bush. In our picture of a male plant in pollen it is possible to distinguish the rows of heavily-laden strobili contrasting yellow against the green of the foliage. It differs from *C. fortunei* in having a somewhat shorter leaf, ending in an abrupt point, and it can stand much colder conditions than its Chinese counterpart. In growth it can be expected to reach to almost 2m (6ft) each way for a ten-year period.   Hardiness 5.

Cephalotaxus harringtonia 'Fastigiata'   Upright Japanese Plumyew

58 This is probably the best-known garden member of this family and quite a distinct one with its strongly vertical growth habit, looking not unlike some coarse-leaved form of Irish Yew. The leaf arrangement differs from the usual pectinate one on the spreading forms, in being wholly radially arranged on vertical or near-vertical stems, the two features combining to produce the distinctly erect habit, in colour a dark glossy green. Like the taxus it tends to be a slow starter, probably reaching the 1.5m (5ft) mark in ten years, with an ultimate potential of 3 to 5m (10 to 16ft).   Hardiness 5.

Chamaecyparis lawsoniana   Lawson False Cypress

59 A highly-variable species which in its first century of cultivation has given rise to more than 200 recorded named cultivars by way of seedling variants or vegetative sports. A hedgerow of seedling lawsons makes an interesting study in variability of individual plants — one usually finds that no two plants are identical in colour, habit or foliage. Its growth habit is further influenced by climate and soil and the best specimens are generally found in cold-winter low-humidity areas well inland where there is good shelter from strong prevailing and salt-laden winds. In such conditions we can find majestic trees of narrow pyramidal form over 30m (100ft) high, bearing little resemblance to the untidy, loose-growing specimens found in warmer high-humidity coastal areas where they are also prone to attack by cypress canker disease.   Hardiness 5.

Chamaecyparis lawsoniana 'Albovariegata'

60 A compact rounded bush that may be classed among the dwarf conifers, this is one of the several variegated forms of *C. lawsoniana*, and is of similar foliage to the tree-sized cultivar 'Argenteovariegata'. Growth approximates 70cm (28in) in height by 50cm (20in) wide for ten years. The white variegation is liable to suffer damage from frost in exposed locations, but given suitable shelter this cultivar is an attractive little ornamental.   Hardiness 6.

Chamaecyparis lawsoniana 'Albospica'

61 Of similar name and colouration to the preceding 'Albovariegata', this cultivar differs in being spattered liberally with smaller patches of white, mainly on the tip growths of the plant. This white growth has a congested nature, almost as if distorted by a virus, which could well be the explanation for its unusual behaviour. Of semi-dwarf gowth, it can in time reach 3m (10ft), but is not likely to make more than one-third of this in the first ten years, at which age it has begun to take on a broad pyramidal form. The white parts do not seem liable to frost-damage as is the preceding conifer.   Hardiness 6.

58 *Cephalotaxus harringtonia* 'Fastigiata'. Winter. Hamilton, New Zealand.

59 *Chamaecyparis lawsoniana.* Autumn. Reefton,
New Zealand.

60 *Chamaecyparis lawsoniana* 'Albovariegata'. Spring. Surrey, England.

62 *Chamaecyparis lawsoniana* 'Alumii'. Winter.

61 *Chamaecyparis lawsoniana* 'Albospica'. Spring.
Glasgow, Scotland.

Chamaecyparis lawsoniana 'Alumii'

62 Probably the earliest recorded blue-green cultivar in the lawson group, 'Alumii' was first listed in 1891 and has enjoyed great popularity as an ornamental conifer until 1960, when the more compact blue forms such as 'Columnaris' came on the scene. It eventually grows too large (10m /33ft high) to be called a shrub ,and the first ten years are the most useful ones for home garden use, in which time it should reach 3m (10ft) by 1m (3ft) wide. As with most of the larger members of this species, growth is slower and tighter in colder regions. There is a plant in Mr Geoffrey Pilkington's collection at Haslemere, Surrey, on which he has the name 'Alumii Nana'. It appears similar to 'Alumii' but being reputedly more compact and slow-growing should be better for the garden.   Hardiness 5.

63 *Chamaecyparis lawsoniana* 'Aurea Densa'. Spring. Surrey, England.

64 *Chamaecyparis lawsoniana* 'Aureovariegata'. Foliage.

Chamaecyparis lawsoniana 'Aurea Densa'

63 One ought to acquire the beautiful compact slow-growing garden gem, 'Aurea Densa', early in life in order to have enough time in which to appreciate it as a mature plant. It is one of three similar dwarf golden seedlings raised at Red Lodge Nurseries, Chandlers Ford, England, around 1910, the other two being 'Lutea Nana' and 'Minima Aurea,. I feel that 'Aurea Densa' takes first prize among them. The specimen illustrated, at the time about thirty-five years old, possessed a solid 8cm (3in) thick truck that tapered upwards to the tip of the bush, to a total height if no more than 1.2m by 1m (4ft by 3ft) wide, a real sturdy specimen clothed in golden yellow. Because of reflection of the glaucous bloom in the foliage, the illustration does not quite depict the true golden colour of this cultivar.   Hardiness 5.

Chamaecyparis lawsoniana 'Aureovariegata'

64 Another variegated lawson, this form grows into a tree of 12m (40ft) in a thirty-year period, and has about 20 per cent of its foliage patched in bright creamy yellow, standing out clearly against the dark green foliage. Illustrated is a typical spray containing variegation, the green parts also serving to illustrate typical *Chamaecyparis lawsoniana* leaf detail. The tree grows in a broad conical shape similar to the type, at about half the growth rate, and rather easily reverts to type. Such all-green growths should be speedily removed at their source. The cultivar commonly known in New Zealand as *Chamaecyparis lawsoniana* 'Armstrongii' appears to be identical to this one, if not the same.   Hardiness 5.

Chamaecyparis lawsoniana 'Blom'

65 While most of the blue upright lawsons grow too large for use in a rockery or pebble garden, 'Blom' is sufficiently compact and slow-growing to be used in such plantings for at least ten years, reaching to 2m (6ft) in this time by 40cm (15in) at the widest part. It can be described as a much refined form of 'Alumii' (of which it is a sport), a lovely blue-green colour the shape of a candle-flame, with fine adult-type foliage arranged in vertical planes. Because of its slower growth and sturdy trunk it is better able to withstand wind and exposure than its faster-growing brothers. When first introduced in 1942 it was classified as *C. lawsoniana* 'Erecta Blom', and this name is still used by some nurseries.   Hardiness 6.

Chamaecyparis lawsoniana 'Columnaris'

66 One of the finest blue forms of this species, 'Columnaris' was released about twenty years ago in the Netherlands and has steadily gained in popularity as a garden plant ever since. It is of narrower habit than 'Alumii', of a better blue colour, and the upward-facing sprays of foliage form an erect and symmetrical plant of beauty and distinction. A ten-year plant can be expeced to reach 2.5m (8ft) in height by 80cm (30in) in width in warmer climates, but growth is noticeably slower in England, resulting in a narrower plant than the one illustrated, but no doubt hardier and more permanent. It is frequently but incorrectly referred to as 'Columnaris Glauca'.
          Hardiness 5.

65 *Chamaecyparis lawsoniana* 'Blom'. Autumn. Te Kuiti, New Zealand.

66 *Chamaecyparis lawsoniana* 'Columnaris'. Winter. Gore, New Zealand.

67 *Chamaecyparis lawsoniana* 'Dow's Gem' (foreground). Spring. Haslemere, Surrey, England.

68 *Chamaecyparis lawsoniana* 'Duncanii'. Winter.

Chamaecyparis lawsoniana 'Dow's Gem'

68 An attractive low-growing wide-spreading conifer, with pale grey-green open, thujoid-type foliage, 'Dow's Gem' is of American origin, having been raised at the Dow nursery, Oakdean, California. The branch tips droop gracefully and produce a spreading, weeping effect that is pleasing to the eye. Of medium growth rate, 'Dow's Gem' should make a diameter of 1.2m (4ft) in ten years, by almost 80cm (3ft) high — an ideal plant for contrast among erect evergreens. It has also been known under the names of 'Dow's Variety' or 'Noble's Variety'. The more compact green lawson in the background is 'Hybrida', one so similar to 'Nidiformis' that only an expert could tell the difference.

Hardiness 6.

Chamaecyparis lawsoniana 'Duncanii'

67 Quite distinct among the lower-growing lawsoniana forms with fine bluish-green threadlike foliage, 'Duncanii' is of New Zealand origin and was introduced by Messrs Duncan and Davies Ltd, of New Plymouth. It grows approximately twice as wide as it does high in the shape of a bun and in ten years can be expected to have a width of 1.5m (5ft) to a maximum of 3.5m (12ft) for an old plant. It is therefore an ideal conifer for planting on a lawn, or as line and colour contrast among more erect conifers.

Hardiness 5.

69 *Chamaecyparis lawsoniana* 'Elegantissima'. Spring,
Haslemere, Surrey, England.

70 *Chamaecyparis lawsoniana* 'Ellwoodii'. Autumn.
Ashburton, New Zealand.

71 *Chamaecyparis lawsoniana* 'Ellwood's Gold'. Spring.

Chamaecyparis lawsoniana 'Elegantissima'

69   A beautiful cultivar of graceful and refined habit, possessing a well-defined
trunk and growing in the shape of a wide pyramid, 'Elegantissima' is an excellent
garden plant of not-too-large proportion and medium growth rate; in ten years
reaching to 2.5m by 1.3m (8ft by 4½ft). Illustrated is a young specimen in Mr
Pilkington's collection at Haslemere, Surrey, a little more erect than typical because
of the presence of surrounding large trees. The light canary-yellow leaf colour is
constant the year round.   Hardiness 5.

Chamaecyparis lawsoniana 'Ellwoodii'

70   This blue-green colour form of the Lawson False Cypress has been in cultivation
for only forty years, but in that short time has probably made itself more widely
known than any other member of this group. The compact, tidy, juvenile foliage
is held on an upward-pointing branch system to make a neat and attractive bush
of ideal garden size, in ten years reaching to 2m by 80cm (6ft by 30in) wide. Of
recent years its popularity has waned in New Zealand because it is susceptible to
cypress canker, and once infected a plant becomes disfigured with patches of brown
foliage that is most unsightly. It also tends to grow into a looser, more open plant
in the New Zealand climate, not making the tight attractive form of plants grown
in the United Kingdom where growth is narrower and slower. There are variegated
forms, of which 'Ellwood's White' is one.   Hardiness 6.

Chamaecyparis lawsoniana 'Ellwood's Gold'

71   A very recent arrival in the Ellwood family and one that will probably 'catch on'
quite rapidly as it is easily propagated (like its parent) and wastes no time in forming
into a neat little bush with all tips touched light yellow-gold. It seems a little slower
in growth than its blue-green parent, making about 20cm (8in) a year once established, but less in cold climate zones.   Hardiness 6.

72 *Chamaecyparis lawsoniana* 'Ellwood's Pigmy'. Summer. Te Kuiti, New Zealand.

73 *Chamaecyparis lawsoniana* 'Erecta'. Autumn. Christchurch, New Zealand.

74 *Chamaecyparis lawsoniana* 'Erecta Aurea'. Summer.

Chamaecyparis lawsoniana 'Ellwood's Pigmy'

72 Presumably a cultivariant of 'Ellwoodıı' but not directly traceable to that cultivar, 'Pigmy' has the same foliage and blue-green colour but makes a low bun of only 40cm (15in) in height and width in twenty years growing. It is a reasonably 'fixed' form but sometimes attempts to form a leader, any such strong growths should be removed to keep the plant in its typical compact shape. For this reason all propagation material should be taken from the less vigorous side growths, otherwise one is likely to end up with a plant that looks more like 'Ellwoodii' than 'Pigmy'. An attractive little plant that is ideally suited to the rockery   Hardiness 6.

Chamaecyparis lawsoniana 'Erecta'

73 This conifer can be simply described as a green, erect form of the following cultivar, 'Erecta Aurea'. It has the same leaf arrangement consisting of flattened verical planes of foliage and makes a similar shape for the first few years of life, reaching a height of 2m by 80m (6ft by 30in) wide in ten years' growth. It docs not stop at that, however, and anyone who has admired the 15m (50ft) specimens of 1878 vintage planted in the Bodnant Gardens, North Wales, will agree that this plant can reach quite grand proportions given time and space. The best specimens are usually seen in colder climate areas; as with most members of this species, fast growth produces a broader, loose type of bush that is inclined to 'fall out' when exposed to wind or snow. Also commonly known as 'Erecta Viridis'.   Hardiness 5.

Chamaecyparis lawsoniana 'Erecta Aurea'

74 'Erecta Aurea' is an attractive slow-growing golden lawson that was raised nearly 100 years ago in the Netherlands and is still in wide use as an oranmental. The foliage held in upward-facing planes in the 'bookleaf' fashion similar of many of the *Thuja orientalis* forms and is a rich yellow colour on the outside of the bush throughout the year. It is best planted where there is some shelter from the elements, otherwise the top growths are likely to become burnt off to a 'flat', thus ruining the symmetrical, rounded, sometimes pointed, top. In ten years, a bush of 1m by 50cm (3ft by 20in) wide can be expected, but when grown in harder climatic conditions a a tighter and narrower plant is the result.   Hardiness 6.

75 *Chamaecyparis lawsoniana* 'Filiformis'. Foliage.

Chamaecyparis lawsoniana 'Filiformis'

75 An erect-growing small tree usually possessing a strong straight leader, horizontal branches, cordlike branchlets and loosely-arranged threadlike sprays of mid-green foliage. It is rather similar to the New Zealand-raised cultivar 'Imbricata Pendula' but is easily distinguished from the larger, more weeping foliage of the latter. Neither cultivars look at all attractive when at their younger saleable age and are best supported by a solid stake for a few years after planting until a straight trunk is well established. 'Filiformis' is a medium grower and can be expected to make 2.5m (8ft) in height in ten years.   Hardiness 5.

77 *Chamaecyparis lawsoniana* 'Fleckellwood'. Spring. Palmerston North, New Zealand.

76 *Chamaecyparis lawsoniana* 'Filiformis Compacta'. Spring. California, USA

Chamaecyparis lawsoniana 'Filiformis Compacta'

76 Illustrated is a specimen of considerable age in the James Noble conifer collection at Golden Gate Park, San Francisco. Although at a glance similar to *Chamaecyparis pisifera* 'Filifera Nana', 'Filiformis Compacta' differs in having much finer threadlike foliage of a blue-green colour rather than the yellow-green of 'Fillifera Nana'. It has an average growth rate of 1m wide by 70cm (3ft by 28in) high in ten years.
                                                            Hardiness 5.

Chamaecyparis lawsoniana 'Fletcheri'
Fletcher's False Cypress.

78 Almost too well known to need much description here, 'Fletcheri' originated as a sport in an English nursery and was first introduced in the early 1920s. Its foliage is a bluish-green colour and is of a type intermediate between the adult and juvenile state. It is inclined to be variable in form, with some plants looser and more open than others; selection of propagation material no doubt plays a part in this, as also does climatic conditions, the best plants having been grown slowly in a not-too-warm climate. 'Fletcheri' is capable of reaching a height of 2.5m (8ft) in ten years, by 1m (3ft) broad.   Hardiness 6.

Chamaecyparis lawsoniana 'Fletcher's White'

79 This is a creamy-white variegated sport from the preceding cultivar 'Fletcheri', and is identical in foliage type and growth habit, apart from the possibility that it may be a little slower-growing because there is less green foliage available to the plant for photosynthesis. The rate of growth would be in the vicinity of 1.5m (5ft) high by 50cm (20in) wide in a period of ten years.   Hardiness 6.

Chamaecyparis lawsoniana 'Fleckellwood'

77 One of the creamy-white flecked forms of 'Ellwoodii', similar in shape but of slower browth to its parent, with irregular splashes of colour throughout the plant. Although it also produces some green foliage areas these do not seem to dominate the growth and are easily removed if so desired. This clone originated in New Zealand and was introduced by the South Taranaki nurseries around 1965, and would seem to be quite distinct from 'Ellwood's White, which Mr Welch describes as a slow-growing form with no columnar tendency. It is much in demand for rockery and pebble-gardens and seems to have about half the growth rate of 'Ellwoodii'.   Hardiness 7.

78 *Chamaecyparis lawsoniana* 'Fletcheri'. Spring.

79 *Chamaecyparis lawsoniana*
'Fletcher's White'. Spring.
Wisley, Surrey, England.

80 *Chamaecyparis lawsoniana* 'Forsteckensis'. Spring. Wisley, Surrey, England.

Chamaecyparis lawsoniana 'Forsteckensis'

80 One of the best of the dwarf lawsons, 'Forsteckensis' forms a dense round bush of light green foliage, has a characteristically neat habit of growth, and is admirably suited to planting among rocks. Once it has grown large enough for one's requirements it may be kept easily to size by the yearly removal of the stronger-growing tips that can be seen protruding above the top of the bush, and if this practice is continued the plant becomes a tight compact ball of foliage. There are two forms currently available, one of somewhat looser and larger growth than the other, and our illustration is, I suspect, of this more open form. A ten-year plant of the dwarfer type should be no more than 30cm (12 in) high by 50 cm(20in) wide. It is also met with under its earlier name of 'Forsteckiana'.   Hardiness 5.

Chamaecyparis lawsoniana 'Fraseri'   Fraser's False Cypress

81 One of the less-spectacular among the great variety of lawson cypresses, 'Fraseri' is the plant for those who desire a consistent row of light grey-green conifer, dense in

81 *Chamaecyparis lawsoniana* 'Fraseri'. Autumn.
Ashburton, New Zealand.

foliage but upright-growing in habit, or who need an erect but bushy lawn specimen. It has been around since 1900 and has gained much popularity over the years. This 3m (10ft) bush would be between ten to fifteen years of age.   Hardiness 5.

82 *Chamaecyparis lawsoniana* 'Gimbornii'. Spring.
Wisley, Surrey, England.

83 *Chamaecyparis lawsoniana* 'Gold Splash'. Winter.
Ashhurst, New Zealand.

Chamaecyparis lawsoniana 'Gimbornii'

82 For general neatness of outline and ability to stay this way without any trimming or pruning, 'Gimbornii' must surely be one of the best. A slow, steady growth rate and a·sturdy branching system contribute to the excellent shape of this conifer, which for ten years' good growing would be no more than 80cm (30in) in height and width. The dark bluish-green foliage is lightly tipped in a mauve colour, as close examination of the illustration will show, but this feature is more of an identification point than one of spectacular attraction. The plant originated as a seedling in the van Gimborn Estate, Doorn, Netherlands, and was first released in 1937.

Hardiness 6.

Chamaecyparis lawsoniana 'Gold Splash'

83 Yet another variegated sport from 'Fletcheri' this time of New Zealand origin. As its name suggests, it displays splashes of golden-yellow foliage in contrast to the darker background colour of blue-green. The spring and summer months see the plant at its best; from then on to winter the gold colouring diminishes somewhat but is still discernible among the darker foliage of the type. An interesting plant for the conifer border. 'Gold Splash' can be expected to reach 1.5m (5ft) in height by 80cm (30in) wide in ten years' growth.

Hardiness 6.

Chamaecyparis lawsoniana 'Grayswood Pillar'

84 An extremely narrow columnar cultivar with tightly-packed ascending branches and bluish-green foliage. It began as a sport on the cultivar 'Blue Jacket' at 'Grayswood Hill', the garden and residence of Mr Geoffrey Pilkington at Halsemere, Surrey, England, and our photograph of the original plant at fifteen years shows it at almost 8m (26ft) high yet less than 50cm (20in) in width. The green background is *Chamaecuparis lawsoniana*. This undoubtedly is the narrowest-growing of any in this species, and should be of value in warmer areas where other types tend to grow rather too loosely.

Hardiness 6.

84 *Chamaecyparis lawsoniana* 'Grayswood Pillar'. Spring.
Surrey, England.

Chamaecyparis lawsoniana 'Green Globe'

85 This must be one of the most compact among the dwarf forms of *Chamaecyparis lawsoniana* and for height would make no more than 30cm (12in) in ten years' growth; a real "mini" in the conifer world. This particular cultivar occurred as a seedling among a batch of lawsoniana plants at Palmers' nursery in Glen Eden, Auckland, New Zealand, about twenty years ago, but is not the only one of this type. Another similar form I have seen has a more rounded outline and a bun-shaped habit, but is as yet unnamed. I also noticed in England small plants under the name of 'Gnome' that looked very like 'Green Globe', so it appears that there are several similar variants of this type. 'Green Globe' is a neat little clump of green that is a worthwhile addition to any rockery.

Hardiness 5.

85 *Chamaecyparis lawsoniana* 'Green Globe'. Autumn. Auckland, New Zealand.

87 *Chamaecyparis lawsoniana* 'Imbricata Pendula'. Winter. Invercargill, New Zealand.

86 *Chamaecyparis lawsoniana* 'Hillieri'. Spring. Surrey, England.

Chamaecyparis lawsoniana 'Hillieri'

86 Of the many erect-growing golden lawsons in cultivation, 'Hillieri' is reputed to be the best, having a graceful, tall pyramidal habit well furnished with fine rich golden-yellow foliage. The growth rate is moderate, making about 2m by 1m (6ft by 3ft) wide for a ten-year tree, but on coming of age tends to add more in height than width, as so most of these upright-growing forms of *Chamaecyparis lawsoniana*. It grows best in a position not unduly exposed to the elements, otherwise it is likely to be disfigured by "burn", the brown-foliage effect sometimes seen on this type of golden conifer. Hardiness 6.

Chamaecyparis lawsoniana 'Imbricata Pendula'

87 A cultivar that originated as a seedling in Palmerston North, New Zealand, about 1930, 'Imbricata Pendula' has no immediate parallel among conifers for its graceful weeping habit. The whip-cord type foliage hangs down in long streamers of up to 1m (3ft) and gives a cascading, waterfall effect of great beauty. It is not widely planted even in New Zealand, partly because of difficulty in propagation in the earlier days, but should be more widely planted now that such problems have been overcome. Of moderate growth rate, it would reach to 2.5m (8ft) in ten years, by 1m (3ft) wide with an ultimate height of 6–8m (20–26ft). Hardiness 5.

88 *Chamaecyparis lawsoniana* 'Juvinalis Stricta', Autumn. Palmerston North, New Zealand.

89 *Chamaecyparis lawsoniana* 'Kilmacurragh'. Spring. Bodnant, Denbighshire, Wales.

Chamaecyparis lawsoniana 'Juvinalis Stricta'

88 This one is included more to spark discussion than to assert the rightness of the name. It originated as a seedling in a row of *Chamaecyparis lawsoniana* plants some forty years ago in Rotorua, New Zealand, and is found to make fairly rapidly a tapering ornamental pyramidal bush, well clothed in soft blue-green foliage, and reaching to 2.5m (8ft) in ten years in the temperate climate. It was given the above name by the nurseryman who raised it, but seems to have closer affinities to members of the *C. pisifera* group. Also, it seems identical in foliage to the tree-sized (to 20m 165ft) conifers which was called *Retinospora leptoclada* in the 1930s and whose name is still uncertain, apart from the fact that it is not the *C. thyoides* 'Andelyensis' to which the above name has been transferred. We are looking forward to the un-ravelling of this mystery.   Hardiness 6.

Chamaecyparis lawsoniana 'Kilmacurragh'

89 One of the best columnar green forms among the *Chamaecyparis lawsoniana* groups, Kilmacurragh' is of recent (1951) United Kingdom introduction and has already gained a reputation for being a hardy, erect, and tidy conifer that is capable of withstanding a heavy fall of snow without "falling out" or becoming otherwise disfigured — a weakness that is noticable with 'Erecta' and similar forms. The trunk is solid and usually single, extending right to the tip of the plant with side branches short and sturdy, which features explain its excellent resistance to snow build-up. It is capable of reaching to 3m by 80cm (10ft by 30in) wide in ten years' growth. The bare-looking trunk to the left of the picture belongs to a specimen of *Pinus sylvestris*.   Hardiness 5.

90 *Chamaecyparis lawsoniana* 'Lane'. Spring. Boskoop, Netherlands.

Chamaecyparis lawsoniana 'Lane'   Lane's Golden Lawson

90 A golden lawson that was introduced as recently as 1949, and has rapidly gained popularity as a garden ornamental in the short time it has been available. It has the distinction of being the brightest golden-yellow cultivar of any in this group, coupled with an excellent garden behaviour, being not too rapid in growth and reasonably tidy in habit, forming itself into a slender columnar spire as the plant matures. This plant is sometimes seen labelled 'Lanei' or 'Lane's Aurea'.   Hardiness 6.

Chamaecyparis lawsoniana 'Lutea'

91 A beautiful golden columnar lawson which in its younger state bears little resemblance to the stately form of the illustration. For the first ten years it is usually nothing more than a heap of golden fan-shaped sprays of foliage of roughly 2.5m (8ft) each way; but finally the plant decides to "grow up" and then produces top growth of a more weeping type of foliage which usually flowers and seeds freely. From this stage on the growth is predominantly in an upward direction with little or no increase in width to become, in fifty years, a beautiful column of golden foliage of up to 20m (65ft) in height. Development of this erect growth is dependent, however, on favourable climatic conditions, namely a free supply of water, a cool temperature range, and freedom from wind and salt spray. Good tall specimens are rarely seen in areas subject to strong prevailing winds.   Hardiness 5.

92 *Chamaecyparis lawsoniana*
'Luteocompacta'. Spring.
Wisley, Surrey, England.

Chamaecyparis lawsoniana 'Lycopodioides'

93 A thread-leaved form of lawson that forms a symmetrical conical bush of 1.5m high by 80cm wide (5ft by 30in) in ten years' growing, ultimately reaching about 5m (16ft). The foliage, of a dark bluish-green colour, is curiously twisted and curled, giving rise to the use of the name 'Lycopodioides', not to be confused with the quite different *Chamaecyparis obtusa* of the same name. It is of seedling origin, around the year 1890 in the Netherlands.   Hardiness 5.

Chamaecyparis lawsoniana 'Luteocompacta'

92 Although both its name and our illustration suggest that this is a compact dwarf form, it does eventually make a small-to-medium-sized tree, densely conical in shape and tipped on all extremities with clear golden yellow. One can expect it to be halfway in height at 1.5m (5ft) in ten years, with a base spread of 1m (3ft).   Hardiness 6.

94 *Chamaecyparis lawsoniana* 'Minima'. Autumn. Momona, Dunedin, New Zealand.

Chamaecyparis lawsoniana 'Minima'

94 A delightful rounded bush, consisting of compact green fans of foliage, 'Minima' is a fine plant for rockery or terrace planting and a must for any conifer collector. It has suffered under much confusion of name with the other forms of 'Minima' and 'Nana' but may be distinguished from 'Nana' by comparison of the trunk system. While 'Minima' branches near the ground, with little or no trunk, 'Nana' usually has a clearly-defined trunk that reaches well up towards the top of the bush. The foliage is a decided green, quite distinct from the bluish-green of 'Minima Glauca', with which it is often confused. Of slow growth, the ten-year plant illustrated measured almost 60cm (24in) each way.   Hardiness 5.

93 *Chamaecyparis lawsoniana* 'Lycopodioides'. Spring.

95 *Chamaecyparis lawsoniana* 'Minima Aurea'. Summer.
New Plymouth, New Zealand.

96 *Chamaecyparis lawsoniana* 'Minima Glauca'. Spring.
Wisley, Surrey, England.

97 *Chamaecyparis lawsoniana* 'Naberi'. Spring.
Boskoop, Netherlands.

Chamacyparis lawsoniana 'Minima Aurea'

95 This wonderful golden-yellow form of the preceding cultivar 'Minima' is of similar foliage, form and habit, but with perhaps a slightly slower growth rate of 50cm by 40cm (20in by 15in) in ten years. Its main distinguishing point from the very similar cultivar 'Aurea Densa' is the way the foliage is held in "fans" similar to the green 'Minima', while 'Aurea Densa' is of more uniform over-all appearance. Either cultivar is a slow-growing cone of colour ideal for rockery or screegarden.
Hardiness 5.

Chamaecyparis lawsoniana 'Minima Glauca'

96 Another variation on the 'Minima' theme, this one, by no means worthy of the name 'Glauca', has a somewhat bluish shade to its slightly darker foliage. This simularity with 'Minima' has given rise to names being confused between the two cultivars, so that plants being offered as 'Minima' often in fact turn out to be 'Minima Glauca'. Both are approximately equal in growth rate.   Hardiness 5.

Chamaecyparis lawsoniana 'Naberi'

97 A lawson cypress with a colour behaviour that is distinct among this species, the tips of the leaf-sprays displaying a light sulphur-yellow that takes on a whitish-blue during the winter months. It is a medium grower and makes a well-proportioned conical tree with an estimated height of 2–3m (6–10ft) in ten years.   Hardiness 5.

98 *Chamaecyparis lawsoniana* 'Nana'. Autumn.
Wanganui, New Zealand.

99 *Chamaecyparis lawsoniana* 'Nana Albospica'. Winter.
Hamilton, New Zealand.

100 *Chamaecyparis lawsoniana* 'Nana Glauca'. Summer.

Chamaecyparis lawsoniana 'Nana'

98 At a glance this is a duplication of the cultivar 'Minima', but a closer examination should reveal that it possesses a well-defined trunk that reaches well on towards the top of the bush, causing it to have a definite pointed top. It also has a less tidy profile than 'Minima', due to the pointed shape of the foliage tips at the lateral ends, which project a few millimetres beyond the general outline of the bush. The colour is a rich green, and the growth rate is capable of making a height of 80cm by 60cm wide (30in by 24in) in ten years.   Hardiness 5.

Chamaecyparis lawsoniana 'Nana Albospica'

99 A colourful and compact silvery-white form of 'Nana' with a growth rate of 1m by 70cm (3ft by 28in) in ten years, 'Nana Albospica' maintains its best greenish-white colour only when well nourished, so planting in a rich soil is recommended. Neglected specimens may degenerate to a dull grey-green colour with a loose and open habit that bears little resemblance to the specimen illustrated. Although the name 'Albospica' seems wrongly applied, examination of the inner foliage reveals that variegation is in fact present among the leaves. Many names have been used on this plant over the years, among them 'Nana Alba', 'Albospica Nana', and 'Argentea Compacta'.   Hardiness 6.

Chamaecyparis lawsoniana 'Nana Glauca'

100 This would be the most widely-grown form among the four of these very similar members of the 'Nana' and 'Minima' clan, and is easily enough recognised as 'Glauca' when grown in good conditions. If given a little starvation, the resulting yellowing of the foliage may produce a colour very like that of 'Nana'. This is probably one of the reasons why the two cultivars have become confused; but the coarser foliage of 'Glauca' is a further identification, and should serve to avoid confusion. They are otherwise identical in growth and hardiness.

101 *Chamaecyparis lawsoniana* 'Nidiformis'. Winter.
Auckland, New Zealand.

102 *Chamaecyparis lawsoniana* 'Pembury Blue'. Summer.
Hants, England.

Chamaecyparis lawsoniana 'Nidiformis'

101 Not unlike a giant bluish-green bird's-nest, and complete even to the depression in the centre, 'Nidiformis' is an excellent ornamental of graceful habit and useful garden proportions. A ten years' growth period would produce a plant of 1.5m (5ft) across by 1m (3ft) high if planted in the open, but it will draw up higher in semi-shade to make a plant of more equal proportions. It is sometimes listed as *Chamaecyparis* x *nidifera* because of its supposed hybrid parentage of *Chamaecyparis lawsoniana* and *Chamaecyparis nootkatensis*.   Hardiness 5.

103 *Chamaecyparis lawsoniana* 'Pottenii'. Winter.
Ashburton, New Zealand.

Chamaecyparis lawsoniana 'Pembury Blue'

102 Of very recent introduction, this cultivar seems to have outdone all its rivals in being the bluest of all lawson cypresses. It is somewhat similar in habit to its nearest competitor, the very popular 'Columnaris', but grows rather wider and looser in habit than that cultivar, making an erect bush that can be expected to measure 3m by 1m wide (10ft by 3ft) in ten years. It is its best in the cool climates that all members of this species seem to prefer.   Hardiness 5.

Chamaecyparis lawsoniana 'Pottenii'

103 Quite distinct among the many green forms of *Chamaecyparis lawsoniana*, 'Pottenii' always has a well-groomed appearance, grows in a pointed oval shape, and is abundantly furnished with sprays of medium-green foliage which nods at the extreme tips. It is best grown as a lawn specimen or used as a background tree where it can grow to its full height of 6m (2ft). For ten years' growth it should reach 3m (10 ft) in height by 1m (ft) wide. Colder climates produce a narrower and more erect specimen.   Hardiness 5.

104 *Chamaecyparis lawsoniana* 'Pygmaea Argentea'. Spring. Wisley, Surrey, England.

105 *Chamaecyparis lawsoniana* 'Rogersii'. Spring. San Francisco, USA.

106 *Chamaecyparis lawsoniana* 'Silver Queen'. Spring. Auckland, New Zealand.

Chamaecyparis lawsoniana 'Pygmaea Argentea'

104 In type very similar but even of slower growth than the 'Nana' forms, 'Pygmaea Argentea' makes little more than 40cm (15in) in height and width for ten years' growth, while the inner foliage is a dark green; in spring and summer the outer margins of the leaf sprays are conspicuously creamy-white. Mr H. J. Welch in *Dwarf Conifers* aptly describes this effect as "the appearance of having been turned upside down when wet into a barrel of flour". It is an outstanding little gem to grace any rockery, but a little shelter from the worst of the elements will help to prevent burning at the tips. This cultivar is probably the same as that named 'Backhouse Silver'.

Hardiness 6.

Chamaecyparis lawsoniana 'Rogersii'

105 Of intermediate growth rate, 'Rogersii' would eventually grow too large for most rock gardens, and is more suited as a colour contrast plant in a planting of other evergreens. The blue-green colour is constant through the seasons, and the leaves are noticeably small, scale-like and imbricated. Young plants grow in a globular shape and in ten years should reach a diameter of 80cm (30in), but subsequent growth is more in an upward direction to make the pyramidal shape as in our illustration. Formerly known as 'Nana Rogersii', the 'Nana' has been dropped to avoid confusion with the other cultivars using that name.

Hardiness 5.

Chamaecyparis lawsoniana 'Silver Queen'

106 A highly-ornamental conifer of silvery greenish-white foliage, 'Silver Queen' is at its brightest while making new growth in the early summer months, but at any time of year it provides excellent colour highlight among a planting of darker evergreens. It makes a broad-based pyramidal shape which for ten years would reach to 3m (10ft) high by 1.2m (4ft) wide at ground level, with an ultimate height of 8m (26ft) when full-grown.

Hardiness 5.

107 *Chamaecyparis lawsoniana* 'Smithii'. Spring.
Haslemere, Surrey, England.

108 *Chamaecyparis lawsoniana* 'Snow Flurry'. Winter.
Christchurch, New Zealand.

109 *Chamaecyparis lawsoniana* 'Stewartii'. Winter.

Chamaecyparis lawsoniana 'Smithii'

107 Another delightful golden upright lawson, 'Smithii' begins life as a rather untidy shrub with planes of foliage directed in no particular direction, but after a few years begins to form into the tall golden pyramid of the illustration. The growth rate is moderate at approximately 3m (10ft) for a ten-year plant by 1.2m (ft4) wide at the base, with subsequent growth mostly in an upward direction. As for most lawsons, warmer conditions produce a looser-growing specimen.   Hardiness 5.

Chamaecyparis lawsoniana 'Snow Flurry'

108 'Snow Flurry' is a creamy-white variegated sport that occurred on a juvenile-leaved form of *Chamaecyparis lawsoniana* and was first introduced by the South Taranaki Nurseries, Hawera, New Zealand, in the mid-1960s. It is slower growing than its 10m (33ft) parent, which is just as well, and although well suited to rockery planting for a few years, would eventually outgrow such a position. Some of the original plants are now about 2m (6ft) high by 1m (3ft) wide at ten years, and it is presumed that growth will continue at this rate. The white parts are easily sun- or wind-burnt, or some shelter would be needed for this plant to look at its best.
                                                                                      Hardiness 7.

Chamaecyparis lawsoniana 'Stewartii'

109 Stewart's golden lawson is a fine specimen tree that grows in an erect pyramidal shape right from the start, usually with a distinct trunk and leader, leaving it till later in life to fill out around the base. The outer golden leaf tips droop slightly, giving the plant its elegant appearance. Since its introduction in 1920 it has become widely planted, mainly because it is one of the hardiest of the golden lawsons, and its freedom from the foliage burn which can be a big problem with golden conifers in some climates.   Hardiness 5.

Chamaecyparis lawsoniana 'Tamariscifolia'

110 This compact lawson starts life in a very informal manner with no leader, and branches that seem to have no particular ambition but to grow outwards and upwards in any direction they find convenient. As the plant become older it forms into a rounded shrub, often with a depression in the centre, and after ten years' growth the once-untidy bush is a uniform rounded specimen measuring 1.2m (4ft) across by 70cm (28in) high, a thing of beauty and at its best in a setting among large rocks. The illustration is of a plant twenty years old; grown fully exposed it has formed into an excellent rounded shape.   Hardiness 5.

110 *Chamaecyparis lawsoniana* 'Tamariscifolia'. Spring. Dunedin, New Zealand.

112 *Chamaecyparis lawsoniana* 'Versicolor'. Autumn.

111 *Chamaecyparis lawsoniana* 'Tharandtensis Caesia'. Autumn. Nelson, New Zealand.

Chamaecyparis lawsoniana 'Tharandtensis Caesia'

111 A compact bluish grey-green conifer that looks not unlike a colour variation of *Chamaecyparis lawsoniana* 'Forsteckensis'. It is reasonably dwarf in habit, attaining a height of 70cm by 80cm (25in by 30in) in ten years' growing, but any vigorous leader growths that project beyond the outline of the bush should be removed, or the plant is likely to put on excessive height and lose its dwarf characteristics.
Hardiness 5.

Chamaecyparis lawsoniana 'Versicolor'

112 A broadly pyramidal conifer which from a couple of metres away appears to be of a yellow-green colour, is found on close examination to be uniformly variegated with cream and green throughout the foliage. This makes it of value for many forms of floral work where the decorative effect of the foliage can be seen at close quarters, and it also makes a good garden specimen featuring graceful weeping branch tips. Unlike many of the lawson cultivars, this form reproduces from seed almost true to type. A ten-year plant would measure 3m by 1.5m (10ft by 5ft) wide. Hardiness 5.

Chamaecyparis lawsoniana 'Westermanii'

113 'Westermanii' eventually grows to a tree of 10m (33ft) or more, and is distinct from the other golden lawsons in the way in which the thin and flexible lemon-yellow tips project outwards and downwards in a graceful semi-weeping fashion. It makes a fine pyramidal specimen for planting on a spacious lawn, or in more crowded circumstances as a coloured backdrop for a planting of lower-growing evergreens. In ten years it is capable of reaching to 3m by 1.4m (10ft by 4½ft) in width.
Hardiness 5.

113 *Chamaecyparis lawsoniana* 'Westermanii'. Winter.

114 *Chamaecyparis lawsoniana* 'Wisselii'. Autumn. Nelson, New Zealand.

115 *Chamaecyparis lawsoniana* 'Witzeliana'. Spring. Ampfield, Hants, England.

Chamaecyparis lawsoniana 'Wisselii'

114 In the nursery this charming bluish-green conifer looks so perfect for putting in that select nook in the rockery, but unfortunately it does not stay that way for all time but steadily keeps on adding the millimetres each year. Pruning may control this to some extent, and one can produce an effective columnar form or a wide vase-shaped bush by pruning selectively. Left alone, 'Wisselii' will reach to 2m (6ft) in height by 1m (3ft) wide in ten years and continue at this rate or faster; the 15m (50ft) tall (more or less) specimen at Nymans, Handcross, Sussex is a fine example of how large this cultivar may grow. It was first introduced in 1893 from the Netherlands. A dwarf form known as 'Wisselii Nana' has been developed, but is known to revert to 'Wisselii' rather easily.   Hardiness 5.

Chamaecyparis lawsoniana 'Witzeliana'

115 A columnar lawson of striking dark green colour and neatly erect habit, 'Witzeliana' is an excellent "vertical effect" conifer of strong character, of value for formal or informal plantings. It is slower growing, darker and more compact than the similar 'Erecta', making height to 2m by 50cm (6ft by 20in) in ten years.   Hardiness 6.

Chamaecyparis lawsoniana 'Yellow Transparent'

116 An interesting sport in that it is a clear yellow development from the *Chamaecyparis lawsoniana* 'Fletcheri', 'Yellow Transparent' shows its colour best with the light shining through the foliage. The colour is at its brightest during and after fresh growth, and winter finds it more brownish than yellow in colour. In growth it seems slower than its parent, giving it a ten-year height of 1.8m by 80cm (5¾ft by 30in) wide.   Hardiness 6.

Chamaecyparis nootkatensis 'Aurea'
Golden Alaska Cedar.

117 The Nootka or Alaska Cedar is a native of the northwest coast of America and is noted for its extreme hardiness and ability to thrive in damp low-lying ground and along the banks of streams. It grows to 30m (100ft) in its native habitat, but the golden-foliaged cultivar shown here is of slower and more compact growth and produces its brightest show of colour in the spring and summer. The adult foliage is distinct from that of the *C.lawsoniana* group in being altogether more coarse and possessing a raspy feel to the touch. This slower-growing golden form would make a height of 2m by 80cm wide (6ft by 30in) in ten years.   Hardiness 4.

116 *Chamaecyparis lawsoniana* 'Yellow Transparent'.

117 *Chamaecyparis nootkatensis* 'Aurea'. Spring. Boskoop, Netherlands.

118 *Chamaecyparis nootkatensis* 'Pendula'. Spring. Haslemere, Surrey, England.

119 *Chamaecyparis obtusa.* Leaf and cone details.

Chamaecyparis nootkatensis 'Pendula'

118 This weeping form of the Alaska Cedar is a beautiful tree, ideally suited to waterside planting, by reason not only of its aesthetic suitability to such location, but also of its physical ability to grow happily in such 'wet-feet' conditions. It makes a fine weeping specimen tree of up to 10m (33ft) reaching to 3m by 1m (10ft by 3ft) in the first ten years.   Hardiness 4.

Chamaecyparis obtusa   Hinoki Cypress

119 One of the five most important trees in Japan, *C. obtusa* is found there in vast natural and planted forests, the timber being of excellent durability, easily worked and capable of taking on a high quality finish. In its native state it can reach to 50m (165ft), given a century or two, but as an ornamental the greatest interest has been shown in the compact and dwarf forms, most of which originated in Japan, along with the age-old practice of artificial dwarfing or bonsai culture. Of note among identification features of this species are the obtuse leaf scales, whitish X-markings on the leaf reverse, and globose cones 10mm ($\frac{1}{3}$in) in diameter. This species and many of the cultivars take on a brownish colour during winter.   Hardiness 3.

120 *Chamaecyparis obtusa* 'Albovariegata'. Summer. Hastings, New Zealand.

121 *Chamaecyparis obtusa* 'Caespitosa'. Spring. Washington, DC, USA.

122 *Chamaecyparis obtusa* 'Coralliformis'. Spring. Washington, DC, USA.

Chamaecyparis obtusa 'Albovariegata'

120 This slow-growing variegated Hinoki Cypress with its semi-open habit and irregular splashes of creamy-white has a height potential of 1m (3ft) in ten years, by 50cm (20in) in width. The few conifer books that list this cultivar usually add, "no longer in cultivation", but in New Zealand there are several old specimens up to 4m (13ft) high and possibly fifty years old, as well as the occasional plant seen in gardens and nurseries. It often goes under the name of 'Tonia', which rather belongs to a more compact but also variegated plant with the habit and dark-green colour of 'Nana Gracilis' (of which it is a sport). Specimens sent to Mr H. G. Hillier brought the reply that this appears to be the cultivar last mentioned in writings by Beissner in 1884, and which was thought to have since become lost to cultivation in Europe. It has a hardiness rating of 4, and turns a decided brown colour in cold areas.

Chamaecyparis obtusa 'Caespitosa'

121 One of the tiniest of dwarf conifers, one of several miniatures raised at the Red Lodge Nurseries near Southampton prior to World War I from seed which set on a plant of *Chamaecyparis obtusa* 'Nana Gracilis'. A ten-year plant of 'Caespitosa' would barely reach a diameter of 10cm (4in) by 7cm (2¾in) high, a flattened irregular mound of rich green, with foliage held in tiny fans pressed tightly one against the other. It is not surprising that most possessors of this midget prefer to grow their specimen in a pot, which also makes it easier to give the plant protection from extremes in exposure to which it seems more sensitive than its larger brothers.

Hardiness 6.

Chamaecyparis obtusa 'Coralliformis'

122 An easily-distinguished member of the *C. obtusa* or Hinoki Cypress group and an interesting plant to have rambling among rocks, with its semi-prostrate habit and curious threadlike growths that twist about in all directions. It builds up into a bush in time, and by ten years should attain a height and width of 70cm (28in).

Hardiness 4.

123 *Chamaecyparis obtusa* 'Crippsii'. Winter.
Ashhurst, New Zealand.

Chamaecyparis obtusa 'Crippsii'
Golden Hinoki Cypress.

123 The well-known Golden Hinoki Cypress is a tree of beautiful form and colour and makes a broad pyramid of bright golden colour throughout spring, summer and autumn, while winter sees it a little less bright yet still a good yellow. Young plants often tend to be of loose and open habit and can be encouraged to furnish better by a shortening back of all the branches. In ten years it is cap-able of reaching 3m by 1.2m (10ft by 4ft) wide, with an ultimate of 10m (33ft).   Hardiness 5.

124 *Chamaecyparis obtusa* 'Fernspray Gold'. Summer.
Rotorua, New Zealand.

Chamaecyparis obtusa 'Fernspray Gold'
Golden Fernspray Cypress.

124 A name has finally been fixed for this beautiful Hinoki, quite distinct from 'Tetragona Aurea', as it is of similar foliage to 'Filicoides' with the same arching near-horizontal fernlike sprays, but in a rich yellow-gold colour. It has for some years been known in New Zealand as 'Tetragona Aurea', but that name has been allotted to the more erect form with upward-facing tips, to be in line with nomenclature in Britain and Europe. It can make a bush of 2m (6ft) in height in ten years, by 1.2m (4ft) wide.   Hardiness 5.

Chamaecyparis obtusa 'Filicoides'
Fernspray Cypress.

125 The Fernspray Cypress is endowed with a unique type of moss-green fernlike foliage of graceful arching form, but unfortunately does not have the right habit to set it off. It is inclined to grow into a rather open, untidy small tree, poorly furnished with foliage; but one may help to overcome this by keeping long growth cut back hard, thus forcing the plant to use its vigour for pro-duction of leaf rather than wood. It is not a dwarf, but by virtue of hard pruning it could almost be kept as one. Normal growth would find it up to 1.5m (5ft) in ten years, by 1m (3ft) wide.   Hardiness 4.

Chamaecyparis obtusa 'Intermedia'

126 Another 'Red Lodge' seedling, which as the name suggests, is an intermediate in form between the tight-growing midget 'Caespitosa' and the looser-growing 'Juniperoides', and like all of these pygmies, in no hurry to get up in the world. A growth rate of 15cm (6in) in ten years is about the maximum for 'Intermedia', which gives it enough size to be able to fend for itself on a rockery, where it will certainly give its owner no worries about outgrowing its location.   Hardiness 5.

125 *Chamaecyparis obtusa* 'Filicoides'. Foliage detail.

126 *Chamaecyparis obtusa* 'Intermedia'. Spring. Washington, DC, USA.

127 *Chamaecyparis obtusa* 'Juniperoides'. Spring. Washington, DC, USA.

128 *Chamaecyparis obtusa* 'Kosteri'. Spring. Wisley, Surrey, England.

Chamaecyparis obtusa 'Juniperoides'

127 'Juniperoides' may be described as being very similar to the well-known 'Nana' but is very slow-growing, and more compact in all its parts. For ten years a height of 15cm (6in) would be as much as one could expect, so a position of security on a rockery and away from where big feet are likely to tread is a must for this little gem. It holds a good rich green colour, and the dainty decurving sprays of foliage give it an air of elegance and charm.   Hardiness 5.

Chamaecyparis obtusa 'Kosteri'

128 In my opinion, this is the most elegant member of the Hinoki Cypress family. 'Kosteri' has a delightfully informal habit of growth composed of large fans of lush green foliage, curiously twisted with one side up and the other down, the whole plant building itself up with layer upon layer of foliage in a most attractive manner. It is inclined to be somewhat sprawling in habit, but with a little training one may produce the more erect type of specimen, as seen in the illustration. In foliage and growth it can be described as an intermediate in form between 'Nana' and 'Pygmaea'. A ten-year specimen would reach to 80cm (30in) in height by the same in width.
                                        Hardiness 5.

Chamaecyparis obtusa 'Lycopodioides'

129 'Lycopodioides' is of a foliage type unique among the Hinoki Cypress family in that it is of quite thick cordlike texture, freely branching from the stems in every direction, so that the whole plant has the appearance of being haphazardly clothed in dense clusters of rich green foliage. It grows in an irregular shape with a sparse and open branching habit but a better shaped bush may be had by cutting back the longer branches and encouraging the plant to bush out. Cockscomb-like fasciated growths are usually present among the foliage or on the growing tips. A slow grower, in ten years it should attain a height of 1m (3ft) by the same in width.
                                        Hardiness 5.

129 *Chamaecyparis obtusa* 'Lycopodioides'. Foliage detail. Summer.

Chamaecyparis obtusa 'Lycopodioides Aurea'

130 This is a colour variation of the preceding cultivar 'Lycopodioides' with a lemon-yellow colour carried on those parts most exposed to the light. It has the same informal growth habit but is a little slower to grow.　　　　Hardiness 5.

Chamaecyparis obtusa 'Mariesii'

131 'Mariesii' is an attractive slow-growing cream-and-white-variegated Hinoki which in time will build up into a pyramidal shrublet of 1m (3ft) in height, and cloak itself in summer in a brilliant creamy-white, moderating to yellowish-green for the winter. It can be classed among the true dwarfs, and in ten years would probably reach little higher than 30cm (12in) by as many wide, tending to grow somewhat too open unless the stronger growths are periodically nipped back to encourage bushing.　　　　Hardiness 5.

131 *Chamaecyparis obtusa* 'Mariesii'. Autumn. Te Kuiti, New Zealand.

130 *Chamaecyparis obtusa* 'Lycopodioides Aurea'. Spring. Haslemere, Surrey, England.

132 *Chamaecyparis obtusa* 'Minima'. Spring. Washington, DC, USA.

Chamaecyparis obtusa 'Minima'

132 The smallest of the 'Red Lodge' seedlings, and probably the most compact conifer in the world, nothing more than a ball of green foliage consisting of a mass of tightly-packed leaves, tetragonal (i.e. four-sided) in section, and rather like a green pincushion to look at. Its growth for ten years would be no more than 6cm (2½in) in height by 10cm (4in) in width, if that. The plant in the photograph is about 25cm (10in) wide and 12cm (4¾in) high and is probably old enough to be a grandfather, growing happily outdoors in the rockery in the Gotelli collection in Washington, DC.　　　　Hardiness 5.

58

CHAMAECYPARIS

133 *Chamaecyparis obtusa* 'Nana'. Autumn. Wanganui, New Zealand.

134 *Chamaecyparis obtusa* 'Nana Aurea'. Summer. Hastings, New Zealand.

Chamaecyparis obtusa 'Nana'

133 Grown by the Japanese for centuries, and in use in the Western world for more than 100 years, 'Nana' is still a much sought-after dwarf conifer for rockery, bonsai or miniature garden use. Some of the oldest specimens have not yet reached a height of 1.5m (5ft) yet approach the age of 100 years, but are wide, bushy and densely-furnished specimens with a grandeur about them that commands instant respect. The foliage is a dark green colour and is haphazardly yet artistically arranged in curved upward-facing fans. 'Nana' normally makes a shrub that is more broad than high, reaching in ten years little more than 25cm (10in) each way. Hardiness 4.

Chamaecyparis obtusa 'Nana Aurea'

134 As the name would suggest, this is a golden-leaved form of the preceding cultivar 'Nana'. It has the same attractive fan-type foliage but is of a more open habit and faster rate of growth. Specimens of 3m (10ft) in height are known to exist and are probably ninety years of age. Spring and summer see the brightest colour display when the new growth of bright golden yellow is being added, and this colour persists until the winter frosts give the more exposed parts a tinge of bronze that adds to the beauty of the plant. A ten-year specimen should reach to 50cm (20in). in height by 30cm (12in) in width. Hardiness 5.

Chamaecyparis obtusa 'Nana Gracilis'

135 This is by far the most widely-planted green form among the 'Nana' group and in fact is often supplied with part of its name missing, as 'Nana', the two names having been confused somewhat in the nursery trade. Adult plants are not difficult to tell apart, however. 'Nana Gracilis', a more vigorous grower, has a potential height of up to 2.5m (8ft) with a width of 1m (3ft), and the leaf sprays, of a lustrous dark green, are arrayed in more loosely-held fans that are rather more flat than cupped, as with 'Nana'. In ten years it can attain a height of 1m by 40cm (3ft by 15in) in width, an essential subject for any rockery, yet not too small for inclusion in the garden border as a rich green contrast to brighter colours. Hardiness 5.

Chamaecyparis obtusa 'Pygmaea'

136 In 'Pygmaea' we have another distinct and attractive form of *Chamaecyparis obtusa* in which the foliage is composed of large open fans held mainly in a horizontal plane with conspicuous orange-brown stems standing out among the green foliage, these stems being always more plentiful towards the top of the plant. In autumn and winter it turns a bronze-green colour with the cold. A ten-year plant can be expected to have reached a height of 45cm (17in) and spread to 70cm (28in) across. A delightfully informal plant, always looking very much at home among rocks and pebbles. Hardiness 5.

Chamaecyparis obtusa 'Repens'

137 'Repens', as its name indicates, is a low spreading form which has an approximate reach of 75cm by 30cm in height (30in by 12in) for a ten-year period of growth. It was developed in a nursery in the Netherlands from a sport that occurred on a plant of 'Nana Gracilis' and carried the same fan type of foliage of a bright green colour. A wonderful ground cover plant, provided one does not have too large an area to cover. Hardiness 5.

135 *Chamaecyparis obtusa* 'Nana Gracilis'. Spring. Adelaide, South Australia.

136 *Chamaecyparis obtusa* 'Pygmaea'. Spring. Washington, DC, USA.

138 *Chamaecyparis obtusa* 'Rigid Dwarf'. Spring. Washington, DC, USA.

137 *Chamaecyparis obtusa* 'Repens'. Spring. Washington, DC, USA.

143 *Chamaecyparis p...*
Boskoop, N...

144 *Chamaecyparis pisife...*
Palmerston Nort...

Chamaecyparis obtusa 'Rigid Dwarf'

138 Formerly known as 'Rigida' but altered to comply with the rules of nomenclature, 'Rigid Dwarf' can be described as like a 'Nana' that has grown stiff and upright, and the fan-shaped foliage is of a dark, almost black-green colour. It is an excellent subject of high ornamental value that is somewhat hindered in becoming a top seller in the trade by its slow rate of increase. Hardiness 5.

Chamaecyparis obtusa 'Sanderi'

139 One may be excused for not including this plant in the Hinoki Cypress group as it looks so totally unlike any other plant of this species. When first introduced it carried the name of *Juniperus sanderi*, and later was reclassified among the *C. obtusa* (whether correctly or not has yet to be proved); however, in appearance and juvenile foliage it is most like *Thuja orientalis* 'Juniperoides' with rather more sturdy stem, branches and leaves and a slower, more regular growth habit. The foliage in summer is a lovely soft blue-green, changing with winter cold to a purplish colour that looks most effective among other low evergreens of contrasting shades of yellow gold or bronze. The average height for ten years would be 1m by 80cm (3ft by 30in) wide. Hardiness 7.

139 *Chamaecyparis obtusa* 'Sanderi'. Autumn. Te Kuiti, New Zealand.

140 *Chamaecyparis obt...*
Washington...

142 *Chamaecyparis pisi...*

147 *Chamaecyparis pisifera* 'Filifera Aurea'. Spring. Palmerston North, New Zealand.

Chamaecyparis pisifera 'Filifera Aurea'

147 The Golden Thread False Cypress, as it is sometimes called, is a conifer of unique and elegant appearance, consisting of a mass of golden threadlike branchlets that weep gracefully downwards at the tips, a most effective shrub for planting in a large rockery or on a ledge where some of the foliage can weep over. In time it grows into a large shrub of up to 3m (10ft) in height, but for a ten-year period a height of 1m by 1.3m (3ft by 4¼ft) in width would be average growth, and for many years it will do excellent service on a rockery before needing to be moved on to larger quarters. Some specimens seem to have extra upright vigour while others are low and spreading; and it is thought that the selection of stronger tip or weaker side-grown cutting material for propagation has a lot to do with this apparent difference in habit.

Hardiness 5.

148 *Chamaecyparis pisifera* 'Filifera Nana'. Summer. Te Kuiti, New Zealand.

Chamaecyparis pisifera 'Filifera Nana'

148 'Filifera Nana' is a somewhat more compact grower than the Golden Thread Cypress, and makes itself very much at home among large rocks, its trailing threadlike foliage creating a weeping effect that is most attractive. It should not be mistaken for the similar but larger parent *Chamaecyparis pisifera* 'Filifera' which grows to almost tree size, and is altogether too large for rockery use, while 'Nana' has a more modest spread of 1m (3ft) in width by 30cm (12in) in height for a ten-year period.

Hardiness 5.

149 *Chamaecyparis pisifera* 'Gold Spangle'. Summer. New Plymouth, New Zealand.

Chamaecyparis pisifera 'Gold Spangle'

149 Of the same leaf colour as 'Filifera Aurea' and in fact a sport that originated from that plant, 'Gold Spangle' is a halfway compromise in foliage between the thread-leaf of 'Filifera' and the larger open leaf of the *C.pisifera* type. It grows in an attractive low rounded bush of a bright golden-yellow colour, too large to be classed as a dwarf but nevertheless an excellent colour plant in a border of assorted conifers. A ten-year plant can be expected to reach a height of 50cm by 1m (20in by 3ft) in width, and it is all the better for regular pruning to keep the plant tight and compact in habit.

Hardiness 5.

150 *Chamaecyparis pisifera* 'Nana Aureovariegata'. Autumn. Dunedin, New Zealand.

151 *Chamaecyparis pisifera* 'Plumosa'. Spring.

Chamaecyparis pisifera 'Nana Aureovariegata'

150 A similar but much more compact edition of *Chamaecyparis pisifera* 'Compressa' (not to be confused with 'Plumosa Compressa') that has the same adult foliage type yet still further reduced in dimensions. It grows into a ground-hugging bun that rarely adds more than 3cm (1in) of growth per year and a ten-year-old specimen would be no more than 30cm wide by 15cm (12in by 6in) high. There are two colour forms in this foliage type; the dark bluish-green 'Nana', and this golden form in which the variegation is not prominent due to the overall golden sheen covering the plant, particularly so in the spring and summer months.   Hardiness 5.

Chamaecyparis pisifera 'Plumosa'

151 'Plumosa' presents the first example in this book of the softer-foliaged forms of Sawara Cypress, intermediate in leaf type between the fully-adult *pisifera* and the soft, juvenile-leaved 'Squarrosa' group. The foliage is finely-divided and soft-looking but has some prickly material and this is particularly noticeable when handling pieces of dried foliage. It makes a well-furnished, conical large bush or small tree, and in ten years should have reached to 3m (10ft) in height with a base width of 1m (3ft).

Hardiness 5.

152 *Chamaecyparis pisifera* 'Plumosa Albopicta'. Foliage.

Chamaecyparis pisifera 'Plumosa Albopicta'

152 One can expect 'Plumosa Albopicta' to grow into an upright bush of about 2m by 1m (6ft by 3ft) in ten years, bearing small-leaved dark-green foliage of typical raspy *C. pisifera* type that is speckled with small patches of creamy-white. The variegation is not outstanding when viewed from a distance but 'Plumosa Albopicta' does have uses as a tub plant, as it is of suitable size and hardiness for this purpose.

Hardiness 5.

160 *Chamaecyparis pisifera* 'Squarrosa Intermedia'. Summer. Norfolk, England.

Chamaecyparis pisifera 'Squarrosa Intermedia'

160 A much compacted edition of 'Squarrosa' in which the foliage, of the same blue-grey colour, is much compressed and congested in character, resulting in a much-reduced growth rate which for ten years would produce a plant little more than 50cm (20in) round and wide. The compact rounded shape in the illustration is typical of 'Intermedia' but it is a conifer that needs to be checked periodically for growth reversion, otherwise one can finish up with a large plant more like 'Squarrosa' if a reverting shoot is left unchecked.   Hardiness 5.

Chamaecyparis pisifera 'Squarrosa Sulphurea'

161 Another variation of 'Squarrosa', this form has the soft, feathery juvenile foliage of the type and in spring and summer is liberally furnished with bright sulphur-yellow colour on all new growth — a bush of attractive form and colour which in ten years may make a height of 2m by 1m (6ft by 3ft) in width. By winter the foliage has lost most of the creamy colour to become a soft green, tinged with bronze on the more exposed parts.   Hardiness 5.

161 *Chamaecyparis pisifera* 'Squarrosa Sulphurea'. Summer.

Chamaecyparis pisifera 'Strathmore'

162 This loose-growing, low spreading *pisifera* looks at first glance more like a young specimen of some Golden Lawson with its leaf arrangement very similar to that species, but one only has to feel the raspy foliage to confirm the species. It is an attractive garden plant with a spread as wide as its height, reaching in ten years to 1.5m (5ft) with no apparent ambitions of forming a leader. The outer foliage sprays are a bright lemon-yellow the year round, and deeper inside the bush it reverts to green. We have been unable to trace this plant to its exact origin, but it came to us from a nursery in Victoria, Australia, and presumably it originated in that country.   Hardiness 6.

Chamaecyparis thyoides 'Andelyensis'

163 *Chamaecyparis thyoides*, also known as the Atlantic White Cedar, is a native of the east coast of the United States and specimens in their native state attain a height of 25m (80ft) being noted for their hardiness and ability to grow in swampy ground. The much more compact cultivar 'Andelyensis' was raised in France over 100 years ago and has the more moderate maximum height of 3m (10ft). In years past it has been a popular compact ornamental but is now largely superseded by columnar forms of more recent introduction. The foliage is predominantly adult in type, held in fans, and very free in flower and cone production, while some juvenile foliage is usually in evidence lower down on the bush. A specimen of ten years of age would attain a height of 1m by 30cm in width (3ft by 12in), of columnar shape with generally more than one leader. 'Andelyensis Nana' is yet slower growing than this cultivar, a flat-topped leaderless bush seldom reaching to more than 1m (3ft) and carrying a greater proportion of juvenile foliage.   Hardiness 4.

162 *Chamaecyparis pisifera* 'Strathmore'. Winter. Palmerston North, New Zealand.

163 *Chamaecyparis thyoides* 'Andelyensis'. Spring.
Wisley, Surrey, England.

164 *Chamaecyparis thyoides* 'Ericoides'. Winter.
Napier, New Zealand.

Chamaecyparis thyoides 'Ericoides'

164 'Ericoides' is an upright-growing conifer of wholly juvenile foliage, firm to the touch but not really prickly, and has a growth rate capable of reaching 2m by 1m in width (6ft by 3ft) in ten years. It is best suited to cool climates where growth is noticeably more compact and tidy. The period of brightest colour is during the late autumn and winter when it turns an attractive plum-purple, but when new growth commences in the spring this gives way to green, leaving but just a trace of the bronze. 'Ericoides' has often been wrongly placed in the genus *Thuja* where there are several specimens that look as though they could be twin brothers to this one; but as the ancestral records place it among the *Chamaecyparis thyoides* it should not be removed from there without good reason.   Hardiness 5.

Chamaecyparis thyoides 'Glauca'.

165 A colour selection of the type, bearing adult *thyoides* type leaf in glaucous blue-green with a looser, more open growth habit than 'Andelyensis'. It is rather slow growing, to 2m (6ft) in ten years, and is one of the few conifers that will grow in swampy conditions if so required. This one has also gone under the name 'Kewensis'.   Hardiness 4.

165 *Chamaecyparis thyoides* 'Glauca'. Spring.
Wisley, Surrey, England.

172 *Cryptomeria japonica* 'Elegans'. Winter. Nelson, New Zealand.

Cryptomeria japonica 'Elegans'

172 A juvenile-leaved form of Japanese Cedar, an erect-growing tree densely clothed in soft, non-prickly needle-type foliage. It usually has a single well-defined trunk and a maximum height of 12m (40ft) for the oldest specimens I have seen. As this variety has been in cultivation for more than 100 years they could well have been of sixty or seventy years of age. When young it seems to be a faster-growing tree and capable of reaching 3m (10ft) in ten years by 1.2m (4ft) in width, adding height at a more leisurely rate thereafter. Winter sees the plant at its most colourful, when the foliage is a rich purple-brown, a colour that lasts well into the spring until the next season's growth turns the tree bronze-green. Hardiness 6.

173 *Cryptomeria japonica* 'Elegans Aurea'. Winter. Ashburton, New Zealand.

Cryptomeria japonica 'Elegans Aurea'

173 This variation among the 'Elegans' group of cryptomeria possesses the same juvenile-type foliage and erect bushy habit of the parent plant, but instead of turning the purplish winter colour remains a light yellow-green.—In growth rate, 'Elegans Aurea' is similar to 'Elegans Compacta'—to 2.5m/by 1.5m wide (8ft by 5ft) in ten years. Hardiness 6.

174 *Cryptomeria japonica* 'Elegans Compacta'. Winter.

Cryptomeria japonica 'Elegans Compacta'

174 This is a more compact edition of the cultivar 'Elegans' and differs from its larger parent in being lower-growing with less inclination to form a strong leader. The needles are also somewhat longer in this variation, and in winter the colour is bronze rather than purple, with the stems and inner foliage remaining green. Although labelled 'Compacta' it still has plenty of vigour, the 2m (6ft) high specimen illustrated being probably no more than eight years old at the time it was photographed. Hardiness 6.

175 *Cryptomeria japonica* 'Globosa'. Autumn. Auckland, New Zealand.

Cryptomeria japonica 'Globosa'

175 This is a low-growing bun-shaped cryptomeria that is generally twice as wide as it is high, a ten-year specimen being about 40cm (15in) high and 70cm (28in) in width. The leaves are small and closely packed along the branchlets in a manner very similar to the taller-growing cultivar 'Lobbii', which no doubt explains why the plant is often seen labelled 'Lobbii Nana'. It is unfortunate that this cultivar could not change names with 'Globosa Nana' as it is the lower-growing of the two, but in any case can be distinguished from the larger by the rusty-red colour that it assumes during winter. For all this it is an excellent plant for rockery or terrace with its neatly rounded outline and gently-nodding branchlets.   Hardiness 6.

176 *Cryptomeria japonica* 'Globosa Nana'. Spring. Wellington, New Zealand.

Cryptomeria japonica 'Globosa Nana'

176 It would sometimes be easier to keep track of the botanical names of some of our conifers if we had no understanding of the meaning of Latin. For when one gets a plant labelled 'Globosa Nana' that grows bigger than 'Globosa' one begins to wonder who made the mistake. The explanation is simply that the two plants were named years apart by different people who had little knowledge of the other plant at the time. This one was christened 'Globosa Nana' and the name describes the plant well enough, but it will grow to 3m (10ft) high and as many wide, a beautiful rounded bush of flexible rich-green foliage, clothed right to ground level. It takes at least thirty years to grow a bush to this size and the first ten are the slowest with seldom more than 1m (3ft) to show for it.   Hardiness 6.

Cryptomeria japonica 'Jindai-Sugi'

177 Although this cultivar is often confused in name with 'Bandai-Sugi' there is no need for uncertainty. 'Jindai-Sugi' is larger and more open in growth with shortened internodes and nodding tips, the foliage type being regular throughout the bush. In ten years it can make a 1.2m (4ft) bush 80cm (30in) wide. It is a pleasant little shrub which retains its green colour throughout the year.   Hardiness 5.

177 *Cryptomeria japonica* 'Jindai-Sugi'. Spring. Washington, DC, USA.

178 *Cryptomeria japonica* 'Knaptonensis'. Summer.
Palmerston North, New Zealand.

179 *Cryptomeria japonica* 'Lobbii'. Summer.
Waikato, New Zealand.

Cryptomeria japonica 'Knaptonensis'

178 One of the tiniest members in the cryptomeria family and a real collector's piece, consisting of a mass of congested creamy-white foliage which in ten years will reach no more than 35cm (14in) in height. It has tendencies to revert, as our photograph would suggest, and any propagation material must be selected from predominantly white foliage in order to produce plants true to type. It should be grown in a well-sheltered position to prevent burning of the white parts by sun or frost.

Hardiness 6.

Cryptomeria japonica 'Lobbii'

179 'Lobbii' is a variation of the Japanese Cedar which forms a columnar symmetrical tree, slower-growing than the species, and with denser and more compacted foliage similar to that seen on the cultivar 'Globosa' already described. An attractive erect-growing garden conifer, it can be expected to reach in ten years a height of 3.5m (11½ft) by 1m (3ft) wide and maintain a rich green colour throughout the year.

Hardiness 5.

180 *Cryptomeria japonica* 'Monstrosa Nana'. Spring. Hilversum, Netherlands.

Cryptomeria japonica 'Monstrosa Nana'

180 This is a compact cryptomeria with a growth rate of 1m (3ft) high and the same in width for a ten-year period. 'Monstrosa Nana' is largely composed of normal needle-type foliage, from among which arise thickened stems of heavy growth topped with bunches of monstrous-type congested foliage. It is green for most of the year, turning bronze in the winter. The cultivar 'Monstrosa' is of similar habit but grows to 3m (10ft) and bears a similar but larger foliage.

Hardiness 6.

181 *Cryptomeria japonica* 'Nana'. Spring. Wilts, England.

182 *Cryptomeria japonica* 'Nana Albospica'. Spring. Washington, DC, USA.

Cryptomeria japonica 'Nana'

181 'Nana' is a compact low-growing conifer with nodding tips composed of foliage that is sometimes very fine and congested in growth, along with larger and more open-type growth with longer needles. It forms a bush of about 1m (3ft) wide and high, given about twenty-five years to do it in, and is distinct from the very similar cultivar 'Pygmaea' in that it remains green for the winter while 'Pygmaea' turns a reddish-bronze colour. Hardiness 5.

Cryptomeria japonica 'Nana Albospica'

182 Of similar habit to the preceding 'Nana', this cultivar is easily distinguished by its creamy-white variegated foliage, seen here in early spring with bud movement evidenced by specks of white at the growing tips, and which will soon extend to re-cloth the plant for the coming summer in a fresh dress of creamy-white. It is hardy enough to be grown outdoors in winter in all but the coldest climates, with the extent of the last winter's damage to be seen in the pinkish-bronze colour on the top. In ten years it would be a bush of 40cm (15in) high, 30cm (12in) wide. Hardiness 6.

Cryptomeria japonica 'Spiralis'

183 An unmistakable cultivar, 'Spiralis' is obviously so-named because of the way many of the leaves twist themselves round the branchlets, giving spiral appearance not unlike that of a wood screw. It is not only grown for its curiosity value, as it is also an excellent ornamental shrub, forming itself into a cone-shaped bush with a flattish top which in ten years would be about 50cm (20in) high and as many wide. A similar cultivar named 'Spiraliter Falcata' also has spiral-type foliage that is much more reduced in size, but grows to a taller, rather untidy bush of open habit and little ornamental value. Hardiness 5.

183 *Cryptomeria japonica* 'Spiralis'. Spring. Wisley, Surrey, England.

184 *Cryptomeria japonica* 'Vilmoriniana'. Summer. Waikato, New Zealand.

Cryptomeria japonica 'Vilmoriniana'

184 This little globular cryptomeria is one of our most popular rock garden subjects and consists of a tightly-held bundle of compacted foliage that for a ten-year plant would be about 50cm (20in) wide and 40cm (15in) high. Yearly growth is added by means of short leaders that project upward beyond the rounded surface of the bush, giving the plant its characteristic knobbly appearance. In winter it turns brownish-green and the rest of the year it is rich green, an excellent rockery conifer.

Hardiness 5.

185 *Cunninghamia lanceolata*. Spring. Hilversum, Netherlands.

Cunninghamia lanceolata   China Fir

185, 186 One finds *Cunninghamia lanceolata* to be a tall graceful tree of unusually long sharp-pointed leaves of up to 6cm (2¼in) long, glossy dark-green above and with two white bands on the underside. It is a tree of character that serves well as a lawn specimen, attaining a height of 4m (14ft) in ten years by 2m (6ft) in width and usually clothed in foliage to ground level. In Southern China where it is a native it is known to grow to 25m (80ft). It was first introduced into Britain in 1804. The cultivar 'Glauca' has a distinct glaucous bloom to the leaves and is said to be somewhat hardier than the type.   Hardiness 7.

Cupressocyparis leylandii

187 This interesting hybrid between *Chamaecyparis nootkatensis* and *Cupressus macrocarpa* has great promise as a fast-growing ornamental or shelter tree. The growth rate is quite outstanding, the 4m (14ft) specimen in the photo being a mere six years old, while average growth for a thirty-year plant is 20m (65ft) with a possibility of 30m (100ft) under ideal conditions. It has inherited the extreme hardiness of its Alaska Cedar parent and is most like that tree in leaf and habit, resembling *Cupressus macrocarpa* only in cone and seed detail. It appears to be free of diseases, will grow in almost any soil type, will tolerate 'wet feet' and has good promise as a timber tree, all features which indicate that this versatile hybrid is assured of a very bright future. Five important clones have been named, some of which are narrow and columnar in habit ('Green Spire', 'Naylor's Blue', and 'Stapehill'), while the other two are more open in growth (Haggerston Grey' and 'Leighton Green'), like the one illustrated.   Hardiness 4.

Cupressus cashmeriana   Kashmir Cypress

188 This most beautiful and elegant of all cypresses has a charm all its own and with its graceful weeping branchlets of silvery grey-green and erect pyramidal habit, is the ideal lawn specimen conifer for the medium to large garden. Growth is reasonably fast in young trees, and any surplus can be easily pruned away with no detrimental effects, so that one can produce a narrower or wider specimen as desired. Supposedly from Tibet, its native habitat has never been established with certainty. A ten-year-old specimen can be expected to reach 5m (16ft) in height by 2m (6ft) wide. To bring out the full beauty of this tree it should be planted where it will not be exposed to strong prevailing winds. Although one of the most graceful, it is unfortunately one of the least hardy of the ornamental conifers.   Hardiness 8.

186 *Cunninghamia lanceolata*. Foliage and cones.

Cupressus funebris   Chinese Weeping Cypress

189, 190 This stately weeping pyramidal tree of the considerable size potential of 20m (65ft) or more may attain quite a wide spread if given space to do so, but when, as is usually the case, it is closely planted with other trees of similar stature its habit

187 *Cupressocyparis x leylandii.* Spring. Temuka,
New Zealand.

188 *Cupressus cashmeriana.* Summer. Palmerston North,
New Zealand.

189 *Cupressus funebris.*
Winter. Toowoomba,
Queensland, Australia.

190 *Cupressus funebris.* Foliage and cones.

becomes predominantly erect. It has an average growth rate of the order of 5m (16ft)
in ten years by 2m (6ft) in width and is easily distinguished from the similar *C.
torulosa* by comparing the feel of the foliage, which, on *C. funebris*, has a raspiness
about it. Found growing wild in Central China, it is also commonly planted near
tombs and temples in that country.   Hardiness 7.

191 *Cupressus glabra.* Spring. Southport, Queensland, Australia.

192 *Cupressus glabra.* Cones, foliage and male strobilii.

Cupressus glabra   Smooth Arizona Cypress

191, 192 This is the more predominantly blue of the two forms of Arizona Cypress and up till recently most plants sold under the name of *C. arizonica* have in fact been this species, *C. glabra*. It is very variable in form and colour and can range from a muddy grey-green to shades of bluish-mauve, several of the more outstanding forms having been named; they are propagated by grafting or cutting as garden cultivars. All forms of *C. glabra* have good resistance to drought and for this reason are valued for shelter in drier areas. Capable of reaching 4m (13ft) in ten years with a width of 2m (6ft).   Hardiness 6.

193 *Cupressus glabra* 'Compacta'. Summer. Winchester, England.

Cupressus glabra 'Compacta'   Dwarf Arizona Cypress

193 This is probably the only truly dwarf member of this species in cultivation, and it makes a beautiful conical globe of tightly-compacted glaucous foliage which in ten years would have a height of about 45cm (18in) by 40cm (15in) wide. The foliage is of the typical adult type with a quadrangular cross-section to the leaf in common with the other members of this family. Normally classified as *C. arizonica* 'Compacta' or 'Nana', it is now felt that it belongs under the heading of *C. glabra* along with the rest of the cultivars in this species.   Hardiness 6.

194 *Cupressus glabra* 'Hodginsii'. Winter. Methven, New Zealand.

195 *Cupressus lusitanica* var. *benthamii*. Foliage, flower and cones.

196 *Cupressus macrocarpa* 'Aurea'. Autumn. New Plymouth, New Zealand.

Cupressus glabra 'Hodginsii'   Hodgin's Arizona Cypress

194 One of the more outstanding selections from this very variable species, 'Hodginsii' was introduced by Messrs Hodgins Nurseries of Melbourne, Australia, and is prized for its silvery glaucous foliage and erect pyramidal shape, clothed in foliage to ground level. Slower in growth than the type, it should make 4m (13ft) in ten years by 2m (6ft) wide. Three golden forms of *C. glabra* now becoming available in Australia and New Zealand are 'Aurea', 'Gold Pyramid' and 'Cannie's Golden'. The latter cultivar seems to possess the best combination of golden foliage with good compact habit. Two blue forms of recent release are 'Blue Pyramid' and 'Gareei', the latter being a Californian introduction.   Hardiness 6.

Cupressus lusitanica var. *benthamii*   Bentham Cypress

195 This most widely-grown member of the *C. lusitanica* family is a popular garden and farm-shelter tree of considerable ornamental value and is now much preferred to *C. macrocarpa* for these purposes. Its many virtues include a rapid growth rate of up to 60cm (24in) a year, healthy disease-free appearance, and its habit of spreading densely at ground level and providing protection for plants and farm stock from ground-draughts. The foliage is attractive both from a distance and close up, being fernlike and closely interspersed with yellow pollen-laden flower buds. A recently raised golden form, as yet unnamed, is at present under trial in New Zealand and promises to become an excellent garden cultivar.   Hardiness 7.

Cupressus macrocarpa 'Aurea'   Golden Monterey Cypress

196, 197 The Monterey Cypress is widely grown in Australia and New Zealand as a shelter tree and many excellent garden forms have come to light as chance seedlings or coloured sport growth on established trees in this area. This cultivar was derived in Australia from a selected green clone then called *C. lambertiana* 'Horizontalis', so-named by reason of its horizontal branch habit, the tree itself being erect and pyramidal in shape. The somewhat misleading adjective 'Horizontalis' has thankfully been dropped for this golden form, and reserved for another low-growing type more aptly suited to the name. This is an excellent conifer for large lawns, background planting or farm beautification, the bright yellow-gold extremities of the foliage contrasting with the darker green inner parts where less light penetrates. In growth it is capable of reaching 5m (16ft) in ten years by 3m (10ft) in width.   Hardiness 7.

197 *Cupressus macrocarpa*. Golden foliage mutation on an old tree.

198 *Cupressus macrocarpa* 'Aurea Saligna'. Spring.
Melbourne, Australia.

199 *Cupressus macrocarpa* 'Donard Gold'. Spring.
San Marino, California, USA.

Cupressus macrocarpa 'Aurea Saligna'

Weeping Golden Cypress

198 This form, 'Aurea Saligna', also known as 'Conybeari', is a graceful erect pyramidal tree that is clothed in long cascades of weeping threadlike golden-yellow foliage. It is a popular garden ornamental in South Australia and Victoria and is now also becoming available further afield in limited quantities. It is a first-class feature tree in a landscaped setting, and its growth rate averages about 30cm (12in) a year. Shelter from strong wind is recommended to preserve symmetrical shape. A tree that grew in the Christchurch Botanic Gardens named 'Filipendula' seemed very similar if not identical to this one but was blown out during a storm in 1968.

Hardiness 7.

Cupressus macrocarpa 'Donard Gold'

199 This is one of the best of the golden Monterey Cypresses, having a pure rich golden-yellow colour and a compact upward-facing branch system that tends to maintain the plant in its characteristic narrow conical shape. Also of similar shape and colour is an Australian-raised cultivar, *Cupressus macrocarpa* 'Brunniana Aurea'; the many fine specimens in gardens around Melbourne and Sydney attest its popularity as a garden conifer. Yet another promising golden form recently released is 'Goldcrest', which is of European origin. A growth of 4m by 1.5m in width (13ft by 5ft) would be average for ten years for either cultivar.

Hardiness 7.

200 *Cupressus macrocarpa* 'Horizontalis Aurea'. Spring. Southport, Queensland, Australia.

Cupressus macrocarpa 'Horizontalis Aurea'

200 Yet another golden form but this time a complete change of habit to something more akin to that of a Pfitzer Juniper than its Monterey Cypress parent. Once again this is an Australian cultivar and is an excellent low spreading shrub of brighter colour and faster growth than any of its juniper rivals. In ten years it can be expected to have a spread of 3m (10ft) and a height of 1m (3ft), building up more in height as it ages but easily kept within bounds by pruning any over-ambitious branches. The cultivar 'Gold Spread' appears to be very similar to this one.

Hardiness 7.

201 *Cupressus macrocarpa* 'Pygmaea'. Spring. San Francisco, USA.

202 *Cupressus sempervirens* 'Gracilis'. Summer. Auckland, New Zealand.

203 *Cupressus sempervirens* 'Stricta'. Spring. Beverly Hills, California, USA.

Cupressus macrocarpa 'Pygmaea'

201 One of the few dwarf forms to be named and propagated, 'Pygmaea' began life as a seedling in 1929 in a nursery in Surrey, England. It is a compressed bun-shaped miniature edition of the parent tree and in England makes little more than 15cm (6in) in height, but this specimen in the James Noble collection at Golden Gate Park, San Francisco, has more than doubled that size, probably because it is back in the more congenial climatic conditions of its home territory. Other miniature forms are 'Globosa' and 'Minima', the latter of juvenile-type foliage.   Hardiness 7.

Cupressus sempervirens 'Gracilis'

202 A New Zealand-raised cultivar of *Cupressus sempervirens* 'Stricta' which is far superior to seedling types, having fine threadlike foliage, fresh green colour and absence of bad habits such as "falling out" or "bushiness". As it is cutting-grown the buyer may with confidence put in a row of these and know that they will remain uniform in habit — a circumstance one cannot be sure of when dealing with seedling-raised plants. A ten-year plant should reach 3m (10ft) in height by 70cm (28in) wide.   Hardiness 7.

Cupressus sempervirens 'Stricta'   Italian Cypress, Pencil Pine

203 This erect-growing form of *C. sempervirens*, which in its native state is normally a spreading tree, has long been grown in the Mediterranean area; seedling-raised plants coming reasonably true to type if the seed is taken from selected upright forms. This method has been standard practice in nurseries for many years but now that it has become easier to produce this species from cuttings, the trend has been towards the latter method of propagation in order to produce a selected type of good form and colour. One such form is sold in California under the name of *Cupressus sempervirens* 'Glauca' and the plant illustrated could be one of these tall columnar specimens. In this case its superb vertical accent is effectively set off by a base planting of Hetz junipers. The average height in ten years would be 4m by 80cm (13ft by 30in) wide.   Hardiness 7.

204 *Cupressus sempervirens* 'Swane's Golden'. Autumn Palmerston North, New Zealand.

205 *Cupressus sempervirens* 'Swane's Golden'. Close-up of male and female strobilii.

Cupressus sempervirens 'Swane's Golden'

Swane's Golden Pencil Pine

204, 205 This superb golden form of Italian cypress is of Australian origin, being introduced by Messrs Swane Bros Nurseries of New South Wales around 1960, and is now a highly popular conifer in that country and is produced in thousands by their and other Australian, nurseries. It is a true golden colour throughout, compact and slow-growing, rarely exceeding 2m (6ft) in height, and should be planted where it is fully exposed to sunlight to bring out its best yellow-gold colour. Over-rich soils are to be avoided with all forms of Pencil Pine, as in such conditions they are apt to lose their characteristic tightness of habit and are more prone to wind damage. A height of 2m by 40cm (6ft by 15in) wide would be an average after 10 years' growth.   Hardiness 7.

206 *Cupressus torulosa*. Spring. Brisbane, Australia.

207 *Cupressus torulosa*. Foliage and cones.

208 *Dacrydium biforme.* Spring. Dunedin, New Zealand.

Dacrydium biforme

208 The genus *Dacrydium* includes twenty different species of evergreens from forest trees down to the tiniest of shrublets and is found chiefly in the countries of the South Pacific, ranging from Thailand through to Chile, with its widest representation in New Zealand. *D. biforme* is one of these New Zealand natives and is mainly found in alpine conditions. In time it may make a tree of 8m (25ft), but as an ornamental is used to best advantage as a shrub, as it is slow-growing and still likely to be under 2m (6ft) by the time it is ten years old. It makes an interesting many-branched bush of rugged outline and light-green, smooth adult foliage. Juvenile leaf is usually present lower in the bush, sometimes predominating in shade-grown plants, and consists of closely-set needle-type 8mm (⅓in) leaves, quite soft to the touch.

Hardiness 6.

209 *Dacrydium cupressinum.* Summer.

Dacrydium cupressinum   Rimu

209 This is the well-known New Zealand native rimu tree which in its earlier years makes an excellent garden ornamental with its pendulous bronzy-green branchlets, reddish-brown in winter in exposed positions but a deep rich green when grown in semi-shade. Although it is capable of growing to 60m (200ft) in the bush, this fact need not deter any person from planting one as an ornamental as he will never live to see it to that size, average growth being seldom more than 30cm (12in) a year. It is also a valuable timber tree but it is now becoming scarce as most of the old forest giants have fallen to the saw. As the rimu does not take well to transplanting, nursery specimens usually begin life in the bush, are collected when between 5cm and 15cm high (2in and 6in) and grown on to size in containers.

Hardiness 6.

210 *Dacrydium laxifolium.* Autumn. Wellington, New Zealand.

Dacrydium laxifolium   Mountain Rimu

210 This is probably the smallest conifer in the world. It begins as a rambling, prostrate, wiry-stemmed shrublet that eventually builds itself up into a ground-covering mat 12cm (5in) in height and in time spreads outwards to cover 50cm (20in) in ten years. A native of alpine areas of New Zealand, it is variable in colour from olive-green to grey-blue, and a selected bluish form is at present under trial with a view to giving it a clonal name. This and other colour forms take on a rich purplish hue with winter cold.

Hardiness 5.

Cupressus torulosa   Bhutan Cypress

206, 207 A tall, handsome, pyramidal tree from the West Himalayas that is known there to reach a height of 50m (165ft) and is popular in Australia as a fast-growing vertical accent tree. The trend in nurseries is to raise this species from cuttings using one good erect form as a stock plant to obtain uniformity of habit. The result can be seen in the many beautiful avenues of symmetrical trees in Victoria and other Australian states. One such cultivar is known as 'Arctic Green'. As a garden plant it quickly grows to ornamental size yet not too fast to become an embarrassment, and a height of 4m (13ft) could be considered normal after ten years' growth, by 1.2m (4ft) wide.

Hardiness 7.

211 *Diselma archeri.* Foliage.

212 *Fitzroya cupressoides.* Foliage.

213 *Fokienia hodginsii.* Foliage.

Diselma archeri

211 A bushy or loose-growing shrub or small tree, endemic to Tasmania and found there in mountain country at altitudes around 1,000m (3,300ft). It has minute scale-like rich-green leaves closely pressed against and concealing the slender branches, and bears tiny cones composed of only two pairs of scales, with male and female strobilii carried on different bushes. Although little known in the garden conifer world it has possibilities as an ornamental, and is estimated to reach to 2m (6ft) in ten years. It is closely allied to the genus *Fitzroya* and was, in fact at one time classified under that name.   Hardiness 6.

Fitzroya cupressoides

212 A native of Chile where it is known to grow to 50m (165ft) in height and 10m (30ft) in girth, but in colder climates usually of much humbler proportions, and it can in fact be kept to bush proportions given some annual pruning, as it is not a rapid grower. In foliage it has few similarities with other conifers, being composed of leaves variable in size and up to 5mm ($\frac{1}{4}$in) in length, set in whorls of three on the stem with two white stomatic bands marking the upper surface, the outer stems and branchlets taking on a weeping attitude. Cones, borne singly on the tips, are of the cupressus type, measure up to 10mm ($\frac{1}{3}$in) in diameter and break into nine segmenst when ripe.   Hardiness 6.

Fokienia hodginsii

213 A little-known genus, resembling *Chamaecyparis* or *Calocedrus* in foliage, which was discovered in 1908 in China in the district of Fokien and from which the name was derived. There are only two recorded species, and the other, *F. kawaii*, is so similar to *F. hodginsii* that it is not certain whether they are actually distinct. It grows to a pyramidal tree of 12m (40ft) in height by 1m (3ft) in girth, and carries flattened thuja-like foliage in medium green, bearing globose cones that open to a diameter of 2cm ($\frac{3}{4}$in).   Hardiness 8.

214 *Gingko biloba*. Autumn. Palmerston North, New Zealand.

215 *Glyptostrobus lineatus*. Foliage in autumn colour.

Gingko biloba   Maidenhair Tree

214 A tree which may to the layman seem out of place among conifers nevertheless belongs here by virtue of the similarity of its flowering characteristics to other conifers. It is a unique tree in many respects and is in fact the only surviving member of a large order of plants that was once wide spread but now exists only as fossilised remains. This most elegant tree, so-named because each leaf resembles on a giant scale the pinules of the maidenhair fern, provides excellent shade from early spring to fall and then changes slowly from its fresh green to a uniform bright golden-yellow colour that never fails to impress. Young plants may put on up to 1m (3ft) of growth in a season, but with age the tree slows down to an annual increment of about 20cm (8in) a year. One of the largest specimens in England is 30m (100ft) high and was planted over 200 years ago.   Hardiness 4.

Glyptostrobus lineatus   Canton Water Pine

215 A small deciduous conifer that bears a close resemblance to *Taxodium distichum* but differs in having glaucous foliage and pearshaped cones up to 2cm ($\frac{3}{4}$in) long, borne on short stalks. It is suitable only for mild temperate climates, yet sheds its leaves in winter, turning a rich rusty-red before the fall, and may be expected to average 40cm (15in) of growth annually. Its outstanding feature is the ability to grow in or near water, and in its native province of Canton, South China, is usually found in damp situations on the banks of streams.   Hardiness 8.

Juniperus chinensis

216 A tree that is very variable in habit in the wild state, sometimes exceeding 20m (65ft) in height in China and Japan. The plant commonly sold under the above name is a small erect conical tree with strong leader growth, usually reaching to 3 or 4m (10 or 13ft) in ten years but increasing at a slower pace thereafter. Specimens grown in windy locations often take on a picturesque weatherworn appearance, sometimes bare to the trunk on the windward side. The greater part of the foliage is adult, but inside and lower down on the bush one can usually find several sprays of prickly juvenile leaves, a feature of many members of this species. Glaucous green berries may be found on female trees, are rounded and irregular in shape, contain from two to five seeds each and average 1cm ($\frac{1}{3}$in) in diameter.   Hardiness 4.

216 *Juniperus chinensis*. Winter. Dunedin, New Zealand.

217 *Juniperus chinensis* 'Ames'. Spring. Washington, DC, USA.

218 *Juniperus chinensis* 'Aurea'. Summer. Palmerston North, New Zealand.

219 *Juniperus chinensis* 'Fairview'. Spring. Dundee, Illinois, USA.

Juniperus chinensis 'Ames'   Ames Juniper

217 A typical member of the Chinese Juniper group, 'Ames' has fine, predominantly juvenile foliage that is prickly to the touch and tapers off towards the top of the bush in a few adult scale-like leaves, with generally a few bluish-white berries among them. An attractive evergreen, it forms an upright broad-based pyramid that needs no trimming or shaping and may be expected to reach 2m (6ft) in height by 60cm (24in) wide in ten years' growth. The illustration shows the spring colour of an adult specimen growing in the Gotelli conifer collection in Washington, DC.   Hardiness 5.

Juniperus chinensis 'Aurea'   Golden Chinese Juniper

218 The difference between the adult scale-like upper foliage and prickly juvenile foliage is clearly shown in the illustration of a four-year-old specimen of this delightful golden juniper. These foliage differences stand out on younger plants of this cultivar and give a two-coloured effect of golden adult foliage and yellow-green juvenile leaves that is quite rare. It gets away to a slow start in life, making at the most 2m by 80cm broad (6ft by 30in) in ten years, but steadily adds height in the form of adult foliage so that an old plant of 6m (20ft) would be composed almost entirely of the adult type of leaf and may not be more than 1m (3ft) wide.   Hardiness 6.

Juniperus chinensis 'Fairview'   Hetz Columnar Juniper

219 Prized for its hardiness and trouble-free habit of growth, 'Fairview' bears the name of the Philadelphia nurseries where it originated as a seedling in the early 1950s. It may be expected to reach 3m (10ft) in ten years in an erect columnar habit of growth that is sometimes improved by trimming. The green colour is constant the year round and summer and autumn sees a crop of silvery-green berries freely displayed among the predominantly adult foliage. Ideal for screen plantings or as a lawn specimen.   Hardiness 4.

221 *Juniperus chinensis* 'Japonica'. Autumn. Christchurch, New Zealand.

220 *Juniperus chinensis* 'Iowa'. Spring. Dundee, Illinois, USA.

Juniperus chinensis 'Japonica'   Prickly Juniper

221 Apparently undecided whether it is a native of China or Japan, our botanical forefathers seem to have been caught with a leg in both countries when they named this prickly member of the *J. chinensis* group. It is quite variable in form and is sometimes seen growing upright with a strong leader, but the typical form is a shrub or 1.2m (4ft) high by as many wide for six years' growth, with several irregular branches rising outward from the base, clothed in very prickly juvenile-type leaf that eventually gives way to a drooping tip growth of adult foliage. It is a handy shrub that lends itself to being influenced into a variety of artistic shapes.   Hardiness 5.

Juniperus chinensis 'Iowa'   Iowa Juniper

220 A recent introduction to the already extensive range of junipers available in the United States, this is another selection by Professor F. J. Maney at the Iowa State College, and bears the name of that American State. The illustration of the container-grown specimen at the D. Hill Nursery Company, Dundee, Illinois, shows the typically erect but informal habit of growth that consists of bluish-green juvenile foliage with adult-type leaves. Growth in ten years would reach 2m by 80cm (6ft by 30in) wide. A handsome garden specimen that is ideally used to give an upright accent among a planting of low-growing evergreens.   Hardiness 4.

Juniperus chinensis 'Kaizuka'

Hollywood Juniper

222 This juniper is immensely popular in California, used there extensively for landscaping, as single specimens, or as shown here, attractively planted in a crowded row. The rich-green foliage and delightfully informal upright habit of growth are the main virtues of this plant, plus the fact that it can withstand conditions ranging from full sun in California to cold as low as —30°C (—20°F) (Zone 5). It has a medium rate of growth, to 3m (10ft)< in ten years by 1.2m (4ft) wide, but slower in colder climates. The upright shape may be modified by systematic removal of the leading growth to produce a plant wider than high, but a plant like this should never be trimmed or shorn and any cuts should be made well out of sight down by the heavier wood near the base of the plant. The leaves are scale-like and quite smooth to touch, and the rich colour is constant throughout the year. Of Japanese origin, it is also known as *J. chinensis* 'Torulosa' and is still sold under this name.

222 *Juniperus chinensis* 'Kaizuka'. Spring. Los Angeles, USA.

223 *Juniperus chinensis* 'Kaizuka Variegated'. Spring.
Los Angeles, USA.

224 *Juniperus chinensis* 'Keteleeri'. Autumn. Berries
and foliage.

Juniperus chinensis 'Kaizuka Variegated'
Variegated Hollywood Juniper

223 An interesting variant of the Hollywood Juniper that originated on a plant of 'Kaizuka' in the Monrovia Nursery, Azusa, California. It does not have the informal habit of its parent plant but prefers to be predominantly narrower and columnar in habit, without the spread of lateral branches at its base. It is also slower-growing than 'Kaizuka' and this specimen in a garden in Los Angeles is 1.8m (almost 6ft) high by 30cm (12in) wide at an estimated age of nine years. The foliage is scale-like, smooth to the touch and attractively accented with patches of creamy-yellow. The colour remains constant throughout the year. Also known as *J, chinensis* 'Torulosa Variegata' and 'Variegated Kaizuka'.   Hardiness 5.

Juniperus chinensis 'Keteleeri'

224 A hardy fast-growing pyramidal juniper that has become a popular garden plant since its raising almost seventy years ago. It quickly forms an erect darkish green bush, in ten years reaching 3m by 1m wide (10ft by 3ft), trims well and makes an admirable hedge. Each autumn sees it loaded with a crop of blue-green berries, 1–2cm ($\frac{1}{3}$–$\frac{3}{4}$in) in diameter, highly decorative in themselves, and holding their beauty for at least three to four weeks after cutting. It is probably the most heavy-fruiting of any of the female forms in this species.   Hardiness 5.

225 *Juniperus chinensis* 'Maney'. Spring. Dundee, Illinois, USA.

Juniperus chinensis 'Maney'   Maney Juniper

225 A versatile spreading juniper with fine bluish needle-type foliage that holds its branches upwards at an angle away from the centre, the Maney Juniper will occupy a space of 2m (6ft) across by 1m (3ft) high after ten years' growth. A fully exposed position is desirable to bring out a full blue colour in this plant and keep its shape to the desired low spreading profile. Taken just before the spring growth period, this plant at the D. Hill Nursery Company, Illinois, will later turn a richer blue as the foliage matures. It was selected by Professor F. J. Maney at Iowa State College and subsequently named after him.
Hardiness 3.

226 *Juniperus chinensis* 'Mountbatten'. Spring. Dundee, Illinois, USA.

227 *Juniperus chinensis* 'Obelisk'. Spring. Haslemere, Surrey, England.

Juniperus chinensis 'Mountbatten'　　　　　　Mountbatten Juniper

226 An attractive erect-growing shrub with a dense tidy habit of growth, this juniper originated as a seedling in a nursery in Canada and is valued in that country for its hardiness. The leaves are predominantly juvenile, prickly, and of a grey-green colour. This potted specimen in the D. Hill Nursery Company, Dundee, Illinois, shows the plant in early spring but before commencement of fresh growth. It may be expected to grow to 2 to 3m (6 to 10ft) in height by 1m (3ft) wide in a period of ten years, and ultimately to 5m (16ft) if not kept to size by trimming.　　　　　Hardiness 3.

Juniperus chinensis 'Obelisk'

227 A new and attractive addition among the Chinese junipers, 'Obelisk' may attain a height of 3m by 80cm wide (10ft by 30in) at the base. It tapers upwards in an irregular manner towards a pointed top that often has the curious tendency to lean a little to one side. The illustration is of a young plant of 1m (3ft) high; with age it will fill out and become somewhat smoother in outline. The juvenile-type leaf is quite large (to 2cm/⅜in) for this type, prickly, and tends to point outwards displaying the whitish inner leaf surfaces, lightening the bluish-green of the plant. It was raised from seed in 1946 at the Boskoop, Holland, nursery of F. Grootendhorst & Son.　　Hardiness 5.

Juniperus chinensis 'Pyramidalis'　　　　　　Pyramidal Juniper

228 At a glance very hard to distinguish from *J. chinensis* 'Stricta', this variety has the doubtful distinction of being the more prickly of the two. Apart from a few adult tips, all the foliage is juvenile and sharp to touch and of a blue-green colour. An average ten years' growth would see it to 2m (6ft) high, but it may eventually ascend to a dense pyramid of 5m by 2m at the base (16ft by 6ft), but does not object to a yearly trimming to keep it down to size.　　　　　　　　　Hardiness 5.

228 *Juniperus chinensis* 'Pyramidalis'. Summer. Norfolk, England.

229 *Juniperus chinensis* 'San José'. Spring. Washington, DC, USA.

230 *Juniperus chinensis* 'Stricta'. Summer. Palmerston North, New Zealand.

Juniperus chinensis 'San José'   San José Juniper

229 One of the lower-growing forms of *J. chinensis*, 'San José' has a definite place in the ground-covering department, having no ambition to grow more than 30cm (12in) high while spreading to 2m (6ft) across. It is of medium growth rate, at its best fully exposed to the elements, is very hardy, and is adaptable to growing on steep banks where adverse conditions prevail. The sage-green foliage is of both whipcord and juvenile type.   Hardiness 4.

Juniperus chinensis 'Stricta'

230 A handsome ornamental juniper, 'Stricta' is an ideal garden plant for the first fifteen years of its life, in which time it should be approaching a height of 2.5m by 1.2 m wide (8ft by 4ft). Younger plants display the excellent blue colouration as depicted in this illustration of a four-year plant; with age it becomes more green than blue. The foliage is only slightly prickly, a factor that serves to distinguish this cultivar from the preceding *J. chinensis* 'Pyramidalis', and is all juvenile except for the erect-growing tips. For reasons yet unknown it has until recently been sold in New Zealand under the name of *J. procera*, or *J.p.* 'Africana', with sometimes 'Glauca' added for good measure, and one may still find plants being offered under these names.   Hardiness 6.

Juniperus chinensis 'Variegata'

231 Apart from the creamy-yellow splashes of colour among the prickly foliage, young plants of this cultivar are identical to the preceding *J. chinensis* 'Stricta'. This similarity does not continue with age, however, and the ten-year-old specimen illustrated now bears as much adult foliage as it does juvenile, a trend that continues as the plant ages. Maximum height would be 6m (20ft) for an old plant, but 2m by 80cm wide (6ft by 30in) is the size of the plant illustrated, and pruning to keep a plant to size is beneficial in maintaining clean foliage growth. Variegation is to be found in either type of foliage and seems to be fixed within the plant as cuttings rooted from all-green foliage will, given time, usually produce creamy flecks true to type. It is commonly seen under the name 'Albovariegata'.   Hardiness 5.

231 *Juniperus chinensis* 'Variegata'. Spring. Auckland, New Zealand.

232 *Juniperus communis.* Berries and juvenile-type foliage.

Juniperus communis   Common Juniper

232 A very aptly-named Juniper, native to most of the countries of Northern and Central Europe extending as far eastward as Korea and Japan and in the other direction throughout the British Isles and on to the USA and Canada. In foliage it is distinguished by its wholly-juvenile leaf type, usually sharp-pointed and awl-shaped with a broad white band of stomata in the concave upper surface. Male and female strobilii are usually found on different plants, the female plants bearing globose berries up to 12mm (½in) in diameter, green when young and usually heavily covered in glaucous bloom. These ripen slowly, taking up to three years to turn dark blue or black, and are sometimes harvested in their green state for the extracting of oil for medicinal purposes and for the flavouring of gin and foodstuffs.   Hardiness 2.

233 *Juniperus communis* 'Compressa'. Spring. Wisley, Surrey, England.

Juniperus communis 'Compressa'

233 This living miniature with a yearly growth of no more than 5cm (2in) is just made-to-order for rockery planting, seldom reaching a height of more than 80cm (30in) and always the perfect little upright specimen, a tightly compressed replica of the Irish Juniper. The tiny dark-green 5mm (⅕in) long leaves are of juvenile type in common with other members of the *J. communis* family, with a white stomatic band marking the inner side of the leaf, and are closely packed together throughout the bush. As most of this species are prone to damage by red spider mite, it is worthwhile applying a protective spray during the summer. In ten years a height of 40cm (15in) should be reached by 10cm (4in) in width.   Hardiness 4.

Juniperus communis 'Depressa Aurea'

234 A beautiful spreading juniper that starts growth in the spring with bright butter-yellow foliage, then slowly changes to yellow-bronze as the foliage becomes mature, shading to rich bronze on some parts of the bush. The almost horizontal branches are held just above the ground at a slightly ascending angle, the tips decurving gracefully. Ten years' growth should produce a plant 1.2m (4ft) in bredth by 30cm (12in) in height, and it will continue at this rate unless kept in check by pruning, a practice that is in any case recommended for plants of this age to help maintain a consistant growth of younger foliage.   Hardiness 4.

234 *Juniperus communis* 'Depressa Aurea'. Autumn. Wanganui, New Zealand.

235 *Juniperus communis* 'Depressed Star'. Summer. New Plymouth, New Zealand.

Juniperus communis 'Depressed Star'

235 Briefly described as a green form of the preceding juniper, it differs also in having a less dominant branching system, making the plant in effect more of a ground cover than a low shrub. Several of these planted at 70cm (28in) spacings would soon grow together, providing a dense mat of clean-looking glaucous green foliage to a height of 30cm (12in) or more. The white stomatic band on the topside of each leaf and present with each member of the *J. communis* group is clearly displayed on this cultivar. It gives the plant a frosted appearance when viewed in certain light conditions. In ten years it is capable of spreading to 1.2m (4ft) wide by 40cm (15in) high.   Hardiness 4.

236 *Juniperus communis* 'Echiniformis'. Spring. Washington, DC, USA.

Juniperus communis 'Echiniformis'

236 Of similar foliage to 'Compressa', 'Echimiformis' is a slow-growing, irregularly bun-shaped bush that is probably more of a collector's item than a "must have" for the rockery. Most specimans of this cultivar in fact spend the first ten years of their life in a pot, by which time they would measure about 30cm (12in) across by 15cm (6in) in height. The plant illustrated is one of the specimens at the Gotelli collection of Dwarf and Slow Growing Conifers in Washington, DC, and is probably thirty years old or more.   Hardiness 4.

237 *Juniperus communis* 'Hibernica'. Spring. Canberra, Australia.

Juniperus communis 'Hibernica'   Irish Juniper

237 This is the well-known hardy Irish Juniper, often met with under its other name of *J. communis* 'Fastigiata', and an excellent tall columnar conifer that needs no trimming to make it "behave". One sees many inferior loose-growing forms offered under either of the above names, the reason often being careless selection of cutting-material, usually from parts of one of the more compact cultivars, such as 'Suecica Nana', which have reverted to the more open-growing type. An erect pillar of 2m by 40cm (6ft by 15in) should be the end result in ten years' growth of this cultivar.   Hardiness 4.

238 *Juniperus communis* 'Hornibrookii'. Spring. Wisley, Surrey, England.

Juniper communis 'Hornibrookii'

238 Is a prostrate grower and an excellent subject for the rock garden where it will spread itself some 1.3m (4¼ft) in diameter in the first ten years of life, at a height of 25cm (10in) or so. As the plant grows older it begins to build up in height with a corresponding reduced rate of spread, resulting in an old specimen looking much different in habit to its younger fully-prostrate twin brother. The leaves are short and quite prickly, having also a characteristic twist to them that tends to display the white stomatic bands along the inner keel, this effect being more noticeable towards the centre of the plant. Hardiness 4.

239 *Juniperus communis* 'Repanda'. Autumn. Dunedin, New Zealand.

Juniperus communis 'Repanda'

239 A fast-growing clean-looking prostrate juniper that is an excellent ground cover plant, forming in ten years a low mound of mid-green foliage with a diameter of 2m by 25cm high (6ft by 10in), and with 'Hornibrookii', previously described, shares the same habit of building itself upwards with age. The foliage is quite soft to the touch, the branches flexible and light brown in colour, and the leaves, no more than 6mm (¼in) in length, tend to lie close to the stems, giving the plant a neat and well-clothed appearance.   Hardiness 4.

240 *Juniperus communis* 'Silver Lining'. Spring. Devizes, Wilts, England.

Juniperus communis 'Silver Lining'

240 A prostrate juniper that previously had been classified as a form of var. *saxatilis* but has now been given the above cultivarietal name by Mr Welch, to whom we are much indebted for his work in the sorting out of many conifer name problems. It is rather like the cultivar 'Hornibrookii' in habit and type, but carries a larger (to 8mm/⅓in) leaf with conspicuously glaucous stomata that are visible in those leaves directly facing the viewer, giving a silvery effect which no doubt was the reason for the above name. It is a reasonably fast grower and can be expected to cover about 1.5m (5ft) in ten years.
Hardiness 4.

241 *Juniperus communis* 'Suecica'. Spring. Boskoop, Netherlands.

242 *Juniperus communis* 'Suecica Nana'. Spring. Christchurch, New Zealand.

243 *Juniperus communis* 'Vase'. Spring. Dundee, Illinois, USA.

Juniperus communis 'Suecica'　　　　　　　Swedish Juniper

241 This is the plant mentioned earlier under the heading 'Hibernica'. Though similar in leaf detail and general appearance, it is faster growing, and makes a wider and more open bush than that cultivar. It is found wild in Scandinavia and East Russia and it is possible that more than one form has found its way into the trade, thus creating some confusion through non-uniformity of type. In ten years it is capable of reaching to 2.5m (8ft) in height by 70m (28in) in width. 　　Hardiness 3.

Juniperus communis 'Suecica Nana'

242 In the scale of compactness among the *J. communis* cultivars this one must take second place behind 'Compressa', mentioned earlier, as it can reach a height of 2m (6ft) if given sufficient time. Young plants however have the appearance of being more compact because of the extreme closeness of the foliage, giving an impression that the plant has been shorn regularly. It has a tendency to occasionally throw out vigorous reverting growths from the top or sides and if not removed promptly will soon ruin the uniform shape of the plant. It would be very convenient if cuttings taken from such growths produced plants true to the compact parent type, but in fact they do not, as many a nurseryman has found to his dismay. Any such plants should be labelled 'Suecica' without the 'Nana' added. It appears that this is the same plant as the one known as 'Columnaris' and it is likely that this name will prove to be the one finally accepted for this cultivar. 　　Hardiness 3.

Juniperus communis 'Vase'　　　　　　　Vase Shape Juniper

243 This juniper has the rare habit of holding its branches upwards at a more or less uniform angle of 60 degrees from the ground to produce a specimen having a wide flattish top with a depression in the centre, this giving rise to the apt name of Vase Juniper. It was introduced by the D. Hill Nursery Company, of Dundee, Illinois, USA, and it is of typical prickly juvenile *J. communis*-type leaves, the general colour effect being a soft bluish-green. It is an excellent hardy juniper, much used as a foundation plant in the USA and Canada. A ten-year-old plant would be 1.7m (5½ft) high and as many wide. 　　Hardiness 3.

Juniperus conferta   Shore Juniper

244 Coming from Japan where it is found among sand dunes in coastal areas, *Juniperus conferta* could be used more this way in other countries. It is no trouble to grow it inland apart from some risk of damage to the foliage in heavy frost areas. In ten years it should form a mat 2m (6ft) wide, building up in places to 30cm (12in), the outer tips prostrate and weaving round large rocks or trailing over ledges. It is very similar in all respects to *J. taxifolia* var. *lutchuensis* but has longer, sharper needles than that variety. This variety has in the past been propagated from seed but the cutting method is now the more common.
Hardiness 5.

244 *Juniperus conferta.* Spring. London, England.

Juniperus davurica 'Expansa'

245 A robust wide-spreading low shrub that at first glance looks more like a ground-cover plant. It does however possess a strong rigid horizontal branching system that maintains the foliage a little above the ground. I imagine it to be the ideal plant for those who like to regularly push-hoe around their shrubs as with this one there would be no embarrassment of getting tangled up with ground-hugging branches that may have rooted down into the soil. This plant has been plagued by more than one name change; the two most used in the past are *J. squamata* var. *parsonii* or *J. chinensis* var. *parsonii*. In ten years a spread of up to 1.7m (5½ft) wide by 60cm (24in) in height may be expected, with a greater build-up in height as the plant ages.   Hardiness 4.

245 *Juniperus davurica* 'Expansa'. Spring. Washington, DC, USA.

Juniperus davurica 'Expansa Variegata'

246 This is the better of the two known variegated forms of the preceding juniper and like that one carries a mixture of adult and prickly juvenile foliage in roughly equal proportions. These two foliage types can be clearly seen in the photograph along with the creamy-white variegations which are evenly distributed throughout the bush. This one is still around under its old name of *J. squamata* 'Variegata'. It has a growth rate similar to the green one. The other variegated form, known as *J. davurica* 'Expansa Aureospicata', has butter-yellow variegations, carries mainly juvenile foliage, and has a less vigorous growth habit.   Hardiness 4.

246 *Juniperus davurica* 'Expansa Variegata'. Spring. Dundee, Illinois, USA.

247 *Juniperus deppeana* 'Conspicua'. Spring. Dural,
NSW, Australia.

248 *Juniperus horizontalis* 'Admirabilis'. Spring.
Washington, DC, USA.

Juniperus deppeana 'Conspicua'   Alligator Juniper

247 A beautiful silvery-blue juniper that is much prized as a garden plant in
Australia, where it usually goes under the name of *J. pachyphloea* 'Conspicua'. Some
further research may need to be done on this one as this particular clone has
predominantly adult foliage while the botanical authorities claim it to be a juvenile-
leaved form. Nonetheless it is an excellent garden conifer for warmer climates and
makes a height of 1.8m by 60cm wide (almost 6ft by 24in) in ten years' growing. On
older trees the reddish-brown bark is divided into small squarish scaly plates giving
rise to the name of Alligator Juniper. It is a native of Mexico.   Hardiness 7.

Juniperus horizontalis 'Admirabilis'

248 There are almost twenty named clones of the hardy
prostrate-growing *J. horizontalis* from North America
and there is much confusion over correct naming within
this group. There is no such problem with 'Admirabilis',
as it is reasonably distinct in its habit of lying its main
branches flat on the ground while holding the side
branches and foliage upwards and away from the ground,
giving the plant an average height of 12cm (5in) on level
ground. The foliage is all juvenile, green and heavily
bloomed, giving an overall colour effect of greyish-green.
It is lush-growing ground-cover of high ornamental value
that can spread to a diameter of 3m (10ft) in ten years.
This form is a male clone, but is otherwise similar to
'Emerson', a female clone.   Hardiness 4.

249 *Juniperus horizontalis* 'Bar Harbor'. Winter. Dunedin, New Zealand.

Juniperus horizontalis 'Bar Harbor'

249 One of the finer-leaved forms of *J. horizontalis* that
shares with 'Admirabilis' the habit of holding its side
branches upwards and away from the ground, giving a
lush "deep-pile carpet" effect. It has thin, flexible main
stems that easily follow the contours of the ground or
weave gracefully between rocks, but its most outstanding
feature is the mauve it assumes in the autumn after having
been touched by the cold of the first frosts. This colour is
clearly seen in the photograph which is quite unretouched.
At other times of the year it is a greyish-green colour with
a brownish tinge to the tips. An average spread of 40cm
(15in) a year can be expected.   Hardiness 4.

250 *Juniperus horizontalis* 'Douglasii'. Winter. Nelson, New Zealand.

Juniperus horizontalis 'Douglasii'   Waukegan Juniper

250 This is another strong-growing ground-cover juniper, similar in growth habit to 'Bar Harbor', having the same tendency for the branchlets to hold themselves in a haphazard, semi-erect manner away from the sparsely-clad main stems. The compact partly-juvenile foliage, of a greyish blue-green in the growing seasons, turns a richer purplish-blue as winter cold sets in. Once again this is a first-class ground-cover plant that averages 40cm (15in) of growth a year, building up a little to 30cm (12in) in height as the plant matures.   Hardiness 4.

251 *Juniperus horizontalis* 'Glauca'. Winter colour on vigorous tip growth.

Juniperus horizontalis 'Glauca'   Blue Creeping Juniper

251 Here we have a completely prostrate variant of *J. horizontalis* that lays its foliage flat on the ground in overlapping layers to a depth of a few centimetres but building up with age, completely covering the earth in a living carpet of blue-green foliage. The main branches are sturdier and straighter-running than with other cultivars, and the foliage is mainly scale-like or whipcord in type, with occasionally a few juvenile leaves further in the plant. A width of 2m (6ft) would be average growth for a ten-year plant.   Hardiness 4.

252 *Juniperus horizontalis* 'Glomerata'. Spring. Washington, DC, USA.

Juniperus horizontalis 'Glomerata'

252 A drawf among the other wide-spreading carpet-like members of the *J. horizontalis* family, 'Glomerata' has little more ambition than to send up short 15cm (6in) high green tuft-like growths of foliage from its prostrate main stems to result in an annual rate of spread of little more than 10cm (4in). It is a green colour in the growing season but changing, in common with other members in this group, to purplish for the winter.   Hardiness 3.

259 *Juniperus x media* 'Blaauw'. Autumn. Auckland,
New Zealand.

260 *Juniperus x media* 'Blue Cloud'. Autumn. Palmerston North, New Zealand.

Juniperus x media 'Blaauw'   Blaauw's Juniper

259 This is an attractive blue-green juniper that throws up strong branches from its
base at an angle of roughly 60 degrees to the ground, densely clothed in fine scale-like
foliage on very short branchlets. This specimen in the Eden Gardens, Auckland,
New Zealand, would be five years old, 70cm (28in) high and as many wide. Growth
slows down and the plant fills out with age so that the ultimate reach would be 1.5m
(5ft) in ten years. This photograph shows the autumn colour of the plant, while in
spring it is more green than blue, due to the growth of new foliage. This plant was
originally known as *J. chinensis* 'Blaauw's Variety', and introduced from Japan by
the firm of Blaauw & Co., Netherlands.   Hardiness 5.

Juniperus x media 'Blue Cloud'   Blue Cloud Juniper

260 One may be forgiven for thinking that there are too many very similar bluish
Pfitzer-type junipers around, but this one has its distinguishing characteristics and
need not be confused with any other. It has a lower profile altogether than the
Blue Pfitzer, and lends itself well to mass planting to do very effectively the work of
a ground cover. The thin, almost-horizontally-set branch tips twist and snake in an
unusual yet picturesque way, with little of the arching or nodding habit of the other
Pfitzers, and the colour, as its name suggests, is a soft bluish-grey. One may expect a
1.5m (5ft) spread and 50cm (20in) height from a ten-year-old plant.   Hardiness 4.

261 *Juniperus x media* 'Globosa Cinerea'. Spring. Wisley,
Surrey, England.

Juniperus x media 'Globosa Cinerea'

261 This is another importation from Japan, very similar in foliage and habit to
Blaauw's Juniper but differing from that cultivar in not having the same vigorous
leader growth, thus giving the branch tips a more rounded appearance. The colour is
a blue-green but leaning more toward green than 'Blaauw', and yellowish-green in
winter. This specimen, photographed at Wisley, England, shows the plant in early
spring growth. In ten years a plant should reach a height of 1m by 70cm wide
(3ft by 28in). It was mis-named 'Globosa' by the original Japanese suppliers, and it
was later realised that the typical globose habit of the original imported plants was
due to the skilled use of the pruning knife rather than natural growth habit.

Hardiness 5.

262 *Juniperus x media* 'Gold Coast'. Summer. Los Angeles, USA.

Juniperus x media 'Gold Coast'
Gold Coast Juniper

262 This seems to be the ultimate in golden Pfitzer-type junipers, and probably the one that will eventually supplant most of the other golden forms when it becomes well known. To quote from the Monrovia Nursery catalogue: "Foliage has most outstanding golden colouring to be found, retained and deepens better than any other gold-tipped varieties. Moderate grower, making trimming almost unnecessary." It is a patented plant and must be sold with the patent tag attached. The foliage is fine and lacy, and in growth it is more bushy and compact than the type.   Hardiness 5.

263 *Juniperus x media* 'Hetzii'. Spring. Los Angeles, USA.

Juniperus x media 'Hetzii'   Hetz Blue Juniper

263 A beautiful juniper with silvery blue green foliage, it is often confused with the similar *J. x media* 'Pfitzeriana Glauca'. Two features set it apart from that plant, however — its generally more upright habit of growth to 2m (6ft) wide and high in ten years, and the smoother feel of its scale-like foliage, which is less prickly than that of the 'Blue Pfitzer' juniper. Usually a few juvenile leaves are to be found towards the inside of the plant. It is a fine hardy conifer for colour accent, showing up well against the darker evergreen colours of green and brown.
                    Hardiness 4.

264 *Juniperus x media* 'Mint Julep'. Summer. Auckland, New Zealand.

Juniperus x media 'Mint Julep'

264 First introduced by the Monrovia Nursery Company, California, in 1961, 'Mint Julep' has rapidly gained popularity in California for its qualities as a vigorously growing, spreading conifer with rich mint-green foliage. Similar to 'Pfitzeriana' but of a more compact habit and with a neater outline, it is a tidy grower that needs no trimming to keep it in shape, which would be roughly 1.2m (4ft) wide by 70cm (28in) high for a ten-year-old plant. Very hardy, it will display its rich green foliage equally well in full sun or in partial shade.
                    Hardiness 4.

265 *Juniperus x media* 'Old Gold'. Spring. Washington, DC, USA.

Juniperus x media 'Old Gold'

265 A beautiful conifer that has rapidly gained popularity since its introduction in 1958. 'Old Gold' originated as a sport on 'Pfitzeriana Aurea' at the nursery of F. Grootendhorst & Son, Boskoop, Netherlands, and it has shorter tip growths of a less vigorous character than its parent, giving a compact plant of 70cm (28in) high by 1.5m (5ft) wide in ten years' growth. Foremost among its qualities is the delightful gold colour that is held in the foliage throughout the year.   Hardiness 5.

266 *Juniperus x media* 'Pfitzeriana'. Spring. Los Angeles, USA.

Juniperus x media 'Pfitzeriana'
Pfitzer Juniper

266 A juniper that was introduced to cultivation over 100 years ago, 'Pfitzeriana' has of recent years become so widely known that it almost seems unnecessary to describe it here. The illustration shows a typical plant at its most attractive age, ten years old, 2m (6ft) across by 1m (3ft) high; with the upward-facing branch habit that droops modestly at the tips. The semi-adult type foliage has scales holding out a little from the stem, giving a prickliness that is noticeable when touched, while further into the bush some juvenile-type leaf is usually in evidence. It is occasionally met with under the name of *J. sabina* 'Knap Hill'.   Hardiness 4.

267 *Juniperus x media* 'Pfitzeriana Aurea'. Spring. Shrewsbury, England.

Juniperus x media 'Pfitzeriana Aurea'
Golden Pfitzer Juniper

267 Another delightful variation in the 'Pfitzer' juniper family, this golden form originated in the D. Hill Nursery at Dundee, Illinois, in 1923, and has proved itself a popular addition to the conifer world. Of somewhat flatter growth than 'Pfitzeriana', it displays on its outer growths and stems during summer a rich golden colour that gives the plant a beautiful gold-dusted appearance. It is capable of spreading to 2m (6ft) wide by 50cm (20in) high in ten years, but may easily be kept to size by removing 30cm (12in) or so from the leading growths each year, taking care to make the cut below an overhanging shoot where it will not show. Winter colour is a yellowish-green.   Hardiness 5.

269 *Juniperus x media* 'Pfitzeriana Glauca'. Spring. Los Angeles, USA.

Juniperus x media 'Pfitzeriana Glauca'　　　Blue Pfitzer Juniper

269 This exciting form of the green Pfitzer juniper is identical in leaf type and habit, but comes dressed in soft silvery-blue, a colour that is seen at its best against a background of dark redwood panelling or evergreen hedge. It may grow to a large shrub, 2m (6ft) wide by 1m (3ft) high in ten years; the attractive arching growth habit as illustrated is typical of an older specimen, and is a feature not usually present in young nursery-size plants. It should not be confused with the similar-looking *J. x media* 'Hetzii' — the prickly feel of the foliage is enough to distinguish it, while 'Hetzii' is rather softer. In colder regions the foliage turns a purplish-brown colour with the onset of winter.　　　Hardiness 4.

268 *Juniperus x media* 'Pfitzeriana Compacta'. Spring. Los Angeles, USA.

Juniperus x media 'Pfitzeriana Compacta'　　　Nick's Compact Pfitzer

268 This slower-growing and more compact green Pfitzer, Nick's Compact, as it is commonly known, has a preference for a more upright habit of growth, 1m (3ft) being the height for a ten-year plant, by the same in width. It is of ideal dimensions for the more compact present-day garden, possessing the graceful arching branch habit of its larger parent without the disadvantage of such a wide spread. It can be distinguished from young plants of 'Pfitzeriana' by the greater proportion of juvenile leaf among the foliage.　　　Hardiness 4.

270 *Juniperus x media* 'Pfitzeriana Kallay'. Spring. Dundee, Illinois, USA.

Juniperus x media 'Pfitzeriana Kallay'　　　Kallay Pfitzer Juniper

270 With the recognition of the fact that the green Pfitzer Juniper really gets too large for many situations (some of the older specimens reach 3m by 6m/10ft by 20ft wide), this cultivar known as Kallay's, Ohio selection, has been introduced as the answer to the problem. With its more modest spread of 1m by 40cm (3ft by 15in) high for an eight-year plant, 'Kallay' promises a behaviour more in keeping with smaller present-day gardens than was its famous predecessor. Of typical Pfitzer foliage, rich green, it has a greater predominance of juvenile foliage than the type.　　　Hardiness 4.

271 *Juniperus x media* 'Plumosa Albovariegata'. Spring. Wisley, Surrey, England.

Juniperus x media 'Plumosa Albovariegata'

271 An interesting variant among the 'Plumosa' junipers, this one follows the typical spreading growth habit of the group but at the more leisurely pace of 1m (3ft) wide by 2m (6ft) high for a ten-year period. The creamy-white variegation which is liberally distributed among the grey-green scale-like foliage consists of very small flecks of colour and is better appreciated on a young plant viewed at close range. For this reason it has probably greater potential as a bonsai or potted specimen than as a garden plant.   Hardiness 5.

272 *Juniperus x media* 'Plumosa Aurea'. Autumn. Gore, New Zealand.

Juniperus x media 'Plumosa Aurea'
Golden Plume Juniper

272 A fine juniper of high decorative value and in much demand as an ornamental, 'Plumosa Aurea' has been in cultivation in the western world for over eighty years and in that time has laboured under a variety of names such as *J. japonica* 'Aurea', *J. procumbens* 'Aurea' and *J. globosa* 'Aurea', and variations thereof. Young plants usually throw a strong growth to one side of the plant but later rectify this by throwing a stronger one in the opposite direction and thus build themselves up until in ten years a specimen could be 1.8m (almost 6ft) across by 80cm (30in) high with plumes of golden foliage rising upwards in a highly-decorative manner. Growth is slow while a plant is becoming established and for this reason larger specimens are rarely available. The foliage is very fine, scale-like and smooth, and adaptable to bonsai use, as were some of the earliest plants imported from Japan under the name of 'Globosa'. The illustration shows a plant in the typical golden-bronze of late autumn colour.   Hardiness 5.

273 *Juniperus x media* 'Plumosa Aureovariegata'. Spring. Dundee, Illinois, USA.

Juniperus x media 'Plumosa Aureovariegata'

273 Not just a slight change of name, but of different colour and habit than 'Plumosa Albovariegata', this is the better garden plant of the two. The green of the foliage is rich and dark, contrasting well with the creamy-yellow variegation which is irregularly distributed in an artistic manner and in places dominates a spray of foliage, giving a colour-splashed effect that can be appreciated at a glance. Growth is not fast, making it excellent for use among rocks, and 1m (3ft) wide by 30cm (12in) high would be the dimensions of a ten-year-old plant, with perhaps another 30cm (12in) in height for a full-grown specimen.   Hardiness 5.

274 *Juniperus x media* 'Shimpaku'. Brooklyn, New York, USA.

Juniperus x media 'Shimpaku'

274 Seen here as a bonsai plant at the Brooklyn Botanical Gardens, New York, this smallest-growing member of the 'Plumosa' group is ideally suited to dwarfing, yet also has its place as an ornamental in the rock garden, among pebbles or as a potted patio plant. There, if left untrimmed, it will grow into a compact grey-green miniature edition of the larger 'Plumosa' juniper. Clearly shown is the fine threadlike foliage typical of this group, quite smooth to the touch and lacking in juvenile leaf. Growth would be less than 70cm (28in) wide by 30cm (12in) high.   Hardiness 4.

275 *Juniperus occidentalis* 'Glauca'. Spring. Washington, DC, USA.

Juniperus occidentalis 'Glauca'
Sierra Silver Juniper

275 A rugged juniper from the high Sierras of Colorado, USA, this selected colour form and only known cultivar of *J. occidentalis* adopts a twisted growth habit and makes a bold erect pyramid of lavish grey-green. At its best left untrimmed in its handsome rough outline, it is the ideal plant to provide vertical accent of strong character, among a planting of lower-growing evergreens. It is recorded that the comparatively-large seeds of this species are eaten by the Indians.   Hardiness 5.

276 *Juniperus procumbens*. Autumn. New Plymouth, New Zealand.

Juniperus procumbens
Japanese Garden Juniper

276 Would that all conifers had a simple straightforward descriptive name like this one. Discovered in the mountains of Japan over 100 years ago and used ornamentally in Western gardens ever since, *J. procumbens* is an excellent fast-growing ground-cover plant which may if left to itself spread to 6m (20ft) across in thirty years, but can easily be kept to size by an annual trimming. It rarely builds up higher than 30cm (12in) on flat ground without assistance, but is amenable to being trained upwards should the gardener wish. The growing tips tend to hold themselves upwards, and the illustration shows a plant, having been led to the top of one side of a rock, now disinclined to weep down the other until the force of gravity gets the better of it. The foliage is composed of pointed juvenile-type leaves arranged in threes on the stem, and the bluish-green colour is constant throughout the year.
Hardiness 4.

277 *Juniperus procumbens* 'Nana'. Spring. Washington, DC, USA.

278 *Juniperus recurva* var. *coxi*. Winter. Christchurch, New Zealand.

Juniperus recurva var *coxii*   Coffin Juniper

278 This graceful weeping form of *J. recurva* was introduced from the Burmese highlands in the 1920s, and soon gained popularity as a garden plant. Although specimens have been recorded up to 25m (80ft) in height, it is not too fast growing in cooler climates for garden use and it is admirably suited to planting in a large rock setting, as a lawn specimen or in association with water. It may be expected to reach 3m (10ft) in ten years by 1m (3ft) wide. The juvenile-type leaves are so closely laid along the stems that they have a threadlike appearance and outer branches weep down gracefully. The durable aromatic timber is prized in Burma and China for the construction of coffins.   Hardiness 7.

Juniperus procumbens 'Nana'

Dwarf Japanese Juniper

277 More compact in all its parts than the preceding, *J. procumbens* 'Nana' is ideally suited to the rock-garden or positions where space is limited, and should not spread further than 1.2m (4ft) in ten years, by 30cm (12in) high. The two plants illustrated, at the Gotelli collection in Washington, DC, show fresh spring growth of a bright-green colour which will later change to the excellent bluish-green typical of this form. Not altogether confined to prostrate growing, 'Nana' also makes a wonderful bonsai subject. Once the leader is trained up as a trunk and hardened by a year's growth, the branches can then be led horizontally to hold a "treetop" of miniature foliage. Introduced from Japan by the D. Hill Nursery Company, Illinois.   Hardiness 4.

Juniperus rigida   Needle Juniper

279 This is one of those conifers that should be clearly labelled "Handle with Care"; not because of fragility on behalf of the plant, but because the needles are unbelievably sharp and any person handling a quantity of this species would soon find himself obliged to wear gloves for protection. Nonetheless, it is an interesting conifer with a graceful drooping habit of growth forming a bush of 2m (6ft) high by 1m (3ft) wide for a good ten years' growth, highlighted by a spring flush of buff-coloured shoots as illustrated, and turning a brownish-green once growth has stopped. It is a native of Japan and has been much cultivated by the Japanese in temple gardens.   Hardiness 5.

279 *Juniperus rigida*. Spring. Devizes, Wilts, England.

280 *Juniperus sabina* 'Arcadia'. Spring. Washington, DC, USA.

Juniperus sabina 'Arcadia'

280 A rich green form of the Savin juniper, 'Arcadia' is a spreading conifer of rugged constitution and proven hardiness which has also been found resistant to the juniper blight that often troubles members of this group. It carries predominantly scale-like foliage held on strong near-horizontal branches, making a handsome spreading shrub of character and distinction. Raised from seed imported from the Ural Mountains in Russia by the D. Hill Nurseries, Dundee, Illinois, USA, it was selected as worthy of name by F. J. Grootenhorst & Sons, Boskoop, Netherlands. 'Broadmoor' and 'Skandia' also have the same origin. A spread of 1.2m by 50cm (4ft by 20in) high would be average growth for a ten-year plant.

Hardiness 4.

281 *Juniperus sabina* 'Blue Danube'. Autumn. Gore, New Zealand.

Juniperus sabina 'Blue Danube'

281 Aptly named, and of Austrian origin, 'Blue Danube' is a juniper of the *J. tamariscifolia* type that prefers to lie its main branches along the ground, where they freely take root, while holding branchlets and tips upward at a 30-degree angle. It is a useful ground-cover plant or low shrub of an attractive silvery bluish-green colour, but inclined to turn brownish in severe winters. Capable of a 1.5m (4ft) spread in ten years by 30cm (12in) high, it can be kept to size by removing excess outer growth.

Hardiness 3.

282 *Juniperus sabina* 'Broadmoor'. Spring. Los Angeles, USA.

Juniperus sabina 'Broadmoor'

282 Another excellent hardy juniper from the same Russian source as 'Arcadia' and 'Skandia', 'Broadmoor' can be described as a refined form of the well-known 'Tamariscifolia', with reduced leader vigour and foliage of soft bright green. Older plants tend to build up in the centre and eventually form a tidy and ornamental mound spreading to 1m (3ft) across by 30cm (12in) high for a ten-year plant, full sun being desirable to keep the plant at its compact best. A 1963 introduction from the D. Hill Nurseries, it will probably exceed 'Tamariscifolia' in popularity once it becomes fully known.   Hardiness 3.

283 *Juniperus sabina* 'Erecta'. Autumn.

Juniperus sabina 'Erecta'

283 One of the more typical members of the savin group, 'Erecta', as its same suggests, has an upright growth habit, the steeply ascending branches being clothed in fine, soft rich-green foliage. Of medium growth rate, to 1m by 70cm (3ft by 28in) in ten years, it has a loose and flexible habit and graceful arching tips and is or value grown *en masse* as a foundation planting or as a medium-sized untrimmed hedge or low screen.   Hardiness 4.

284 *Juniperus sabina* 'Skandia'. Spring. Washington, DC, USA.

Juniperus sabina 'Skandia'

284 Another of the Russian savin junipers selected from seed collected in the Ural Mountains, 'Skandia' was likewise introduced by the D. Hill Nursery Company, Dundee, Illinois, USA. The hardiness of this juniper is its foremost quality, and its ability to maintain the excellent mid-green colour through adverse conditions. Its greatest use is for ground-cover as illustrated, or for planting as a group. A growth spread of at least 1m (3ft) in ten years can be expected.   Hardiness 3.

285 *Juniperus sabina* 'Tamariscifolia'. Spring. Los Angeles, USA.

Juniperus sabina 'Tamariscifolia'
Tamarix Juniper

285 A conifer that stands out among all others as a distinct and recognisable form, 'Tamariscifolia' has been in cultivation for 200 years and will doubtless continue to be grown for a long time yet. It is technically a botanical variety, being found in the wild in Southern Europe, and is therefore often found listed as var. *tamariscifolia*. Illus-trated is a young plant with typical rounded top, branches arching out from the centre carrying the upward-facing branchlets of rich deep-green foliage, which is quite prickly to handle; the tiny leaves are mainly of juvenile type and sharp. Poorly-nourished plants usually revert to adult foliage and fade to an unattractive dull green. It can be expected to make a tidy mound of foliage of 1.5m (4ft) wide by 50cm (20in) high in ten years and can be kept to this size if required by a yearly pruning. Two similar cultivars, 'Broadmoor' and 'Buffalo', have recently been introduced as compact-growing editions of 'Tamarisci-folia'.   Hardiness 5.

286 *Juniperus scopulorum* 'Blue Heaven'. Spring.
Los Angeles, USA.

287 *Juniperus scopulorum* 'Grey Gleam'. Spring.
Washington, DC, USA.

288 *Juniperus scopulorum* 'Platinum'. Summer.
California, USA.

Juniperus scopulorum 'Blue Heaven'

286 The Rocky Mountain Juniper, as its common name suggests, is a native of the mountain areas of Western North America, and comes in a wide range of shapes, sizes and colours, some of the larger forms reaching to 12m (40ft) in their native state. 'Blue Heaven' is undoubtedly the most outstanding among the thirty-five-odd recorded garden cultivars and it makes an erect compact pyramidal bush of breath-taking silvery-blue foliage, maintaining this colour throughout the year. It is currently enjoying much popularity as a specimen plant in the United States and no doubt elsewhere in the world when it becomes better known. Of medium growth to 1m (3ft) in five years by 30cm (1ft) wide, it is mostly propagated by grafting. It often carries numerous clusters of berries of the same silvery-blue colour as the foliage.
Hardiness 3.

Juniperus scopulorum 'Gray Gleam'

287 Narrow, columnar, and symmetrical, with attractive silvery grey-green foliage, 'Gray Gleam' is a shrub of durability and permanence that looks smart at all times of the year, and particularly so in winter, when, instead of turning dull, the silvery colouring becomes even more accentuated. It is a slow grower, making about 1m by 25cm wide (3ft by 10in) in five years, and will maintain a uniform erect shape without need of trimming. In the United States the sale of this plant is protected by Plant Patent No. 848. No berries may be expected on this plant as it is a male form.
Hardiness 5.

Juniperus scopulorum 'Platinum'

288 A beautiful erect-growing pyramidal juniper that provides eye-catching vertical accent at all times of the year in a lush silvery-blue colour. It was introduced early in the 1960s by a Kansas, USA, nursery and is protected in that country by Plant Patent No. 1070. Included in the illustration are three plants of *J. sabina* 'Buffalo', a prostrate juniper of 'Tamariscifolia' type that has a more ground-hugging habit of growth. The photograph was kindly supplied by the Monrovia Nursery Company, Azusa, California. 'Platinum' is a medium-slow grower and can be expected to reach 1.8m (almost 6ft) in ten years by 80cm (30in) in width, and retain its shape without need of trimming.
Hardiness 5.

289 *Juniperus scopulorum* 'Repens'. Spring. Adelaide, South Australia.

Juniperus scopulorum 'Repens'

289 One of the few prostrate members of the *J. scopulorum* family, 'Repens' differs also in having 5mm (⅕in) long awl-shaped leaves in contrast to other members whose leaves are mostly scale-like and adult in type. It is fairly slow growing, to a 1.2m (4ft) spread in ten years, following the contours of the ground or stonework well and with short semi-erect side-branches giving it a height of 15cm (6in) or so. The bluish-green foliage and brown stems make a pleasing colour contrast. Plants named *J. scopulorum* 'Palmeri' or 'Prostrata' seem to be identical to this one.   Hardiness 4.

290 *Juniperus squamata* 'Meyeri'. Summer. Auckland, New Zealand.

Juniperus squamata 'Meyeri'   Meyer Juniper

290 The species *J. squamata* is a native of the mountain areas of Eastern Asia, and is represented in civilisation by some nine named cultivars, the most outstanding of which is 'Meyeri'. The eye-catching bluish colour of this shrub is the key to its popularity, making it an excellent contrast subject among the bronze and yellow shades of other conifers. In growth behaviour it is very variable, the general habit being to spread outwards and upwards in roughly equal proportions, to 2m (6ft) in ten years, but it is strongly advised to limit this growth by a yearly pruning; this practice encourages bushing and overcomes the tendency of the plant to display its brown withered inner leaves. A new cultivar, 'Blue Star', developed in the Netherlands promises to be a tidier grower than its larger parent.   Hardiness 4.

291 *Juniperus squamata* 'Pygmaea'. Spring. Wisley, Surrey, England.

Juniperus squamata 'Pygmaea'

291 As its name would suggest this is one of the smallest members of the *J. squamata* family, and has its place on the rockery where it will grow into a squat dense little bush as wide as it is high. The 6mm (¼in) long leaves are similar to those on 'Wilsoni', but the tips do not display the decurving habit so prominently as on that cultivar. A ten-year bush would measure approximately 1m (3ft) each way.   Hardiness 4.

292 *Juniperus squamata* 'Wilsoni'. Spring. Dunedin, New Zealand.

Juniperus squamata 'Wilsoni'

292 This splendid cultivar can be described as a more refined silvery grey-green version of its best-selling Meyer juniper brother, and displays prominently the typical *J. squamata* feature of nodding tips, a characteristic of all members of this species. It is slower growing, to 1.3m (4¼ft) each way in ten years, and can vary in habit from a spreading bush as illustrated to one more compact and erect, depending on branching habit or pruning treatment earlier in life. The 6mm (¼in) awl-shaped leaves carry two bluish-white bands on the inner side, these bands tending to give the bush its silvery effect when viewed in certain lighting conditions. *J. squamata* 'Loderi' is similar in foliage but grows symmetrical and erect, with a more definite leader. Hardiness 4.

293 *Juniperus taxifolia* var. *lutchuensis*. Summer. Palmerston North, New Zealand.

Juniperus taxifolia var. *lutchuensis*

293 An excellent ground-cover juniper that has often been confused with the very similar *J. conferta* already mentioned, it has in the past been grown under the name (among others) of *J. conferta* var. *maritima*. Of the two cultivars this is the one I prefer to grow with its softer, less-prickly leaves, richer green foliage and contrasting light-brown stems. It is clean-growing, covers the ground well, can be trimmed to keep it low or confined, yet is reasonably fast growing, to 3m (10ft) wide in ten years by 25cm (10in) at its highest point on level ground. It will also if so required cascade very happily down the face of a bank or rock wall. A cultivar known in California as *J. conferta* 'Blue Pacific' looks very like this one and could well prove to be the same plant, or perhaps a selected bluish form of it. Hardiness 5.

294 *Juniperus virginiana* 'Burkii'. Autumn. Ashburton, New Zealand.

Juniperus virginiana 'Burkii' Burk Red Cedar

294 *Juniperus virginiana* is a native of North America where it is widely distributed east of the Rocky Mountains and is represented in the trade by sixty recorded cultivars, some of which are now no longer grown. It was known in cultivation in England as early as 1664. 'Burkii' is among the most popular of these cultivars and is widely grown in Europe where the colder winters turn the normally blue-green foliage a rich steel-blue colour. It makes a narrow pyramid of up to 2m (6ft) in ten years by 1m (3ft) at the base, and can easily be kept to this size or smaller if desired with an annual trimming. Hardiness 5.

295 *Juniperus virginiana* 'Canaertii'. Foliage.

296 *Juniperus virginiana* 'Glauca'. Spring. Dundee, Illinois, USA.

Juniperus virginiana 'Canaertii'

295 An erect-growing dark green form that has been in cultivation for more than 100 years and is still popular in colder areas for its hardiness and ability to retain its green colour throughout the winter. The outer foliage is fine, smooth and adult in type with some juvenile leaf usually to be found on older branches or further on in the bush, and a crop of bluish-white berries is always an attraction during autumn, contrasting well against the darker foliage. In ten years, it is capable of reaching to 3m by 1m (10ft by 3ft) in width.   Hardiness 4.

Juniperus virginiana 'Glauca'   Silver Cedar

296 Another well-known cultivar that has been around for more than 100 years, deservedly popular with its fine smooth grey-blue foliage, attractively-informal open habit and medium growth rate, reaching to approximately 3m (10ft) in ten years on a bush 1.5m (5ft) wide at the base. It is best grown in a fully exposed position, and is easily trimmed if a more formal outline is desired. This, as well as most other *J. virginiana* cultivars, is propagated by grafting.   Hardiness 4.

297 *Juniperus virginiana* 'Globosa'. Spring. Wisley, Surrey, England.

Juniperus virginiana 'Grey Owl'

298 'Grey Owl' is a low spreading bush with a habit similar to that of *J. x media* 'Pfitzeriana', of which it possibly is a hybrid, being a seedling from a plant of *J. virginiana* 'Glauca' that was growing near a plant of 'Pfitzeriana'. The yellowish branches contrast well with the silvery grey-green leaf, and the outer foliage is thread-like and open, becoming more densely furnished toward the centre. A ten-year plant may be expected to spread to 1.5m by 45cm high (5ft by 18in) and is seen at its best spreading its foliage across a large flat rock. The name of *J. sabina* 'Grey Owl' is often wrongly applied to this plant.

Juniperus virginiana 'Globosa'

297 This compact bush of rich green begins in a somewhat irregular globose shape which with age fills out to become very regular and rounded in outline, looking almost as if it had been carefully trimmed that way. The foliage, which is mainly adult in type, is a compact mass of short twigs and tips and in colder areas turns a brownish winter colour. It is a slow-growing plant which in ten years would measure about 80cm (30in) in height and as many in width.   Hardiness 4.

298 *Juniperus virginiana* 'Grey Owl'. Summer. Norfolk, England.

299 *Juniperus virginiana* 'Hillii'. Winter. Gore,
New Zealand.

Juniperus virginiana 'Hillii'

299 Raised by the D. Hill Nursery Company, of Dundee,
Illinois, around the year 1916, this cultivar has steadily
gained popularity over the years and is prized in colder
climate areas for its hardiness and attractive winter
colour of rich purple-blue. It bears awl-shaped leaves,
slightly prickly, of a bluish-green colour at other times of
the year and makes a broadly pyramidal bush of up to
2m (6ft) in ten years by 1m (3ft) in width.   Hardiness 4.

300 *Juniperus virginiana* 'Kosteri' Spring. Auckland,
New Zealand.

Juniperus virginiana 'Kosteri'

300 It is questionable whether this plant belongs in the
J. virginiana group as it exudes a distinctive savin odour
when the foliage is crushed, and this feature indicates
that it probably belongs either in the *J. sabina* or *J.
x media* groups. I suspect that many plants labelled
J. sabina 'Knap Hill' and many labelled *J. x media*
'Pfitzeriana', are this cultivar. The difference can be seen
in the lower more spreading growth habit of 'Kosteri',
and the more greyish-green foliage colour. Regardless of
the name mix-ups, it is an excellent flat-growing conifer
with a wide spread, to 3m by 1m (10ft by 3ft) high in
ten years.   Hardiness 4.

Juniperus virginiana 'Silver Spreader'

301 The cultivar 'Silver Spreader' is one of the few really
low-growing members of the mainly erect-growing
J. virginiana family, others being 'Chamberlaynii' and
'Horizontalis', both prostrate grey-green forms, and
'Grey Owl' already mentioned. It was introduced early in
the 1960s by the Monrovia Nursery Company, Azusa,
California, who kindly supplied the illustration for this
book. It is a first-class low accent shrub in a silvery grey-
green colour that will cover a 2m (6ft) circle in ten years
at a height of 50cm (20in).   Hardiness 5.

301 *Juniperus virginiana* 'Silver Spreader'. Spring. California, USA.

Juniperus virginiana 'Skyrocket'

302 Probably the most fastigiate narrow-growing conifer in cultivation, 'Skyrocket' was originally discovered in 1949 growing wild in the USA, was propagated but unnamed by a nursery in Indiana, and was first listed in a nursery catalogue under the species *J. virginiana* in Holland in 1957. The foliage is fine and adult in type of a lustrous silvery-blue-green. In ten years a height of 2m (6ft) may be expected, at a width of 30cm (12in). By then it will be a narrow erect column that will stand out in any garden setting. Some authors prefer to classify this juniper among the *J. scopulorum* cultivars, a point that is still not clear.   Hardiness 5.

302 *Juniperus virginiana* 'Skyrocket'. Spring. The Hague, Netherlands.

303 *Keteleeria davidiana*. Foliage.

Keteleeria davidiana

303 The keteleerias are monoecious evergreen trees native to China and Formosa and are represented in cultivation by the four recorded species *K. davidiana, K. evelyniana, K. formosana,* and *K. fortunei,* with possibly one or two other species not yet fully identified but rather similar to *K. davidiana.* They most closely resemble the genus *Abies* with similarities in leaf and upward-facing cones, and in their native state are known to grow as high as 40m (130ft) with a well-buttressed base to the trunk. Generally they are more tolerant of dry conditions than species of *Abies.* The name commemorates a French nurseryman, J. B. Keteleer, and was first applied to the genus in 1866. Propagation is by seed or cuttings.
K. davidiana, the hardiest member of this genus and probably the one best known although by no means common, makes a fine pyramidal tree when young, but opens up and becomes more round-topped with age. The leaves are pointed, up to 5cm (2in) long, shining dark green on the upper surface and sometimes bluish and pale on the underside, with a prominent keel on both surfaces. The upward-facing cylindrical cones 10–20cm (4–8in) in length and up to 5cm (2in) in width are reddish-brown in colour, maturing pale brown.   Hardiness 3.

Larix decidua   European Larch

304, 305 Along with the genera *Gingko, Metasequoia* and *Taxodium,* the larches belong the that class of conifers which completely shed its leaves in the autumn and remains bare throughout winter. In doing so *Larix decidua* (previously known a *L. europea*) turns a rich golden-yellow colour that is quite eye-catching — whole forests in colour are an unforgettable sight. Spring and bud-burst sees it re-clothed in beautiful fresh green, so that there is ample compensation for its not being evergreen. Apart from its ornamental value it is an excellent timber tree, and produces a straight tall trunk with very little taper, and the trunks of younger trees are often used in the construction of ornamental rustic fences complete with bark, which tends to remain attached, whether the wood is split or used in the round
Hardiness 2.

Larix decidua 'Pendula'   Weeping European Larch

306 The European Larch has been in cultivation for more than 200 years and there are at least twenty recorded variations of form and colour that have appeared from time to time, most of which are seldom met with these days. Probably the best known of these cultivars is 'Pendula', a weeping form, several of which have been found in the wild in the past. They are usually propagated by grafting on to *L. decidua,* a more pendulous effect being obtained if the graft is made some 2m (6ft) above ground level. This gives an excellent weeping specimen with a straight trunk which will gradually build up in height as the plant ages.   Hardiness 2.
(Photo by Clarence E. Lewis.)

304 *Larix decidua.* Autumn. Christchurch, New Zealand.

305 *Larix decidua.* Cones and foliage.

306 *Larix decidua* 'Pendula'. Summer. Michigan, USA.

307 *Larix x eurolepis.* Spring. Nelson, New Zealand.

308 *Larix x eurolepis.* Cones and foliage.

Larix x eurolepis   Hybrid larch. Dunkeld Larch

307, 308 This interesting hybrid between *L. decidua* and *L. leptolepis* originated in Dunkeld, Scotland, around the year 1900 and is of considerable interest to forestry growers because so far it has been free of the aphid and fungus attack that is so destructive to many other larch species. Coupled with this feature is its outstandingly vigorous growth, outstripping both parents in this respect. From a garden point of view it is more glaucous in foliage than its parents, and the cones which are borne in profusion are a highly-decorative reddish colour, ripening to a warm brown. In ten years it is capable of reaching 5m (16ft) in favourable conditions.   Hardiness 2.

309 *Larix leptolepis.* Spring. Wisley, Surrey, England.

Larix leptolepis   Japanese Larch

309 This is a native of Japan, actually from the island of Hondo, where it grows wild on mountain slopes between 1,000m and 2,000m (3,300ft and 6,600ft). It is quite capable of making a tree of up to 30m (100ft) in height of a similar shape to the European Larch. The illustration of a plant, by no means typical in shape, growing in the rock garden at Wisley, shows the beauty of fresh spring foliage and also how the shape of a tree may be altered and it be kept to garden size with a little systematic pruning. Autumn is also a time of beauty when the leaf before falling turns an eye-catching whitish buff colour that is most unusual, to say the least. Normal growth for a ten-year tree would be 3m by 1.5m (10ft by 5ft) wide. There are some ten recorded cultivars, two of which have attractive weeping forms but most are no longer in cultivation. Some botanists prefer to classify this as *L. kaemferi*. Hardiness 5.

310 *Libocedrus bidwillii.* Spring. Christchurch, New Zealand.

Libocedrus bidwillii

310 The genus *Libocedrus* now covers only five species of evergreen shrubs and trees native to New Zealand and New Caledonia, and the Incense Cedar, formerly known as *Libocedrus decurrens*, has now been placed in a separate genus, *Calocedrus*, along with *C. formosana* and *C. macrolepis*. *L. bidwillii*, the hardiest of the five, is native to mountain areas of altitudes up to 2,000m (6,600ft) in New Zealand, and varies in shape from a rounded green bush to an erect tree as illustrated, and specimens are known to reach as high as 20m (65ft). It is however, not a fast grower, 3m (10ft) in ten years being average, carrying fine fernlike adult foliage as well as some juvenile leaf, and may be used effectively as a focal point in garden landscape work.

Hardiness 6.

Libocedrus plumosa   Kawaka

311 A beautiful conifer, attractive even when less than 1m (3ft) high by reason of its lush green fernlike leaves held in arching horizontal sprays, becoming densely furnished as the tree grows so that all trunk and branch structure is completely hidden. It is symmetrical in growth, averaging 3 to 4m (10 to 13ft) in ten years by 1m (3ft) in width, and although specimens to 30m (100ft) are known, it seldom reaches half that as a garden plant. It grows well in sun but is happier in semi-shade, making a taller, narrower specimen. In all, a wonderful garden conifer where climate permits.

Hardiness 8.

Metasequoia glyptostroboides   Dawn Redwood

312, 313 A beautiful deciduous conifer, native to remote mountainous areas in China where it is recorded as reaching heights of up to 35m (115ft). It has been available to the horticultural world only since 1946, and before that was thought to have been extinct, the only evidence of its existence being in fossil form. Once discovered, it soon became widely distributed among nurseries as "the living fossil". It is easily propagated from seeds or cuttings, and is now a popular garden conifer of beautiful form and fresh spring leafage. In late autumn it is a blaze of rich golden bronze, holding this colour for some weeks before leaf-drop. It is an erect-growing tree with upward-facing branches which in ten years would measure 4m (13ft) in height by 2m (6ft) in width.

Hardiness 6.

Microcachrys tetragona

314 The name *Microcachrys* is of Greek origin meaning "micro catkin" in reference to the minute 2mm (⅛in) male strobilii. *M. tetragona*, the sole member of this genus, is a native of the mountains of Tasmania where it makes a low, straggling, almost-prostrate bush, clothed in fine whipcord evergreen foliage composed of tiny scale-

311 *Libocedrus plumosa.* Spring. Auckland, New Zealand.

312 *Metasequoia glyptostroboides.* Spring. Palmerston North, New Zealand.

313 *Metasequoia glyptostroboides.* Foliage.

314 *Microcachrys tetragona.* Stem and foliage.

like leaves arranged in a tetragonal pattern, i.e. in four ranks, giving a square cross-section to the stem. As an ornamental it has possibilities in a rock setting, being either allowed to sprawl naturally among the stones or pruned back a little to give a bushier effect. In ten years it may be expected to make little more than 1m (3ft) in growth. It bears tiny egg-shaped translucent red fruits. Hardiness 6.

Microstrobos fitzgeraldi

315 The two species of Microstrobos, natives of New South Wales and Tasmania, are moisture-loving shrubs usually found at alpine elevations near the margins of lakes, streams or waterfalls. *M. fitzgeraldi* is a low many-branched shrub with slender semi-weeping branchlets clothed in short olive-green 3mm ($\frac{1}{8}$in) leaves arranged similaterly to those of the genus *Dacrydium*, to which it is closely allied. It is an interesting, little-known conifer that is worth experimenting with in moist or shady situations. An annual growth of 10cm (4in) may be expected from both this low-growing species and the taller, denser and finer-leaved *M. niphophilus*.

Hardiness 7.

315 *Microstrobos fitzgeraldi.* Foliage.

116

316 *Neocallitropsis auraucarioides.* Foliage.

Neocallitropsis araucarioides

316 A genus of only this one species, native to New Caledonia, and so named for its similarities in cone to *Callitris*, but in foliage most like *Araucaria*. It makes a symmetrical, conical tree to 10m (33ft) with horizontal branches and dense covering of fine mid-green foliage consisting of 1cm ($\frac{1}{3}$in) incurved leaves set on the stems in rows of eight. Both male and female strobilii are borne on the same tree.

Hardiness 8.

317 *Papuacedrus papuana.* Upper and lower leaf detail.

Papuacedrus papuana

317 The three species of *Papuacedrus*, natives of New Guinea, were until 1953 all classified under *Libocedrus*, which genus they resemble in foliage. This is much flattened, almost fernlike with some of the individual leaves measuring as long as 1cm ($\frac{1}{3}$in). *P. arfakensis* is known as a shapely conical tree with a potential height of 35m (110ft) and is possibly the hardiest of the three species, being native to the Arfak mountains at altitudes around 2,000m (6,500ft). Slight botanical differences in leaf detail set apart the other two species, *P. papuana* and *P. toricellensis*, either of which are worthy of some experimentation for garden use. Little is known about hardiness but possibly none of them would rate hardier than 8.

318 *Phyllocladus alpinus* var. *minor.* Spring. Leaf and female strobilii.

Phyllocladus alpinus var. minor

318 Of the six species in the genus *Phyllocladus* this is the one most likely to make its way as a garden plant, being more compact than its tree-sized brothers; in ten years it reaches to about 1.5m (5ft), and being an alpine species is hardier than any and therefore more resistant to cold. As a curiosity alone it is rare with its peculiar flattened stems and leaves quite unlike anything else in the conifer world, along with a display of crimson flowers, or more correctly female strobilii, in the spring, maturing to tiny 8mm ($\frac{1}{4}$in or so) cones.

Hardiness 7.

Phyllocladus trichomanoides — Celery Pine

319 A genus comprising six different species and probably one of the most untypical conifers of any, with thick fleshy cladodes, looking rather like pieces of olive-green plasticine, in place of true leaves. This species grows to a tree of up to 20m (65ft) in New Zealand, is moderately hardy and carries a thick bark that yields a high percentage of tannin from which the Maoris obtained a bright red dye.

Hardiness 8.

319 *Phyllocladus trichomanoides.* Spring. Wellington, New Zealand.

Picea abies   Norway Spruce

320, 321 The common or Norway Spruce is the traditional Christmas tree in Europe and Britain. There are large forests of this species in Northern and Central Europe where specimens of 50m (165ft) have been recorded. As it has been a widely-grown tree for many years, a number of different forms have turned up as seedlings, while many of the excellent dwarf cultivars have evolved by means of a condition called "witches broom", where part of the plant forms into a tight birdnest-like clump of dwarf or congested foliage, and these parts when propagated from usually produce a compact or dwarf plant of similar foliage type. There are no less than 133 forms and cultivars of *Picea abies* listed in the *Manual of Cultivated Conifers* by Den Ouden and Boom, some of which however are no longer grown. There is still considerable confusion among the dwarf forms but we hope that research being conducted by Mr H. J. Welch on these cultivars will clarify the position.

Hardiness 3.

320 *Picea abies.* Autumn. Hanmer, New Zealand.

321 *Picea abies.* Cones.

322 *Picea abies* 'Aurea'. With cones. Winter. Taihape, New Zealand.

Picea abies 'Aurea'   Golden Norway Spruce

322 With this colour-variant of the Norway Spruce the leaves are a golden yellow, the colour being more pronounced in the more exposed parts of the tree while those on the inner parts remain a light green. In other respects it follows the type closely, with full-sized leaves and cones and a growth rate that could produce a tree of 6 to 8m (20 to 26ft) in twenty years. Apparently several golden forms have been found over the years and it is possible that there are some variations among these forms. Hardiness 3.

323 *Picea abies* 'Capitata'. Spring. Wisley, Surrey, England.

Picea abies 'Capitata'

323 This is one of the many compact forms of *P. abies* (or *P. excelsa* as this species used to be named), ideally at home in a rockery setting. It is an attractive irregularly-rounded low bush, glossy mid-green for most of the year, and punctuated by a spring display of bright pale green all over the bush as the bud tips burst to add another year's growth. Like most of these dwarf forms it is a slow and steady grower, rarely adding more than 10cm (4in) each year, a ten-year plant measuring about 80cm (30in) wide and 50cm (20in) high. Hardiness 4.

324 *Picea abies* 'Clanbrassiliana Elegans'. Spring. California, USA.

325 *Picea abies* 'Globosa Nana'. Winter. Dunedin, New Zealand.

Picea abies 'Clanbrassiliana Elegans'

324 This beautiful low-growing conical bush, seen here in its brightest fresh spring green, later takes on a darker colour as the foliage hardens up on completion of its annual growth. The leaf sprays have a characteristic downward trend at the tips, this feature helping to distinguish the tree from the taller-growing cultivar 'Clanbrassiliana', the two being often but quite unnecessarily confused. In ten years it may be expected to reach 80cm (30in) in height and as many broad, an excellent border or rockery subject with year-round appeal. Hardiness 4.

326 *Picea abies* 'Gregoryana Parsonii'. Spring. Washington, DC, USA.

Picea abies 'Globosa Nana'

325 This rugged little compact bush of irregular outline and prickly appearance is an ideal rock garden or tub plant, a pleasing light green colour, and slow-growing enough to be regarded as permanent in most situations. It is reputed however to have a habit of occasionally sending out strong leader growth; such growths should of course be removed promptly to keep the plant to its intended compact size. This ten-year-old specimen measured 50cm (20in) wide by 30cm (12in) high.   Hardiness 4.

Picea abies 'Gregoryana Parsonii'
Parsons Norway Spruce

326 *Picea abies* 'Gregoryana' may be described as a low-growing globose bush almost hemisherical in shape when young: with age, becoming somewhat irregular in outline with humps and mounds breaking its attractive uniformity of shape. The form 'Parsonii' illustrated here originated in the Arnold Arboretum in the US and is the less commonly grown of the two, differing in having a more horizontal growth habit and longer side branches. Older plants are very difficult to distinguish from each other. In ten years, a low mound of 70cm by 30cm high (28 in by 12in) would be average growth for this cultivar. Another very similarly-shaped picea, known as 'Echiniformis', is characterised by a more irregular and prickly appearance and slower growth.   Hardiness 4.

327 *Picea abies* 'Inversa'. Spring. Wisley, Surrey, England.

Picea abies 'Inversa'   Drooping Norway Spruce

327 An easily-recognised cultivar with its in-built tendency to trail downwards. For this reason it is best trained up a stake in its early years, or the plant will do no more than sprawl flat on the ground. The exception to this rule is where the plant is intended to trail downwards from a ledge or rock wall, and a spectacular cascade effect can be obtained in this manner. 'Inversa' has foliage of a light mid-green, and this lighter colour and the comparatively thinner branches distinguish it from 'Reflexa' the only other similar cultivar in this species. This plant is also met with under its older name of 'Inverta'. A growth of about 10cm (4in) a year is considered average   Hardiness 4.

Picea abies 'Maxwellii'   Maxwell Spruce

328 A dwarf cultivar that has been around for over 100 years, originating in Geneva, New York, USA, in the grounds of T. E. Maxwell Bros, and now fairly widely grown in the United States and Europe. Dr Boom reports that in Europe the growth habit of 'Maxwellii' differs from that of plants grown in the United States, in that it is more compact, and this feature no doubt contributes towards the confusion over the correct description for this cultivar. As depicted here it is a low-growing compact evergreen of irregular outline, ideal for rockery or border; this twenty-year specimen is 30cm (12in) high by 90cm (35in) wide.
Hardiness 4

328 *Picea abies* 'Maxwellii'. Spring. Washington, DC, USA.

329 *Picea abies* 'Nidiformis'. Spring. Dundee, Illinois, USA.

330 *Picea abies* 'Pygmaea'. Spring. Adelaïde, South Australia.

Picea abies 'Nidiformis'   Bird's Nest Spruce

329 So-called because the semi-erect main branches usually curve outwards and away from the centre of the plant, leaving there a low depression which, with younger plants in particular, resembles a large green bird's nest. Our specimen in a tub at the D. Hill Nursery, Dundee, Illinois, USA, no longer displays this feature, being an older plant and not as uniform in shape as most specimens, which are normally dense rounded low bushes with branches in a series of layers with gracefully outward-curving tips. Like most of the *P. abies* cultivars, it is very attractive in spring when the buds burst in bright fresh green, making up to 5cm (2in) of growth that is at first semi-pendulous, then becoming straighter as the wood hardens. In ten years a plant should have reached 25cm (10in) in height by 70cm (28in) in width.

Hardiness 4.

331 *Picea abies* 'Reflexa'. Spring. Washington, DC, USA.

Picea abies 'Pygmaea'   Pygmy Spruce

330 This true miniature among the Norway Spruces is one of the earliest recorded dwarf forms, being known in cultivation as far back as 1800. It shares with 'Humilis', a similar but more compact cultivar, the distinction of being the slowest-growing member of this family. A plant of thirty years would measure no more than 30cm (12in) wide by 50cm (20in) high. The foliage is tightly packed, irregular in size and vigour, and is sometimes seen to revert to a strong-growing type; such growths are liable to ruin the dwarf nature of the plant unless promptly removed. It is seen here commencing its annual growth of about 2cm ($\frac{3}{4}$in). It is a light grey-green and this will change to darker mid-green as the season continues.

Hardiness 4.

Picea abies 'Reflexa'   Weeping Norway Spruce

331 This curiosity in the conifer world seems to have the desire to grow erect but lacks the rigidity and strength to carry out this ambition. The growing tips have an upward-facing tendency, and do not droop until the second year at which stage they evidently lose heart and take on the typical pendulous habit, with just the occasional one or two remaining upright to give the tree a little yearly increase in height. The plant illustrated has quite a strong trunk up to the 1.2m (4ft) level, no doubt having been trained this way when young; from there on it has been left to fend for itself, spreading in all directions, either weeping, spreading or semi-erect. It makes a beautiful specimen if left as a prostrate shrub and grown on a slope or rock ledge, the dark green stiff-looking leaves setting off beautifully the fresh lime-green new spring foliage. The annual growth increase is about 12cm (5in). Also known as 'Pendula'.

Hardiness 4.

332 *Picea abies* 'Repens'. Spring. San Francisco, USA.

333 *Picea breweriana.* Spring. Exbury, Hants, England.

Picea abies 'Repens'   Creeping Spruce

332 One of the finest of the low-growing cushion-shaped spruces, 'Repens' makes a
clean-looking low mound of uniform foliage type, gaining some height over the
years by holding its branches a little above the horizontal. The apparent weeping
effect in the photo is mainly due to the extreme softness of the fresh tip growth; a few
weeks later this would harden up and assume a more erect bearing. The annual
growth of up to 3cm (over 1in) puts it in the dwarf class, and a thirty-five-year-old
specimen in the Gotelli collection measured 1.7m (5½ft) wide by 50cm (20in) high.
Hardiness 4.

334 *Picea engelmannii.* Spring. San Francisco, USA.

Picea breweriana   Brewer's Weeping Spruce

333 This most beautiful of weeping conifers is a native of the Siskiyou Mountains of
western USA, where it is confined to a few isolated localities, having been first
discovered by a Professor Brewer in 1863. It trails its foliage vertically downwards in
long streamers sometimes 1m (3ft) in length; the slender branches attempt to grow
horizontal but seem to be borne downwards by the weight of foliage. The tree
nevertheless possesses a strong straight trunk with a leader always in dominance,
most noticeably so if grown in crowded conditions where a very narrow, erect tree
is the result. It has a medium growth rate to 3m (10ft) in ten years with a maximum
of 35m (115ft), and is best propagated from seed, which is usually scarce and much
in demand by the nursery trade.   Hardiness 2.

Picea engelmannii   Engelmann Spruce

334 Another beautiful spruce from the mountains of western USA, capable of growing in almost any kind of soil and tolerant of extreme cold, being rated in America as
hardy in Zone 1 which includes temperatures below —46°C (—50°F). The leaf colour
of seedling plants may vary from a glaucous green to steel blue and this specimen in
the James Noble collection in Golden Gate Park is a good example of the blue
colour obtainable; I should imagine it is not inferior to the cultivar 'Glauca' which
was first recorded in 1874. The annual growth is about 15cm (6in), the habit dense
and pyramidal, making in ten years an approximate height of 2m by 1.2m (6ft by
4ft) at the base.   Hardiness 1.

335 *Picea glauca.* Spring. Boskoop, Netherlands.

336 *Picea glauca.* Cones.

Picea glauca   White Spruce

335, 336 Also known in Britain as the Canadian Spruce of which there are twenty-eight recorded cultivars, the White Spruce is in its own right an excellent garden conifer which with its moderate average yearly growth of between 10 and 15cm (4 and 6in) is not likely to outgrow its position as do some of its faster-growing brothers. It is particularly attractive in the spring when the new light-green shoots contrast with the inner matured foliage of darker glaucous green. It thrives best in well-drained moist gravelly soil and in ten years should be a symmetrical pyramid of up to 2m by 80cm (6ft by 30in) wide. A native of Canada and northern USA.

Hardiness 2.

Picea glauca 'Conica'   Dwarf Alberta Spruce

337 Also known as *P. glauca* 'Albertiana Conica', this compact erect-growing garden gem was originally found in the wilds near Lake Laggan, Alberta, Canada, in 1904 and has since found its way to the four corners of the globe. It has merit as a first-class rockery and garden subject. As its name suggests, it forms a neat erect cone of rich grass-green and in ten years should make a height of 80cm by 30cm (30in by 12in) at the base, with a potential height of 2 to 3m (6 to 10ft), but is easily kept smaller with an annual trimming if need be.   Hardiness 4.

337 *Picea glauca* 'Conica'. Spring. Glasgow, Scotland.

338 *Picea jezoensis* var. *hondoensis.* Spring. Hilversum, Netherlands.

339 *Picea jezoensis* var. *hondoensis.* Cones.

Picea jezoensis var. *hondoensis* — Hondo Spruce

338, 339 This beautiful erect-growing symmetrical conifer from the mountains of Hondo, Japan, has more compact foliage and growth than the Yezo Spruce, *P. jezoensis,* and is recommended as the more suited of the two as a garden ornamental. An ideal specimen tree for lawn planting, where it will have sufficient space to display its uniform tall conical shape to the best advantage. Normal leaf colour is a dull mid-green but springtime brings a spectacular colour display with the production of new leaf shoots of light green and young cones in purplish-red, contrasting with the darker mature foliage with its (occasionally seen) inner sides of silvery-blue. Average annual growth, 20 to 30cm (8 to 12in). Hardiness 5.

Picea omorika — Serbian Spruce

340 A handsome tree of tapering spire-like proportions that is habitually narrow and erect, seldom spreading to more than 3m (10ft) at the base yet capable of reaching heights of up to 35m (115ft). It is a native of Yugoslavia where it is confined to a small area on limestone slopes at altitudes between 800 and 1,800m (2,600 and 5,900ft), and like most of the spruces, prefers cold winters. Propagation is from seed with very little variation in type, and growth is of the order of about 40cm (15in) a year to make in ten years a tree up to 2m (6ft) wide at the base but increasing in width very little from then on. Hardiness 4.

340 *Picea omorika.* Summer. Palmerston North, New Zealand.

341 *Picea omorika* 'Expansa'. Spring. Washington, DC, USA.

342 *Picea omorika* 'Nana' Spring. Devizes, Wilts, England.

Picea omorika 'Expansa'   Spreading Serbian Spruce

341 An unusual variant among the six recorded cultivars of this usually tall narrow species, 'Expansa' has the typical foliage of its parent but no ambition to make any vertical leader growth. This peculiarity results in a low spreading shrub which in ten years would be 2m (6ft) across by 80cm (30in) high, the upward-facing branch tips standing at an angle of about 40 degrees away from the ground. An attractive spreading conifer that would be used more if it were better known.   Hardiness 4.

Picea omorika 'Nana'   Dwarf Serbian Spruce

342 A delightful compact member of the species, and a true dwarf having an annual growth of no more than 5cm (2in) and usually less on its less vigorous parts. Seen clearly in the photo are the whitish-blue stomatic bands on the undersides of the leaves, a typical feature of *P. omorika* and most other spruces, which together with the light-green upper colour and paler tips, just commencing their year's growth, make a pleasant combination of colours. It is an attractive garden gem, capable of making a height of 80cm (30in) in ten years' growth by 30cm (12in) in width and a somewhat irregular pyramidal shape that is nevertheless quite picturesque.
                                                                          Hardiness 4.

343 *Picea omorika* 'Pendula'. Spring. Washington, DC, USA.

Picea omorika 'Pendula'   Weeping Serbian Sprue

343 This gracefully-weeping version of *P. omorika* is characterised by longer and more slender downward-hanging branches that come upwards only at their extreme tips, the foliage likewise hanging freely to produce a tall elegant tree with a many-tiered effect. It has the typical tall columnar habit of the species at about half the rate of growth.   Hardiness 4.

344 *Picea orientalis.* Spring. Young cones and emerging buds.

345 *Picea orientalis* 'Gracilis'. Spring. Wisley, Surrey, England.

346 *Picea pungens* 'Glauca'. Spring. Dundee, Illinois, USA.

Picea orientalis   Eastern Spruce

344 A wide handsome pyramidal conifer that is well furnished in healthy-looking dark-green foliage right to ground level, and an ideal specimen for lawn planting where space is not at a premium. A native of Caucasus and northern Asia Minor, it is on record as capable of a height of 60m (200ft) but its growth rate of less than 30cm (12in) a year is not likely to create any immediate space problem, should one decide to plant a specimen on one's lawn. Seen here is foliage detail with the young, rich purple-red cones as they appear in the spring, and these eventually ripen to a brownish colour. This species, of which there are ten known cultivars, has been on record in England since 1770.   Hardiness 4.

Picea orientalis 'Gracilis'   Columnar Oriental Spruce

345 This slower-growing cultivar of *P. orientalis*, with leaves of a lighter grass-green colour has the more modest height potential of 6m (20ft), and an average growth increment of 10cm (4in) a year. It not infrequently spends its earlier years as a tub plant, being suited for this purpose with its rounded pyramidal habit, roughly half as high again as wide, becoming more erect-growing with age.   Hardiness 4.

Picea pungens 'Glauca'   Blue Colorado Spruce

346 The blue-foliaged forms of *Picea pungens* must rank among the most highly-prized of garden conifers, and in most countries where they are grown the demand for large well-shaped specimens usually far exceeds the supply. The name 'Glauca', as applied here, is used in its collective sense as including all glaucous-foliaged forms, and the illustration is of seed-grown specimens, being selected plants from a batch of *P. pungens*, and known to the trade as 'Shiners'. Every effort is made to secure seed from stands of parent trees showing predominantly bluish colouration, but even then less than one-third of these show sufficient blue colour to sell as such. In ten years, a height of 3m by 1.5m (10ft by 5ft) at the base can be expected of this species.   Hardiness 2.

347 *Picea pungens* 'Glauca Pendula'. Spring. Hilversum, Netherlands.

Picea pungens 'Glauca Pendula'

347 A fascinating variation in form that seems to possess on the one hand a desire to make erect leader growth, yet on the other has completely weeping foliage that sometimes turns up at the tips. The result is a plant that is quite unpredictable as to its final shape or form. No doubt a little "help from the audience" in its early years, in the form of staking or pruning, would go a long way towards turning possible confusion into a thing of beauty. It is definitely a plant for the enthusiast, with silvery-blue foliage, equal to the best of the blue cultivars, and a habit that is eye-catching to say the least. It was introduced in 1895 by the Dutch nursery firm of Koster & Company, of *Picea pungens* 'Koster' fame.   Hardiness 2.

Picea pungens 'Glauca Prostrata'
                            Prostrate Blue Spruce

348 Here we have a prostrate version of the Blue Colorado Spruce, quite a collector's item and a wonderful conifer for bank display, or, as illustrated, trailing downwards over a low rock ledge. Although it appears to be completely prostrate the original plant in the Hamburg Botanic Gardens, Germany, is reported to have disgraced itself by sending up an erect main shoot to a height of 6m (20ft). Such embarrassing situations can be avoided by the timely use of the secateurs if the owner should deem such action necessary. Growth is slow; a ten-year plant would measure no more than 2m (6ft) across by 40cm (15in) in height.   Hardiness 2.

348 *Picea pungens* 'Glauca Prostrata'. Spring. Wisley, Surrey, England.

349 *Picea pungens* 'Globosa'. Spring. Washington, DC. USA.

Picea pungens 'Globosa'

349 This compacted version of *P. pungens* originated as a seedling in a Dutch nursery in 1937 and soon became recognised as an ideal plant for the present-day smaller garden, having the excellent blue-grey colour of 'Koster' in a bush of more modest proportions. In ten years it may reach 50cm (20in) high by 70cm (28in) wide, an irregular mass of closely-set branchlets that is highly decorative in a rockery or garden setting. As with most species of *Picea*, a summer spraying against mites is strongly advised to prevent later defoliation of the plant, and this is a particularly necessary practice in warmer areas.
                                                            Hardiness 2.

350 *Picea pungens* 'Koster'. Spring. Christchurch, New Zealand.

351 *Picea pungens* 'Moerheimi'. Spring. Summertown, South Australia.

352 *Picea pungens* 'Thomsen'. Spring. Dundee, Illinois, USA.

Picea pungens 'Koster'   Koster's Blue Spruce

350 Among the thirty-eight recorded cultivars of *Picea pungens*, 'Koster' must take pride of place as the best known and most widely-grown of the blue forms of Colorado Spruce. It is one of the first to have been produced in any quantity, having been catalogued in the Netherlands in 1901, and has ever since been in demand as a specimen garden conifer, eventually finding its way into parks and gardens in the four corners of the globe. Propagation is by grafting, usually on to *P. abies*, and scion wood must be taken from leader growths of the parent tree in order to produce an erect-growing specimen—all these factors tending to make production more difficult and saleable plants more scarce. In ten years' growth an erect pyramid of 2m (6ft) high by 1m (3ft) at the base should be the result.   Hardiness 2.

Picea pungens 'Moerheimi'   Moerheim Blue Spruce

351 A very close rival in popularity to the Koster Blue Spruce, 'Moerheimi' is a selection by the Royal Moerheim Nurseries in the Netherlands and is preferred by many growers for its longer needles and stronger, more erect growth habit, along with the lovely silvery-blue foliage typical of the best of these selected forms of Colorado Blue Spruce. Under ideal conditions it is capable of making a height of (6ft) in ten years by 1m (3ft) in width at the base, and is best grown in a fully exposed location clear of any overhanging shade trees to ensure perfect regularity of form.
                                                            Hardiness 2.

Picea pungens 'Thomsen'

352 This is of much more recent (1932) selection than most other blue spruces, and it is to be expected that 'Thomsen' should have features that outshine earlier-named members of this group. And it does just this by virtue of its superb whitish silvery-blue foliage, more intense than that of any existing glaucous cultivar. Its long, substantial leaves are twice as thick as those of many other forms, and its erect, stately growth habit typical of the best of this group. Among the blue spruces it is doubtful whether there will ever be a more perfect selection than 'Thomsen'. Growth rate and hardiness as for 'Koster'.

353 *Picea sitchensis.* Summer. Palmerston North, New Zealand.

354 *Picea smithiana.* Winter. Taihape, New Zealand.

Picea sitchensis   Sitka Spruce

353 A hardy native of the north American continent that can be found growing from Alaska to North California. It is popular with nurserymen as a fast-growing specimen conifer, and is often the choice of landscapers when an instant specimen effect is required in the 3 to 4m (10 to 13ft) height range. They transplant reasonably well in this size, and will also tolerate soil conditions ranging from pure sand through to heavy bog. Aphis attack often occurs in warm, humid climates and should be controlled by spraying. A popular timber tree in many countries of the world, it can reach 10m (33ft) in its first ten years' growing, making a narrow conical tree that fills out at the top later in life.   Hardiness 6.

Picea smithiana   Himalayan Spruce

354, 355 Closely resembling the beautiful weeping *P. breweriana* in habit, the Himalayan Spruce may be recommended as a good substitute when one is unable to obtain a specimen of the former. It must be borne in mind however that this tree is a native of the mountains of Northern India and cannot be expected to survive winter cold below —17°C (0°F). A beautiful specimen tree with straight erect-growing trunk and leader, ascending branches from which the foliage hangs in cascades of up to 70cm (28in) in length, often terminated by the attractive cones which change from green when young to a mature shining brown. Average height for a ten-year specimen is 2.5m by 1m (8ft by 3ft) at base. Also known as *P. morinda*. Hardiness 6.

355 *Picea smithiana.* Cones.

356 *Pilgerodendron uviferum.* Foliage.

357 *Pinus aristata.* Spring. Haslemere, Surrey, England.

358 *Pinus canariensis.* Spring. Los Angeles, USA.

Pilgerodendron uviferum

356 A genus closely related to *Libocedrus* and at one time classified under that name, as *L. tetragona*, but now recognised as sufficiently different to belong in a genus of its own. It is native to South America, occurring chiefly on the slopes of the Chilean Andes, where it grows to heights of 25m (80ft) and is a valued source of timber. In cultivation in colder climates it is a slow grower, and makes little more than a small tree of stiff and upright habit. The tiny 4mm (⅛in) leaves are closely set in four ranks to give the branchlets a quadrangular appearance, an arrangement very like and often confused with that of *Fitzroya cupressoides*, also a native of the same area.

Hardiness 6.

Pinus aristata   Bristlecone Pine. Foxtail Pine

357 For those who collect dwarf and unusual conifers *P. aristata* is a "must". Not only is it the slowest-growing of any pine but it also has the reputation of being the oldest living tree species on earth. A specimen found recently in Nevada is believed to be 4,900 years old, more than 1,000 years older than the next oldest the giant Californian *Sequoia*. Its potential height of 10m (33ft) or so therefore, should not be a problem to the average gardener when he knows it may take it 1,500 years to get there. As a garden pine it is an attractive dwarf, the bushy darkgreen leaves in clusters of five liberally dusted with a whitish resin exudation giving an overall blue-green effect. Propagation is by seed, and annual growth is approximately 5cm (2in).

Hardiness 5.

Pinus canariensis   Canary Pine

358 A lovely pine in its earlier years, beginning life from seed in a rich glaucous blue colour not unlike that of the blue spruce. A cluster of these blue tips usually appears also at ground level round the leading growth which continues on up for 1m (3ft) or so to do the same at this higher level. The second year's growth sees the appearance in threes of longer green adult needles of up to 25cm (10in) but I imagine that if this foliage along with the leader were removed at regular intervals, the attractive juvenile glaucous effect could be retained for a few more years. The illustration shows a young tree with both types of growth. An excellent pine for temporary decorative tub or garden use that can later be moved elsewhere to continue its growth up to 30m (100ft). In five years it can reach to 5m (16ft).   Hardiness 7.

359 *Pinus cembra.* Spring. Washington, DC, USA.

360 *Pinus cembra* 'Chlorocarpa'. Spring.
Washington, DC, USA.

Pinus cembra   Swiss Stone Pine. Arolla Pine

359 This excellent landscape pine has been in garden use since 1746 and among its
virtue possesses a not-too-rapid growth rate, regular conical shape furnished right to
ground level, and a neat, fully-clothed appearance due to its needles holding on the
tree for up to five years. The needles are proportionately short (5 to 8cm /2 to 3in) and
the overall effect is of a full-grown mature pine tree (which it is), yet less than a
quarter of the size of its forest brothers. In ten years' growing, a tree a little less than
2m (6ft) would be the result. All round, an interesting pine of ideal proportions for
garden use.   Hardiness 4.

Pinus cembra 'Chlorocarpa'

360 A variation from the type that produces cones of a distinct yellow-green colour.
With all members of this species, of which there are thirteen on record, the cones
begin with an attractive purplish colour, and these grow no more than 8cm (3in) long,
maturing to a rich purplish-brown. These never open on the tree and do not fall
until the spring of their third year—the large edible seeds are not liberated until the
cone finally rots or is opened by force.   Hardiness 4.

361 *Pinus cembroides* var. *edulis.* Spring.
Washington, DC, USA.

Pinus cembroides var. *edulis*   Pinyon Pine. Nut Pine

361 *Pinus cembroides* is another compact short-needled pine that lends itself admirably to garden landscape work and provides a mature, seasoned look when even no
more than 2m (6ft) in height. A tree of this size would probably be fifteen years old
anyway, so in this case maturity is more than skin deep. The variety illustrated can
be considered a more consistent form of this somewhat variable species, and the
name *edulis* refers to the 2cm (¾in) rounded, edible nutlike seeds that are carried in
knobbly rounded cones no more than 6cm (about 2¼in) in diameter. These edible
seeds common to all members of the *P. cembroides* group are valued for food
by the Indians of Arizona, California and Mexico.   Hardiness 6.

362 *Pinus cembroides* var. *monophylla.* Spring.
San Francisco, USA.

363 *Pinus contorta* var. *contorta.* Spring. San Marino,
California, USA.

364 *Pinus contorta* var. *latifolia.* Autumn. Waiouru,
New Zealand.

Pinus cembroides var. *monophylla*   One-leaved Nut Pine

362 This variety is distinct from other nut pine forms in having longer (5cm/2in) stiffer leaves of a distinct glaucous blue-green colour, these being held singly instead of in twos, threes or fours as with other members of this group. It is reported to make a tree of 15m (50ft) in its native states of Utah and Arizona, but I imagine that this is a slow process and that a ten-year-old specimen would hardly reach 2m (6ft). In habit it is more irregular than *edulis* and tends to become flat-topped with age, and would be more suited to a garden position where symmetry of form is not essential.   Hardiness 5.

Pinus contorta var. *contorta*   Shore Pine

363 *Pinus contorta* as a species varies widely from a stunted-looking flat-topped small tree of 3m (10ft) to a forest king of up to 70m (230ft), but all bear common identification features such as short, twisted leaves in pairs, long dark reddish-brown buds and small prickly-looking cones. The botanical variety *contorta* shown here is a native of the Pacific coast of North America and belongs to the more compact former class, lending itself well to pruning and shaping in accord with the whims of the gardener, be he Oriental or European. Such a plant in the Huntingdon Gardens looks very much at home alongside the red Japanese bridge. Approximate height for a ten-year plant would be 2m (6ft).   Hardiness 5.

Pinus contorta var. *latifolia*   Lodgepole Pine

364 This is the opposite extreme in growth habit to the preceding variety, a tall tapering tree that may reach 70m (230ft) and not at all in keeping with the name *contorta*. As a young tree it is quite ornamental with its short, thick leaves and tidy growth habit, but will need plenty of room for later expansion. Illustrated is a self-sown seedling, one among many thousands in the desert plateau of central North Island, New Zealand, that have established themselves in this area, the very light seeds having been carried by wind for many kilometres from neighbouring forest plantings. A native of the North American Rockies where there are still vast areas of unmilled forest, it earned its name of Lodgepole Pine through its common use by the Indians as a centrepole for their lodges.   Hardiness 5.

365 *Pinus coulteri.* The Big-Cone Pine.

366 *Pinus densiflora.* Spring. Washington, DC, USA.

Pinus coulteri   Big-Cone Pine

365 An outstanding pine characterised by its huge cones, measuring up to 35cm (14in) in length and often weighing up to 2.3kg (5lb) in the green state — a formidable missile to land on one's head from the top of a 30m (100ft) tree. In its young state it is an interesting garden subject with its very stout, stiff needles of up to 30cm (12in) in length, arranged in threes, the whole tree having a sturdy character about it that is evident throughout its life. A native of dry mountain slopes of California, it makes best growth in reasonably light soils, reaching to 7m (23ft) in the first ten years.   Hardiness 8.

Pinus densiflora   Japanese Red Pine

366 So-called by reason of the reddish colour of the bark when young, *P. densiflora* is a native of Japan and is represented there by no fewer than twenty-three cultivars, very few of which are known outside that country. It is regarded there as the most common of all trees, and is also much planted in forests for timber. It is variable in shape with a tendency to twist and knot, and hence an excellent subject for pruning and shaping in the Japanese style. Although capable of reaching 35m (115ft) it would probably be no more than 3m (10ft) in height in its first ten years' growth, and if pruning is indulged in can be kept at practically any chosen height for the rest of its life.   Hardiness 4.

367 *Pinus densiflora* 'Pendula'. Spring. San Marino, California, USA.

Pinus densiflora 'Pendula'
         Weeping Japanese Pine

367 This is a very prostrate form that can either be left to trail over and among rockwork, or be first trained upwards to form a trunk before letting it revert to its weeping habit. Either way it is an attractive graceful specimen, and it is a pity that it is not more widely available from the nursery trade. The specimen shown was probably twenty years old and measured some 2m (6ft) across.   Hardiness 4.

368 *Pinus densiflora* 'Umbraculifera'. Spring. Dundee, Illinois, USA.

Pinus densiflora 'Umbraculifera' Tanyosho Pine

368 Probably the best-known cultivar of *P. densiflora* in the Western world is the Tanyosho or Umbrella Pine, so-called because of its dense flattish parasol-like top, from which the branches converge to the base, not unlike the ribs of an umbrella. It grows slowly and is an excellent tub or rockery plant for many years before it reaches its ultimate of 5m (16ft) at around thirty-five years of age. They are often coveted for large landscape projects, and offers of up to $1,500 are not unknown for good-shaped specimens of this size.   Hardiness 4.

369 *Pinus griffithii*. Spring. Los Angeles, USA.

370 *Pinus griffithii*. Cones.

Pinus griffithii   Bhutan Pine

369, 370 It is rather confusing when one book lists this as *P. wallichiana* and the other main authority, Den Ouden, prefers the above name. In New Zealand it is known more by its now superseded name of *P. excelsa*; but in all cases the reference is to the Bhutan or Himalayan Pine, one of the distinct features of which is the long, narrow downward-hanging cones, quite smooth and not unlike those of *Picea smithiana* for shape. It eventually becomes a large tree to 40m (130ft) in height, but in its earlier years is a useful and attractive ornamental that possesses the added virtue of being more resistant to atmospheric pollution than other pine species. It is a fairly fast grower, in ten years able to reach to 4 or 5m (13 or 16ft) in height Welch mentions 'Nana' as a dwarf form with shorter, more silvery leaves.

Hardiness 5.

371 *Pinus griffithii* 'Zebrina'. Wahington, DC, USA.

372 *Pinus halepensis.* Spring. Los Angeles, USA.

373 *Pinus heldreichii* var. *leucodermis.* Spring.
Washington, DC, USA.

Pinus griffithii 'Zebrina'   Striped Bhutan Pine

371 Quite a peculiarity among pines, 'Zebrina' is so-named by reason of the barred and striped effect produced by the band of cream colouring which runs across each bunch of downward-hanging needles. It has been around for nearly 100 years, raised at the Croux nursery in France in 1874, but is still by no means common, and according to the books on the subject has not yet been grown in Britain. It is slower growing than the type as may be expected of a variegated plant, to 3m (10ft) in ten years.
Hardiness 5.

Pinus halepensis   Aleppo Pine. Jerusalem Pine

372 Outstanding among the features of *P. halepensis* is its great ability to withstand drought and extended periods of heat, and it is a much-planted tree in its native Mediterranean countries for coastal areas and exposed situations. Of note in younger plants are the short, narrow grey-green needles, usually in pairs, and the ash-grey colour of the branches and branchlets, with age changing from a pyramidal form to a rounded top, bare at the base. The specimen illustrated is rather more than typical in this respect, having been pruned bare for more than half its length of trunk, but nevertheless an attractive focal point on a bank covered with yellow arctotis and prostrate junipers. Growth rate is moderate, to 3m (10ft) in ten years.   Hardiness 7

Pinus heldreichii var. *leucodermis*   Bosnian Redcone Pine

373   *P. heldreichii*, a native of mountains of the West Balkans, is a strong-growing pyramidal tree reaching to 20m (65ft) and is represented in garden form by its smaller alpine counterpart, var. *leucodermis*, an excellent garden plant that has been in nursery cultivation in Europe for many decades. In ten years it would reach to approximately 1.5m (5ft) in height by 70mm (2¾in) at the base, pyramidal in shape with short, stiff dark-green needles, and looking very much the sturdy little alpine pine that it is. Two lesser-known cultivars of *P. heldreichii* are 'Compact Gem' and 'Pygmy', both dwarf growers and also attractive garden subjects.   Hardiness 5.

374 *Pinus monticola.* Spring. Hilversum, Netherlands.

Pinus monticola   Western White Pine

374 This is a native of the mountain areas of Western
North America; specimens there are known to reach
65m (200ft) in height and ages of up to 500 years. It is a
symmetrical straight-growing conical tree that rarely
needs trimming or shaping and is widely used for timber
in its native countries, also for the making of matches.
The long, tapering cones hang downwards from the
branch tips and are a distinct purplish colour when young,
later maturing to a warm brown. In ten years it should
reach to 4m by 2m (13ft by 6ft) at the base, this rate of
spread decreasing as the tree becomes older.

Hardiness 5.

375 *Pinus montezumae.* Spring. Ampfield, Hants, England.

Pinus montezumae   Montezuma Pine

375 This semi-tropical pine from Mexico, with long and
substantial needles of a distinct light blue-green colour,
makes a round-topped tree of up to 40m (130ft) in its
homeland, but considerably less in colder climates. It is
hardy in Zone 8 or possibly 7, and is grown successfully
in Southern England but on the Continent it is more
likely to be a greenhouse plant than an outdoor tree. It
carries its needles in clusters of anything from three to
eight depending on vigour and climate conditions, older
trees having attractive reddish-brown deeply-fissured
bark and reddish branches.

376 *Pinus mugo.* Spring. Dundee, Illinois, USA.

Pinus mugo   Dwarf Mountain Pine

376 *Pinus mugo*, once known as *P. montana*, a native of
the mountain areas of Europe, is highly variable in form
and one photograph is not really equal to representing
this species in a typical way. In its native state it ranges in
size from a low bun-shaped mound to occasional trees of
20m (65ft) high, and positive identification of this species
therefore depends on comparisons of cone, bud, leaf and
bark details rather than shape or size of tree. The dwarfer
forms are highly ornamental slow-growing garden subjects, excellent for large tub or rockery, and most seedling-
raised plants available nowadays are grown from one of
the more fixed-form compact varieties such as *P. mughus*
and *P. pumilio*, or the larger shrubby varieties *rotundata*
or *rostrata*.   Hardiness 2.

377 *Pinus mugo* 'Gnom'. Spring. Boskoop, Netherlands.

Pinus mugo 'Gnom'

377 A selection by the Den Ouden nurseries, Boskoop, Netherlands, as the best from a large quantity of seedling *P. mugo* var. *mughus*, 'Gnom' is probably the most popular named cultivar among the mugo pines today. As with all of this species the needles are in pairs, about 4cm (1½in) in length, closely set on short many-branched stems to form a tight little bush, in ten years about 80cm wide (30in) and 50cm (20in) high. The mass of whitish spring shoots shown in the photograph will eventually mature into the current year's growth, and change to its typical rich black-green colour. Grafting is the usual method of propagation of cultivars such as this. Hardiness 2.

378 *Pinus mugo* 'Mops'. Spring. Boskoop, Netherlands.

Pinus mugo 'Mops'

378 Another lovely low-growing pine, selected and propagated in the same way as 'Gnom', this time at the Hooftman nursery at Boskoop, and it is probably the most compact named cultivar in this group, making bun-shaped little bush about 40cm (15in) high by 60cm (24in) wide in a period of ten years. Still another cultivar from the same nursery is 'Kobold', having very short needles (25mm/1in) possibly not quite so tight a grower as 'Mops', but nonetheless an excellent dwarf pine for tub or rockery growing. There is no great difference to the untrained eye between many of these cultivars but once given cultivarietal names they must continue under these names when propagated vegetatively i.e. by grafting or cuttings. Hardiness 2.

379 *Pinus mugo* var. *mughus.* Spring. Wisley, Surrey, England.

Pinus mugo var. mughus   Mugho Swiss Mountain Pine

379 As variations of habit in *P. mugo* var. *mughus* go, the specimen shown here is what one may expect to find at the larger end of the scale—a many-branched small tree of 2m (6ft) in height. Compare this with the next illustration, and we see the other extreme and the type of plant that every nurseryman hopes to get from every seed he germinates. Either photograph could be used to illustrate either variety, as the sorting-out between var. *mughus* and var. *pumilio* depends largely on the comparison of cone details. Partly mature cones of the former should be a yellow-brown colour, while the cones of the latter have a purplish tint, ripening to brown, and are almost globular in shape. Hardiness 2.

Pinus mugo var. *pumilio*
Dwarf Swiss Mountain Pine

380 A compact and uniformily-rounded bun of short rich green needles is what every nurseryman hopes he will get from every seed packet he sows of the above-named *P. mugo* pine, but in practice he considers himself fortunate to get more than 40 per cent of his plants as uniform as these shown. The strain known as 'Dwarf Tyrolean' is considered to be the most consistent seed source available, and those plants that do not conform to pattern are generally useful for odd tub or rockery plantings — and even though they are a little more open or spreading, they make very attractive garden plants. Plants at the 40cm (15in) size illustrated would be four to five years old.   Hardiness 2.

380 *Pinus mugo* var. *pumilio*. Spring. Dundee, Illinois, USA.

381 *Pinus mugo* var. *rostrata*. Spring. Washington, DC, USA.

Pinus mugo var. *rostrata*

381 Yet another varietal form of *P. mugo*, intermediate between the very dwarf bun-shaped alpine types and the pine-tree shape as we usually know it. The form used for garden purposes seems to be more squat-growing than the type which in its native Pyreneean Alps becomes a tree to 25m (80ft) and is regarded there as a useful source of millable timber. Yet another variety is *rotundata*, more compact than *rostrata* but not as tight as *pumilio*. It is regarded by some that the varieties *rotundata* and *rostrata* belong in a species of their own, *P. uncinata*, because of their larger (6cm/2¼in) cones, and in some books you will find them under the latter heading.
                              Hardiness 3.

382 *Pinus nigra*. Spring. San Francisco, USA.

Pinus nigra   Black Pine

382 A species widely distributed throughout Central Europe, carring common names adopted from respective localities, such as Corsican Pine (var. *maritima*), Crimean Pine (var. *caramanica*), Pyrenean Pine (var. *cebennensis*), or Austrian Pine (var. *nigra*). All are quite distinguishable from one another, and are mainly forest or shelter trees, the Corsican Pine being probably the one most used as a timber tree. The Austrian Pine has value as a seaside tree with great ability to withstand strong winds while growing equally as well in either sand or heavy clay soils. As an ornamental, it does not look at all out of place near one of the gates to the Strybing Arboretum, San Francisco. A growth rate of 2.5m (8ft) in ten years would be average for this species.   Hardiness 4.

383 *Pinus nigra* 'Hornibrookiana'. Spring. San Francisco, USA.

385 *Pinus parviflora* 'Glauca'. Spring. Wisley, Surrey, England.

384 *Pinus nigra* var. *maritima*. Autumn. Hanmer, New Zealand.

Pinus nigra 'Hornibrookiana'

383 One of the few dwarf cultivars of *P. nigra*, this one originated as a witches broom on an Austrian Pine in Rochester, New York, around 1930. It is an excellent garden ornamental of spreading, ground-hugging habit in rich dark green, ideally suited to planting among rocks, and is at its best during spring when displaying its new crop of creamy-coloured young shoots, standing vertically like so many little candles on a cake. Like most conifers derived from witches brooms, this one is a slow grower; a ten-year-old plant would probably measure no more than 1m (3ft) wide by 40m (15in) in height. Grafting is the usual method of propagation.   Hardiness 4.

386 *Pinus parviflora* 'Glauca'. Cone and foliage.

Pinus nigra var. *maritima*   Corsican Pine

384 For those who desire the stillness and majesty of a needle-carpeted forest, this is their pine. These trees were planted in 1904, making them sixty-four years old when photographed, so it would seem that one should not procrastinate when planting one's forest. In Corsica, trees are milled at the average age of 180 years which is about half their usual life span; whichever way you look at it, this tree is suitable mainly for long-term projects, although young 'thinnings' are often used for the making of fence-posts. As can be expected it produces excellent timber while having an adaptability to a wide range of soil types.   Hardiness 4.

387 *Pinus patula.* Spring. Menlo Park, California, USA.

Pinus patula   Weeping Pine

387 A highly-ornamental weeping pine with long (up to 30cm/12in) glossy grass-green needles that hang in graceful clusters from the ascending branches to create (especially in older trees) an elegant cascade. Large trees form an effective shelter and garden backdrop when planted together, while single specimens make an excellent fast-growing focal point. It is an easy matter once the tree has reached sufficient size to limit its spread with an annual pruning. A native of Mexico, it is not hardy in Continental Europe, but is a popular ornamental in California and New Zealand, where it is also under trial as a forest tree. In ten years it is capable of reaching 5m by 3m (16ft by 10ft) at the base.   Hardiness 7.

Pinus parviflora 'Glauca'

385, 386 This attractive blue-foliaged form of the Japanese White Pine could easily be taken for a dwarf when young. It is in any case not a fast grower, annual growth being around the 12cm (5in) mark, and is an excellent garden plant, not likely to outgrow its situation for many years and easily pruned to an attractive shape while keeping the plant to size. Although den Ouden quotes the height as 10 to 20m (33 to 66ft) he does not mention at what age. The needles, in clusters of five, gain the bluish effect from the bright blue-white stomatic bands on the inner sides of each needle, the reverse being a normal green. *Pinus parviflora* in all forms is a popular subject for bonsai-type cultivation. Two more compact cultivars are 'Brevifolia' (upright) and 'Gimborns Pyramid' (spreading).   Hardiness 5.

388 *Pinus pinaster.* Winter. Christchurch, New Zealand.

Pinus pinaster   Maritime Pine

388 The Maritime Pine of the Mediterranean countries has for many years been the world's main supplier of resin, and there are large forests in the south of France devoted to that industry. The resin is extracted from the trunk by tapping, and trees thus used also yield a harder timber once they have reached the end of their useful life, which is usually around eighty years. It is a tree well suited to coastal growing and very much at home in a light, sandy soil. Capable of reaching 5m (16ft) in ten years, it is conical at first but with age becomes rounded at the top, losing most of the lower branches to display more effectively that highly-ornamental, deeply-fissured reddish-brown trunk.   Hardiness 7.

389 *Pinus pinea.* Summer. Wellington, New Zealand.

390 *Pinus pinea.* Cone and seed.

Pinus pinea — Italian Stone Pine

389, 390 Another Mediterranean pine, also commonly known as the Umbrella Pine with its rounded umbrella-like top, this is a picturesque subject where one has room for a tree of this size, which is potentially 25m (80ft) in seventy-odd years. When young and still in juvenile foliage it is a neat conical bush of a lovely bluish colour and short, stiff needles not unlike a young blue spruce, and bearing no resemblance to its round-topped, green-leaved parent. Many young plants are sold in this condition as an ornamental, and it should be possible to keep them this way a little longer by restricting the roots in a tub and pruning away any green needles that appear. Under normal growing conditions the adult green foliage takes over in the third year when the tree is approaching 2m (6ft) in height.   Hardiness 8.

391 *Pinus ponderosa.* Spring. Washington, DC, USA.

392 *Pinus pumila.* Spring. Wisley, Surrey, England.

Pinus ponderosa — Western Yellow Pine

391 A common forest and timber tree and one of the largest specimens being noted at up to 70m (230ft) in its native regions, the mountains of western North America. As a young tree it is interesting with the well-furnished look that goes with pines that hold their needles for the third year before dropping them. It is a three-needle pine that is frequently used as a grafting stock for other three- and five-needled pines. In ten years it is capable of a height of 3m (10ft) and continues to make a tall, narrow tree with straight, clean trunk and spire-like top.   Hardiness 5.

Pinus pumila 'Dwarf Blue'

393 Photographed in the Nisbet collection of dwarf and slow-growing conifers at the Royal Horticultural Society's garden at Wisley, this conifer in 1968 carried the name of *Pinus cembra* 'Pygmaea', but unfortunately that name did not tally with descriptions in the current books on the subject. It does however tally with the description of *Pinus pumila* 'Prostrata', at one time regarded as synonymous with the above, which in Mr Welch's opinion is apparently no different from the better-known and popular compact cultivar 'Dwarf Blue'; it is under this last name that we prefer to leave it. To quote Mr Hillier (who lists it as 'Prostrata'): "A gem among dwarf conifers, my plant in about thirty-five years has reached 21 in by 48in." (53cm high by 122cm wide)   Hardiness 5.

393 *Pinus pumila* 'Dwarf Blue'. Spring. Wisley, Surrey, England.

394 *Pinus radiata.* Spring. Los Angeles, USA.

395 *Pinus radiata.* Cones and foliage.

Pinus pumila   Japanese Stone Pine

392 Also known as the Dwarf Siberian Pine, *P. pumila* may be found in large groves in the mountains of Japan and east Asia, usually in the highest, most exposed situations on windswept plateaux or near the snowline. A five-needled pine with glaucous-green foliage, it has botanically much in common with *P. cembra* but is generally more prostrate and smaller in all its parts. Seedling plants make excellent rockery subjects for many years and in time produce small violet-purplish cones that change slowly over a period of two years to a reddish-brown. Average height for a ten-year specimen would be 60cm (24in).   Hardiness 3.

Pinus radiata   Monterey Pine

394, 395 It is interesting to note how the use to which a conifer is put is entirely dependent on the area in which it is grown. A good example of such treatment is the Monterey Pine which in its native California is of little value as a timber tree—it is planted there chiefly as an ornamental or shelter tree and valued for its cheerful bright green foliage and picturesque growth habit. Conversely in New Zealand, where it makes optimum growth for timber production and is planted in millions yearly for forest use, it is never considered for ornamental use, being rather too common to attract attention for such a purpose. In ideal situations it can add 1m (3ft) in growth per year and be ready for milling in twenty years. It is noted also for its large cones up to 15cm (6in), often in clusters. They are bright green when young and mature to a warm brown. It is a three-needled pine.   Hardiness 7.

397 *Pinus strobus* 'Nana'. Spring. Wisley, Surrey, England.

396 *Pinus radiata* 'Aurea'. Spring. Temuka, New Zealand.

398 *Pinus strobus*. Cones.

Pinus radiata 'Aurea'   Golden Monterey Pine

396 Among the millions of *P. radiata* seedlings raised annually in Australia, New Zealand and South Africa, it is surprising that more cultivars of unusual colour or shape have not occurred. 'Aurea' seems to have been the only cultivar to be considered worth naming to date, and as its name implies its needles are a bright golden-yellow, otherwise conforming fairly closely to typical Monterey Pine specifications. The original tree, in the South Island, New Zealand, now twenty or more years old, has coned and produced seedlings, a high percentage of which displayed good golden leaf colour but for some reason did not survive more than one or two seasons. It seems that the usual methods of grafting or cutting propagation are the only reliable ones for reproducing this attractive colour variant.   Hardiness 7.

Pinus strobus 'Nana'   Dwarf White Pine

397, 398 The dwarf forms of *P. strobus*, the White Pine of eastern North America, are excellent rockery subjects with their compacted growth habit, the needle clusters so close as to completely hide any of the inner branch structure. Such a plant is 'Nana', illustrated, which is intermediate in form between 'Umbraculifera', a round-topped bush with drooping leaves, and 'Prostrata', which prefers to be flat on the ground. Such plants are slow growing and make little more than 6cm (about 2¼in) of growth a year. Propagation is by grafting on to seedling *P. strobus*, which is also the preferred understock for most dwarf three- to five-needled pines   Hardiness 3.

Pinus sylvestris   Scots Pine

399 The Scots Pine, as well as being a popular timber tree in the United Kingdom and Europe, is also in demand as an ornamental whether in its young state — sometimes in a tub (often sold as a Christmas tree), at which stage the shape is pyramidal and the colour blue-green—or later in life when a picturesque rounded top develops, and the lower branches have fallen away to leave exposed the attractive pinkish-orange trunk, seen at its best in a group of the same kind. It is prone to witches broom and in its 200 years in cultivation has produced many named dwarf forms by this means, along with others such as 'Fastigiata' which usually begin as seedling variants, there being more than fifty cultivars now on record, but few of them in general cultivation. To date grafting is the only method of perpetuating such cultivars, but it is possible that the recent cutting methods so successful in New Zealand with *P. radiata* could be applied to these ornamental forms. (The columnar green *Chamaecyparis lawsoniana* seen here is described under Plate 76.)
Hardiness 3.

Pinus sylvestris 'Argentea Compacta'

400 As the name suggests this is a compact grower in silvery grey and a fine plant for rockery or large tub. I have retained the 'Compacta' part of the name as given on this specimen photographed in the Gotelli collection in Washington DC, to keep it distinct from the one Dr Boom lists as 'Argentea', which is a tall-growing silvery form and not a dwarf. The plant is particularly attractive during spring with all the new growths standing erect and almost vertical; these later open out into needles to give the plant its average 40mm (1½in) yearly increase in size.   Hardiness 3.

399 *Pinus sylvestris.* Spring. Bodnant, North Wales.

400 *Pinus sylvestris* 'Argentea Compacta'. Spring. Washington, DC, USA.

Pinus sylvestris 'Beuvronensis'

401 Typical of the Witch's Broom variation of *P. sylvestris*, with its densely compacted form almost completely hiding the branches, *P.s.* 'Beuvronensis' makes a somewhat irregular bush of roughly equal proportions, adding to its stature to the extent of 40mm (1½in) yearly. This makes for a very slow-growing plant which would no doubt need to spend many of its earlier years in a pot before planting out; or one may wish to compromise, as Mr Gotelli did with many of his cherished specimens, by planting the pot and plant together, making it easier to change locations when the plant outgrows its situation. Such plants in any case would need re-potting at least every second year.   Hardiness 3.

402 *Pinus sylvestris* 'Fastigiata'. Spring. San Francisco, USA.

401 *Pinus sylvestris* 'Beuvronensis'. Spring. Washington, DC, USA.

Pinus sylvestris 'Fastigiata'

402 Quite a dramatic variation from the usual Scots pine shape, 'Fastigiata' is slower growing than the type (to 2.5m (8ft) in ten years) with little or no increase in spread, there being on record specimens 10m (33ft) high with a base width of less than 1m (3ft) The needles are an attractive bluish-green, thus making it a useful evergreen ornamental capable of withstanding winters too cold for most other narrow conifers   Hardiness 2

403 *Pinus sylvestris* 'Viridis Compacta'. Spring.
Washington DC, USA.

404 *Pinus sylvestris* 'Watereri'. Spring. San Francisco, USA.

Pinus sylvestris 'Viridis Compacta'

403 This little rounded slow-growing bush that takes many years to attain a height of 1.5m (5ft) is more of a curiosity than a thing of beauty, with its 10cm (4in) long twisted leaves of a distinct grass-green colour. The name 'Globosa Viridis' is also used for this (or a very similar) plant, and it would seem that the names can be regarded as synonymous. Hardiness 4.

Pinus sylvestris 'Watereri'

404 This slow-growing blue form of Scots Pine can build itself up in time to quite a tree, according to Mr Welch, who reports that the original plant in Waterer's nursery, Bagshot, Surrey, at a 100 years of age had reached a height of about 7.5m (25ft). For garden purposes however, it may still be regarded as a dwarf and with its annual growth of only 8cm (3in) one need not be worried about space problems for many years after planting. It is eminently suitable for planting either in a setting of large rocks or bedded in association with other low and medium conifers. Hardiness 2.

Pinus thunbergii   Japanese Black Pine

405 This is one of the commonest pines of Japan as a timber tree and also as an ornamental, having been used over the centuries for bonsai and general garden work. In most cases it is pruned systematically once or twice yearly to control shape or size according to the gardener's desires. *Pinus thunbergii* is not among the fastest-growing pines but can be expected to average 3m (10ft) for ten years' growing without any pruning; it may be reduced to 50cm (20in) or less by pruning. Specimens vary in habit widely, being seedling-raised, but the rugged trunk and branch framework give the tree character, and the rigid thickish needles and conspicuous white buds serve to distinguish it from other pines. Hardiness 5.

Pinus virginiana   Scrub Pine

406 A pine of variable dimensions ranging in height from a shrub of 2m (6ft) to a tree of 30m (115ft) in its native state, the eastern side of North America. It is distinguishable from other pines by its purplish young shoots with a glaucous covering. *Pinus virginina* would not normally qualify for inclusion in this book but this fine bonsai specimen in the collection at the Brooklyn Botanic Gardens, New York, indicates that it is an excellent ornamental when cultivated in this way. It has the virtue of being one of the few trees that will give good results on heavy clay soil where little else will grow. Hardiness 4.

Podocarpus acutifolius

407 This compact version of the New Zealand totara, although capable of making a tree of 10m (33ft), is best cultivated as a shrub by keeping it to size with an annual pruning, which also gives better density of foliage. It makes a fine hedge that trims

405 *Pinus thunbergii*. Spring. San Francisco, USA.

406 *Pinus virginiana.* Bonsai specimen. Brooklyn, New York, USA.

408 *Podocarpus andinus.* Spring. Hilversum, Netherlands.

407 *Podocarpus acutifolius.* Autumn. Wellington, New Zealand.

well and does not need constant cutting with its moderate annual growth of 10cm (4in). The prickly leaves are a deterrent to persons or animals attempting to break through its boundary. The summer colour of light olive-green changes to a bronzy shade for the winter.   Hardiness 6.

Podocarpus andinus   Plum-fruited Yew

408 A native of the South Chilean Andes, this yew may be found growing at altitudes between 1,200 and 2,000m (3,900 and 6,600ft). *P. andinus* earns its common name from the appearance of its rounded plum-like fruits which measure up to 20mm (¾in) in diameter and are a pale yellow colour. In general appearance this shrub has much in common with members of the Yew family (*Taxus*), but is lighter in colour, and apart from being less hardy may be used in much the same way, particularly for hedging. A steady 15 to 20cm (6 to 8in) annual growth is no problem if trimmed or pruned, but given fifty to sixty years with no cutting it can become a tree of up to 20m (65ft) in height.   Hardiness 6.

Podocarpus falcatus   Oteniqua Yellow Wood

409 A native of South Africa that is much prized there for timber production, this tree makes up to 30m (100ft) in height and 6m (20ft) in girth. Its value as an ornamental, however, is not so spectacular, its main use being as a potted plant at which it excels, making a 1m (3ft) specimen in two years or less and possessing sufficient hardiness and tolerance of poor light to withstand the rigours of pot-plant life. A similar closely-related species, *P. gracilior*, with finer leaves, is also popular for the same purpose.   Hardiness 8.

409 *Podocarpus falcatus.* Foliage.

410 *Podocarpus macrophyllus.* Spring. San Francisco, USA.

411 *Podocarpus macrophyllus* var. *maki.* Spring. Los Angeles, USA.

Podocarpus macrophyllus   Yew Podocarpus

410 A native of China and Japan, found in Yunnan at altitudes around 3,000m (10,000ft) *P. macrophyllus* is a popular specimen shrub in California, its informally irregular upright habit and rich grass-green foliage making it a year-round focal point in the garden. In its earlier years it is an excellent pot-plant, tolerating a little shade, and one expects to see this species more widely grown once its virtues become better known. It is a medium grower, taking an average of ten years to reach 2.5m (8ft), although odd specimens are known to remain shrubby

while others in time reach a height of 15m (50ft) It takes well to pruning or trimming, and in Japan it is used successfully for hedging. Six forms or cultivars are recorded, including one dwarf, 'Hillier's Compact', and also white-and-yellow-variegated forms.   Hardiness 7.

Podocarpus macrophyllus var. *maki*
                                    Shrubby Podocarpus

411 A more compact form of Yew Podocarpus which can be recommended where space is limited. It usually branches just above ground level into several near-vertical branches to make a tidy well-furnished shrub in dark glossy green, not unlike a large-leaved form of Irish Yew, and in ten years should be almost 2m (6ft) in height by 80cm (30in) at its widest part. The specimen shown has a longer, more flexible foliage than the usual 5cm (2in) leaf, due mainly to vigorous growth promoted by its well-sheltered, partly-shaded location under the roof overhang of the house. As good subject for tub or garden planting. This variety can be propagated true to type from seed.   Hardiness 7.

Podocarpus nivalis   Alpine Totara

412 A low-growing almost prostrate native of New Zealand, the Alpine Totara is at home in locations up to 2,000m (6,600ft), but in equally at home at lower altitudes set among rocks in the home garden. It bushes out nicely into a ground-covering low shrub, not un-attractive in a soft olive-green, and makes an annual growth of approximately 10cm (4in). It has been known to cross with other species of *Podocarpus* — there is one such example at the Otari Native Plant Museum in Wellington, New Zealand, a hybrid between *P nivalis* and *P hallii* and a colour variant bearing the name 'Bronze' is recorded in Mr Welch's book, *Dwarf Conifers*.
                                        Hardiness 6.

412 *Podocarpus nivalis.* Autumn. Mt Cook, New Zealand.

413 *Podocarpus totara.* Summer. Wellington, New Zealand.

Podocarpus totara   Totara

413 Another New Zealand native, used in that country as a timber tree and an ornamental; younger trees like the one illustrated are clothed in the small prickly leaves right to the ground, but with age become bare at the base, exposing a picturesque branch and trunk structure. Forest giants of up to 200 years old are a majestic sight in their native state with a clean straight trunk to 25m (80ft) or more before branching into top growth, with a base diameter of 2 or 3m (6 or 10ft) thick. The light red timber is much prized for general building, fence posts and other purposes, is straight-grained, easily worked and durable in or out of the ground. Supply is now very limited due to the 100-year minimum milling age of this tree. Average height for a ten-year specimen would be 2.5m (8ft). Hardiness 7.

414 *Podocarpus totara* 'Aurea'. Autumn. Palmerston North, New Zealand.

Podocarpus totara 'Aurea'   Golden Totara

414 Although this may be the first listing of the cultivar in a book of this kind I don't expect it to be the last. It has been around in New Zealand for probably twenty years and is now obtainable from most nurseries, but due to its slow growth in the early years one is not usually able to purchase specimens taller than 25cm (10in) and at this size they do not look very inspiring. After ten years' growing however, it should be past the 2m (6ft) mark, an attractive golden column which can be trimmed to a fully symmetrical shape if need be, the tree being quite amenable to shaping or dwarfing to suit the desires of the gardener. In all an excellent garden conifer that has consistent year-round good looks and is not difficult to grow. Hardiness 7.

415 *Pseudolarix amabilis.* Bonsai specimen. Spring. Brooklyn, New York, USA.

416 *Pseudolarix amabilis.* Cones.

Pseudolarix amabilis   Golden Larch

415, 416 A native of China where specimens are known to reach heights of 40m (130ft) and also a popular subject for Bonsai-type culture, as depicted in the photograph of a fine old specimen in the bonsai collection at the Brooklyn Botanic Gardens, New York. Mr Kalmbacher reports from there that it is a tough tree that can grow well in city parks, something that true larix cannot do. Autumn sees it a wonderful golden colour, hence the common name, and small 5 to 7cm (2 to 2¾in) cones open reddish-brown like small flowers along the branches. Propagation is by seed but this is not usually easy to obtain and often has poor viability, which is probably why the tree is not more widely grown. Previous names used for the Golden Larch are *P. kaemferi* and *Larix amabilis*.   Hardiness 5.

417 *Pseudotsuga menziesii.* Autumn. Richmond, New Zealand.

418 *Pseudotsuga menziesii* 'Caesia'. Cones.

419 *Pseudotsuga menziesii* 'Densa'. Spring. Washington, DC, USA.

420 *Pseudotsuga menziesii* 'Fletcheri'. Spring. Wisley, Surrey, England.

421 *Pseudotsuga menziesii* 'Pendula'. Spring. Washington, DC, USA.

Pseudotsuga menziesii Oregon Pine. Douglas Fir

417, 418 Of the five recorded species of *Pseudotsuga*, *menziesii* (previously known as *P. taxifolia* or *P. douglasii*) is by far the most cultivated, primarily as a timber tree and secondarily as an ornamental, there being no fewer then fifty-six forms or cultivars on record—though many of these seem to be no longer in cultivation. Its virtues as a timber tree are well known, with specimens on record reaching heights of 100m (330ft) at ages of up to 400 years, but it also has shorter-term value as an ornamental, making a first-class evergreen windbreak and garden backdrop, or as a single specimen on a large lawn, the downward-hanging cones which appear at an early age adding to the decorative effect. A blue-foliaged form, *P. menziesii.* var. *glauca*, from the central Rocky Mountains, is slower-growing and more pyramidal in form and if available is to be preferred for garden planting. The average ten-year height for *P. menziesii.* would be 5m by 2.5m (16ft by 8ft) at the base.   Hardiness 6.

Pseudotsuga menziesii 'Densa'

419 One of the lesser-known dwarf cultivars of Douglas Fir, an irregular, dumpy little heap of cheerful, dark-green foliage bearing little resemblance to its towering forest parent, apart from foliage detail. It is clearly a rockery subject and with its annual growth of about 5cm (2in) is not likely to outgrow its position for many years, and if it does become over-large can be quite easily pruned back to size. The needles of this cultivar are about half the length of those of the species.   Hardiness 6.

Pseudotsuga menziesii 'Fletcheri'

420 The fact that it is a seedling of the Rocky Mountain variety *glauca*, which some botanists prefer to list as a separate species, explains why this cultivar is sometimes listed as *P. glauca* 'Fletcheri'. It is probably the most popular of the dwarf Douglas Firs, a first-class garden conifer, and this specimen at the Royal Horitucltural Society's gardens at Wisley was in 1968 1.3m (4¼ft) high at an estimated age of twenty-five years. The irregular shape and the wider-than-high proportions are typical of this cultivar.   Hardiness 6.

Pseudotsuga menziesii 'Pendula'
Weeping Douglas Fir

421 This picture of a Weeping Douglas Fir growing in the Gotelli collection of dwarf and slow-growing conifers in Washington, DC, would appear to be of a dwarf which would remain so for many years. Whether it is the same as the tall-growing weeping specimen of the same name in the Pinetum Blijdenstein in the Netherlands and illustrated on page 375 of den Ouden and Boom's book, *Manual of Cultivated Conifers*, seems doubtful, but not impossible if the one had been given restrictive growing conditions (as Mr Gotelli often arranged) and the other had been encouraged to ascend. For rock gardens the former habit would be excellent on an outcrop, if allowed to cascade downwards, and with its annual 6 to 10cm (2¼ to 4 in) growth would be unlikely to ever get out of hand.   Hardiness 6.

422 *Saxegothaea conspicua.* Foliage.

Saxegothaea conspicua   Prince Albert's Yew

422 A South American native found chiefly in Chile and West Patagonia, where it occurs in dense forests in the lower mountain regions. It is a botanical curiosity in that it is said to form a link between the families *Podocarpaceae* and *Araucariaceae*, resembling the former in foliage and the latter in female strobilii while the ripe fruit suggests that of a juniper. To confuse us further, it looks more like a yew than any of these genera, with leaves of similar 2cm ($\frac{3}{4}$in) length and colour, strongly marked on the reverse with two white stomatic bands. It is also similar in growth habit, slowly making a maximum of 12m (40ft), but much less in colder regions. The unusual generic name was given in honour of Prince Albert after the Prussian province from which he came.   Hardiness 6.

Sciadopitys verticillata   Japanese Umbrella Pine

423, 424 The unusual generic name of this species is simply a combination of two Greek words which, literally translated, mean 'umbrella pine', referring to the way the 'leaves' in whorls of ten to thirty radiate outwards from the stem like the ribs of an umbrella. This remarkable plant has two types of leaf, the real ones being small and scale-like, lying flat along the stems; but anyone not in the know will be forgiven for calling the larger ones 'leaves', as the botanists themselves do not have a technically correct name for them. Slow-growing when young, it can be treated as a dwarf for at least ten years (like the specimen illustrated), but eventually it will get going and make a fine pyramidal tree. In their native Japan very old trees have been known to reach 50m (165ft) in height, and in one province where it is plentiful it is milled for timber.   Hardiness 5.

Sequoia sempervirens   Redwood

425, 426 The giant Californian Redwood is too well known to need much description here, but those who may be confused between this one and the Big Tree, *Sequoiadendron giganteum*, are reminded that this tree has leaves not unlike those of *Taxus*, up to 20mm ($\frac{3}{4}$in) long and arranged in opposite rows on the branchlets, while the latter has small, crowded scale-like leaves of the type seen on species of *Cupressus*. Both grow to majestic forest trees; this one grows the faster, and is the one used most for timber. Specimens are on record as reaching 120m (400ft) in height and ages of 800 years. But one need not be deterred by these figures from planting *Sequoia* as an ornamental, as its annual growth of 45cm (18in) is ideal to provide excellent backdrop foliage, lawn or field specimen in a few years. Good soil and some shelter help to speed the process.   Hardiness 7.

Sequoia sempervirens 'Adpressa'   Dwarf Redwood

427 From the tallest of trees comes one of our finest dwarf conifers, seen at its best in spring and summer when frosted in creamy-white at all growing tips, the contrast becoming moderated in autumn and winter. It would appear that 'Adpressa' is a sport from the taller-growing cultivar once named 'Albo Spica', but the latter is now included under the same heading as 'Adpressa' in den Ouden and Boom, indicating that the two are virtually inseparable. The choice apparently lies with the gardener, and if he desires his plant to remain dwarf, he promptly removes any erect leader-type growths bearing radial-type foliage, otherwise he will finish up with a shrub of considerable height instead of the dwarf described here.   Hardiness 7.

423 *Sciadopitys verticillata.* Winter. Auckland, New Zealand.

424 *Sciadopitys verticillata.* Cones and foliage.

425 *Sequoia sempervirens*. Autumn. Hamilton, New Zealand.

426 *Sequoia sempervirens*. Cones, flower and foliage.

427 *Sequoia sempervirens* 'Adpressa'. Autumn.
Washington, DC, USA.

428 *Sequoia sempervirens* 'Nana Pendula'. Potted specimen. Washington, DC, USA.

Sequoia sempervirens 'Nana Pendula'

428 A slow-growing dwarf cultivar that probably originated as a sport from the tall-growing form 'Pendula', its much-reduced rate of growth tending rather in a horizontal than a vertical direction, but amenable to training upwards if desired. The cultivars of *Sequoia* lend themselves to training, either by staking or cutting, and usually break away and refurnish in new greenery from any heavy cuts. This feature is well demonstrated in the way the stump of the giant redwood will soon re-sprout into a mass of fresh young growth. The small, crowded leaves are a bluish-green colour, noticeably so on the undersides.   Hardiness 7.

429 *Sequoia sempervirens* 'Pendula'. Summer. Rotorua, New Zealand.

Sequoia sempervirens 'Pendula'   Weeping Redwood

429 As the name suggests, this is a weeping form of redwood, capable of growing to 50m (165ft) given time and good conditions. The branches are noticably pendulous, and on old trees spread over the ground. A tall narrow tree that does not occupy excessive space, best seen on a large lawn or in a park. Average annual growth, 30cm (12in).   Hardiness 7.

Sequoiadendron giganteum   Big Tree, Wellingtonia

430, 431 A true giant among trees, with specimens such as the 'General Sherman' in California's Sequoia National Park measuring 100m (330ft) in height with a base diameter of 12m (40ft), surely the largest tree in existence. The age of such trees has proved difficult to determine, estimates ranging between 500 and 1,500 years, while some put the age of the oldest specimens at around 4,000 years. So it would appear that pride of place for the world's oldest tree belongs to the diminutive Bristlecone Pine, *Pinus aristata*, and not as is often reputed to the Big Tree. Quite apart from claims to greatness, this is a fine specimen tree where space is available, thriving best in an area where the annual rainfall is around 1,270mm (50in) and the soil is deep and rich, and making an annual growth of 50cm (20in) in its earlier years.
Hardiness 6.

Sequoiadendron giganteum 'Pendulum'   Weeping Wellingtonia

432 Of the fourteen recorded named forms or cultivars of the Big Tree, the two most likely to be met with are a dwarf form, 'Pygmaeum', and the one described here, 'Pendulum'. This remarkable tree must have he greatest height-for-width ratio of any; the branches hanging (almost clinging) close in to the trunk make a tall tapering spire narrower than any other tree I know of. The growth rate seems to be about half that of its parent, 25 to 30cm (10 to 12in) a year. This would be an excellent ornamental if it were more readily available.   Hardiness 6.

Taiwania cryptomerioides

433 As the name suggests, the genus *Taiwania*, of which there is only one species, is native to the island of Taiwan, but it has also been found growing on the Chinese mainland. There it is known to make a conical tree of up to 60m (200ft) in height with a trunk to 6m (20ft) in girth which is usually bare of branches for the first 20m (65ft) on trees of that size. The juvenile leaf state (illustrated) is not unlike that of *Cryptomeria*, with individual leaves sometimes 2cm (¾in) in length, but often less than this. In contrast, the adult leaf is rarely more than 5mm (⅕in) in length, triangular in shape and for half its length, pressed against the stem of the plant. Short, cylindrical 12mm (½in) cones are borne on the tips of the branchlets. Hardiness 7.

430 *Sequoiadendron giganteum*. Autumn. Blenheim, New Zealand.

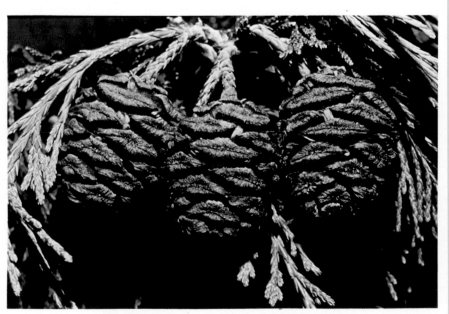

431 *Sequoiadendron giganteum*. Cones and foliage.

432 *Sequoiadendron giganteum* 'Pendulum'. Spring.
North Wales.

433 *Taiwania cryptomerioides.* Juvenile foliage.

434 *Taxodium distichum.* Spring. Brisbane, Australia.

435 *Taxodium distichum.* Cones and autumn foliage.

Taxodium distichum   Swamp Cypress

434, 435 As the above common name would suggest, his tree is happy growing in swampy or damp situations where few other trees will survive, but is also no problem to grow in ordinary garden soil. A deciduous conifer, the tree goes through a colour change in early winter, from yellow to orange-brown, before shedding its leaves completely, refurnishing with the coming of spring in a small delicate fresh-green yew-like leaf, this similarity being the reason for the generic name *Taxodium*. An interesting feature of old trees growing in swampy conditions is the emergence from the ground of numerous knobbly root protuberances known as "cypress knees"; these are usually hollow and may reach as high as 1m (3ft). In ten years a height of 5m (16ft) can be expected, and a spread of 2.5m (8ft).   Hardiness 4.

436 *Taxus baccata.* Autumn. Christchurch, New Zealand.

Taxus baccata   English Yew

436, 437 A tree indigenous to the British Isles that has been in cultivation for centuries—some of the older ones are reputed to be 1,000 years of age. There are 103 forms or cultivars recorded in den Ouden and Boom (*Manual of Cultivated Conifers*), but many of these are no longer grown. *Taxus baccata* has been used extensively for hedging and topiary work, lending itself well to annual close trimming and maintaining colour and shape well throughout the season, but it has not been planted much of recent years because of its comparative slowness in getting established. The average annual growth of 20cm (8in) can, if left untrimmed, add up to a tree 10m (33ft) high and wide in sixty years. Most yews resent being planted in a poorly-drained soil.   Hardiness 6.

437 *Taxus baccata.* Used for topiary. Nymans, Sussex, England.

438 *Taxus baccata* 'Amersfoort'. Spring. Hilversum, Netherlands.

Taxus baccata 'Amersfoort'

438 This slow-growing cultivar of *T. baccata* with its thick, much-shortened little leaves closely packed on the branchlets is quite an oddity among the yews and looks at first sight as though it belongs to a different genus altogether. It can be classed as a dwarf conifer, making an open-growing little shrub of up to 1m (3ft) in ten years, which because of its weak side-branch system never becomes filled between the main leaders. It was named by a Dutch nurseryman, but apparently originated from France some years prior to 1939.   Hardiness 6.

439 *Taxus baccata* 'Aurea'. Summer. Palmerston North, New Zealand.

440 *Taxus baccata* 'Cavendishii'. Spring. Devizes, Wilts, England.

Taxus baccata 'Aurea'   Golden English Yew

439 This golden-leaved form of the English Yew, apart from being a little slower in growth, is of similar form to its green-leaved parent and is equally adaptable to a variety of shapes by pruning and shearing. If it is left untrimmed, one may expect for ten years' growth a bush of 1.5m (5ft) each way with an annual growth of 10cm (4in) which (in common with most species of *Taxus*) is likely to increase as the plant becomes better established. The golden leaf colour is at its brightest during the spring and summer growth months, and this slowly changes to yellowish-green by midwinter and remains this colour until the fresh growth appears. Apparently there are several bushy golden forms covered by the above name, some of these male and others female forms.   Hardiness 6.

Taxus baccata 'Cavendishii'   Cavendish Yew

440 Two very similar spreading yews are 'Cavendishii' and 'Repandens', both capable of reaching a width of 4m (13ft) at less than 1m (3ft) in height, and a dark blue-green in colour. Of the two, 'Cavendishii' is somewhat more irregular and untidy in growth, a little darker in colour, and possesses longer leaves (to 30mm/over 1in) that curve outwards and upwards from the near-horizontal stems. In ten years' growing one should have a plant in the vicinity of 1.6m (5ft) in width and 40cm (15in) in height.   Hardiness 6.

441 *Taxus baccata* 'Elegantissima'. Spring. Ampfield, Hants, England.

Taxus baccata 'Elegantissima'

441 Of similar appearance to the well-known Golden English Yew, 'Elegantisima' is a selected and fixed form of this type and has good compact growth and excellent, bright creamy-yellow colour during the growth months. As it is a female form it has it has the added attraction of a crop of red berries in the autumn.   Hardiness 6.

442 *Taxus baccata* 'Fastigiata'. Spring. San Francisco, USA.

Taxus baccata 'Fastigiata'   Irish Yew

442, 443 The upright-growing columnar Irish Yew needs little description here, as it is well-known throughout the world for its erect habit and rich dark-green foliage, highlighted during autumn with a crop of red berries. When young it is slow growing, taking perhaps ten years to reach 2m (6ft) in height by 40cm (15in) in width, but annual growth seems to increase as the tree becomes older. Eventually it loses its pointed top, with many leaders of equal vigour competing for pride of place, and a regular trimming programme is recommended to keep this tree from getting that 'top heavy' look. The parent plant originated in Ireland around 1780.   Hardiness 6.

443 *Taxus baccata* 'Fastigiata'. Ripe arils and foliage.

444 *Taxus baccata* 'Fastigiata Aurea'. Autumn. New Plymouth, New Zealand.

Taxus baccata 'Fastigiata Aurea'   Golden Irish Yew

444 Of similar habit and growth to 'Fastigiata', this excellent golden form holds its colour well, still holding some golden-yellow foliage on its more exposed parts throughout the winter months.   Hardiness 6.

445 *Taxus baccata* 'Fastigiata Aureomarginata'.
Foliage detail.

446 *Taxus baccata* 'Overeynderi'. Autumn. New Plymouth,
New Zealand.

Taxus baccata 'Fastigiata Aureomarginata'

445 Yet another form of Irish Yew, this variation differs
from the preceding in having the gold colour mainly on
the leaf margins, with a central insert of green The effect
is not noticeable except at close range and one is otherwise likely to mistake it for 'Fastigiata Aurea', particularly during the spring when both are an overall bright
yellow Later in the season this one fades rather quickly,
becoming by winter more pale green than gold in general
colour but still retaining traces of the yellow margin on
some of the outer leaves.   Hardiness 6.

Taxus baccata 'Overeynderi'

446 This seedling of 'Fastigiata', raised in the Netherlands around 1860, is characterised by a smaller leaf than
its parent, and a neater, more uniform habit of growth.
Younger plants at ten years are a narrow pyramidal form
2m (6ft) high and 60cm (2ft) wide but become with time
quite a large bush to 3m (10ft) wide by 5m (16ft) high,
usually tapering at the top to several leader points. An
excellent dark green upright yew that is widely grown in
in the nursery trade and generally preferred to the Irish
Yew for its tidier, more uniform habit of growth.
                                                Hardiness 6.

447 *Taxus baccata* 'Repandens'. Spring. Hilversum, Netherlands.

Taxus baccata 'Repandens'

447 As mentioned earlier under the heading of the
cultivar 'Cavendishii', these two are very similar in habit
and colour, 'Repandens' differing in having a straighter
leaf and somewhat tidier habit of growth. A fine spreading yew that will cover a circle 4m (13ft) in diameter.
                                                Hardiness 6.

448 *Taxus baccata* 'Semperaurea'. Spring. The Hague, Netherlands.

449 *Taxus baccata* 'Standishii'. Spring. Ampfield, Hants, England.

450 *Taxus cuspidata* 'Nana'. Autumn. USA.

Taxus baccata 'Semperaurea'
Evergold English Yew

448 This attractive golden-leaved cultivar is slower-growing than most of the bushy yews and would take many years to realise its potential height and width of 2m (6ft). The picture is of a 40cm (15in) bush growing in front of a miniature building at the Madurodam Model Village at The Hague, and has obviously had regular pruning to prevent it from getting out of scale and dwarfing its surroundings. Its golden-yellow colour is retained through the winter months.   Hardiness 6.

Taxus baccata 'Standishii'

449 This cultivar takes pride of place among upright yews as the most golden-yellow form in existence. It is slower-growing than 'Fastigiata Aurea' and therefore the best cultivar for planting on a rockery, with its minimum tendency to broaden out with age. One should not be surprised to find such slow-growing cultivars expensive to buy, as a 50cm (20in) plant would have been grown by the nurseryman for at least six years, more probably eight or ten.   Hardiness 6.

Taxus cuspidata 'Nana'   Dwarf Japanese Yew

450 The Japanese yew is a popular subject in cold climate areas where *T. baccata* will not survive, and for this reason is much grown in a variety of forms in the gardens of North America. This dwarf form is one of the best of these, making a low spreading bush to 2 to 3m (6 to 10ft) wide and 1m (3ft) high. As it has good shade tolerance it is popular as a foundation plant or around entrances, remaining well clothed in dark-green colour throughout the year.   Hardiness 4.

451 *Taxus x media.* Spring. Washington, DC, USA.

452 *Taxus x media* 'Taunton'. Spring. Dundee, Illinois, USA.

Taxus x media   Anglo-Japanese Yew

451 A hybrid between *T. baccata* and *T. cuspidata* that was first achieved around the turn of the century by a Mr Hatfield of Hunnewell Pinetum, USA. There are now more than twenty cultivars of this popular yew on record. Among the better known are 'Hicksii', a tall bushy shrub that trims well, especially as a hedge, the compact 'Hatfieldii' (named after the hybridiser), as well as fastigiate and spreading forms. It appears to have retained the best features of both parents, and being hardier than the English Yew is popular in North America and the colder parts of Europe.

Hardiness 5.

453 *Tetraclinis articulata*. Foliage.

Taxus x media 'Taunton'   Taunton Spreading Yew

452 'Taunton' is of fairly recent introduction among the media hybrids and is outstanding among low-growing yews for its dense, free-branching habit, requiring little or no trimming, and for its apparent freedom from foliage discoloration in severe winter conditions. In ten years it is capable of reaching to 60cm by 1m (2ft by 3ft) wide.

Hardiness 4.

Tetraclinis articulata

453 A genus that is distinguished from the closely-allied *Callitris* by having only four scales to its rounded 12mm ($\frac{1}{2}$in) cones, the name Tetraclinis meaning 'four-valved'. It is native to Morocco and neighbouring Mediterranean countries, and is known there to make a conical evergreen tree to 15m (50ft) in height. It is often found growing in areas subject to considerable periods of drought. The milled timber is of hardwood quality with uses over the years including roofing tiles and furniture making, and a resin which exudes from the trunk is also popular as a base for the manufacture of varnish. The fine, almost tape-like foliage is very flat, measuring to 2mm ($\frac{1}{12}$in.) at the widest parts. A tree that will stand dry for long periods.

Hardiness 8.

Thuja occidentalis   American Arborvitae

454 Much unnecessary confusion seems to exist between the two species *T. occidentalis* and *T. orientalis*, and no doubt a lot of this arises through the similarity of the two names. They are not difficult to differentiate however, as a comparison between the two close-ups of foliage and cones will confirm. The only tricky cultivars are those with juvenile-type foliage, and of these there are only a few. In all there are over 130 recorded cultivars of *T. occidentalis*, ranging from compact bun-shaped miniatures to trees of 20m (65ft) in height. The inconspicuous brown cones average 8mm (over $\frac{1}{4}$in) in length.

Hardiness 4.

454 *Thuja occidentalis*. Typical thujoid adult foliage and cones.

461 *Thuja occidentalis* 'Filiformis'. Summer. New Plymouth, New Zealand.

463 *Thuja occidentalis* 'Holmstrup'. Spring. Ampfield, Hants, England.

462 *Thuja occidentalis* 'Globosa'. Spring. Boskoop, Netherlands.

Thuja occidentalis 'Filiformis'   Threadleaf Arborvitae

461 Another thuja of outstandingly distinct foliage. The leaf of this cultivar is closely pressed in against the long trailing stem of the branchlets, creating a cord-like effect, rich green in colour and contrasting well with the orange-brown branches and stems. It remains a low and rather sprawling shrub for the first ten years of its life, reaching in this time a height and width of around 80cm (30in), with a maximum of no more than 2m (6ft). In cold winter areas the foliage assumes a brownish tinge. At one time known as *T.o.* 'Douglasii'.   Hardiness 4.

Thuja occidentalis 'Globosa'

462 One of the many excellent low-growing rounded forms of Arborvitae, 'Globosa' is identified primarily by its foliage colour of light greyish-green, combined with its neatly rounded shape composed of closely-packed sprays of haphazardly-arranged foliage. Of average growth rate, it is capable of reaching to 1m (3ft) each way in a ten-year period. This cultivar does not lose its colour during the winter. Other very similar globose forms are 'Froebelii', 'Compacta', 'Tom Thumb', 'Globularis', 'Spillmannii', 'Woodwardii', and 'Umbraculifera'.   Hardiness 4.

464 *Thuja occidentalis* 'Hoveyi'. Autumn. Wanganui, New Zealand.

465 *Thuja occidentalis* 'Little Gem'. Winter. Te Kuiti, New Zealand.

466 *Thuja occidentalis* 'Lutea'. Spring. New South Wales, Australia.

Thuja occidentalis 'Holmstrup'

463 This excellent pyramidal thuja of Danish origin has rich apple-green foliage, and is slow enough in growth to be classed as a dwarf. The compact foliage is arranged in flattened planes typical of this species and is closely packed, providing well-defined substance to the bush, while the strong trunk and leader assure a sturdy pyramidal shape. It is capable of growing to 5m (6ft) in ten years, but a little annual pruning will keep it to more compact dimensions for many years. This is one of the best for retaining a good green colour through the winter, but in colder areas will still "brown" a little. Hardiness 4.

Thuja occidentalis 'Hoveyi'

464 A somewhat larger edition of the rounded globose thuja forms, 'Hoveyi' will in time make a 3m (10ft) high, rounded, higher-than-wide bush with its foliage held in flat planes, much of it vertically and radiating outwards from the centre of the bush. It may be grown as a dwarf for about ten years, at which age it would be approximately 1.5m (5ft) high and 1m (3ft) wide. During he growth seasons it is a medium green, turning brown with the onset of winter cold. Hardiness 4.

Thuja occidentalis 'Little Gem'   Green Globe Arborvitae

465 This compact, flattened mound of rich green is one of the few true dwarfs among arborvitae and has a growth rate less than half that of the 'Globosa' types. It may be expected to be no more than 40cm (15in) high and little more in width after ten years' growing, and is easily recognised by its somewhat untidy appearance caused by the characteristic twist of the sprays and branchlets. It is nevertheless a fine little garden conifer and holds its rich green colour well, becoming darker through the winter. Hardiness 4.

Thuja occidentalis 'Lutea'   George Peabody Arborvitae

466 This cultivar has been with us for nearly a century and is still popular, especially in cold areas where hardiness is an essential feature. During the growth seasons all foliage tips hold bright creamy-yellow colour, maturing to light gold and later a rich golden bronze with the onset of winter cold, with the inner foliage remaining brownish-green. Young plants tend to grow in all directions for a year or so, but eventually a leader takes over and the plant begins to take on the broad pyramidal form typical of this cultivar, in ten years reaching 2.5m (8ft) high at 1m (3ft) base width. A well-exposed situation away from shade is necessary to produce a uniform tight-growing habit. One still finds this cultivar wrongly labelled 'Elegantissima'. Hardiness 4.

Thuja occidentalis 'Ohlendorffii'

467 One of those horticultural curiosities that carry two kinds of entirely different foliage on the same plant. The juvenile type, forming the basic substance of the bush, consists of 12mm (almost ½in) long needles neatly arranged in four rows up the stems, and these are topped by the thin cordlike, four-sided whips of adult foliage in a lighter-green colour, or when in growth, a reddish-brown. It builds itself up into a bush roughly 80cm (30in) each way in ten years, and generally needs a little help from the pruners to retain a tidy shape. The once-used name of 'Spaethii' is still sometimes applied to this plant. Hardiness 6.

467 *Thuja occidentalis* 'Ohlendorffii'. Spring. London, England.

468 *Thuja occidentalis* 'Pyramidalis'. Spring.

469 *Thuja occidentalis* 'Pyramidalis Compacta'. Winter.

Thuja occidentalis 'Pyramidalis'

468 A handsome pyramidal cultivar that is much used to provide good vertical accent in landscape projects. It carries its rich-green adult-type foliage in fan-shaped clusters typical of this species, and may in ten years be expected to grow to a height of 3m (10ft) and base width of 1m (3ft), tapering inwards towards the apex. Subsequent growth is usually in an upwards-only direction and this may continue to a height of 10m (33ft) or more, with a tendency at this age to split into more than one leader.   Hardiness 3.

Thuja occidentalis 'Pyramidalis Compacta'

469 Apparently not originating from the same source as the preceding cultivar 'Pyramidalis', this form is nevertheless very similar, but possesses a narrower and more erect growth habit and softer green leaf colour. In ten years it may be expected to be 2.5m (8ft) in height and 80mm (30in) at the base; it continues to add height annually with no significant increase in width. Of the two, this one is to be preferred for city gardens where space is limited.   Hardiness 3.

470 *Thuja occidentalis* 'Rheingold'. Winter. Nelson, New Zealand.

Thuja occidentalis 'Rheingold'
                                        Rheingold Arborvitae

470 A highly popular low-growing, bun-shaped little shrub, pinkish gold in summer growth and turning a bright golden-bronze for the winter. The differences between this cultivar and the taller-growing 'Ellwangeriana Aurea' have been much disputed, but it is generally agreed that 'Rheingold' tends to have smaller sprays of foliage and a greater proportion of juvenile leaf, and grows much wider than high. The issue is often confused by nurserymen who intentionally propagate only from juvenile leaf to produce a plant of totally juvenile foliage (apart from an odd spray of adult leaf near the top which always appears). Such bushes are excellent garden plants, more low-growing than the type, and can be kept this way by pruning off any adult foliage that may appear, but are still not a different cultivar than that illustrated in the colour plate with its mainly adult-type foliage. A ten-year-old 'Rheingold' may be expected to measure 70cm (28in) high by 1.3m (4½ft) wide.   Hardiness 4.

472 *Thuja occidentalis* 'Umbraculifera'. Spring. Boskoop, Netherlands.

471 *Thuja occidentalis* 'Spiralis'. Spring. Ampfield, Hants, England.

Thuja occidentalis 'Spiralis'

471 Probably the narrowest-growing cultivar among the many pyramidal forms of arborvitae, 'Spiralis' spends its earlier years in a conical shape, attaining a base width of approximately 60cm (2ft) at a height of 3m (10ft) in its tenth year, with most of the growth from then on being in an upward direction at an average rate of 25cm (10in) a year. The curved, often spirally-arranged, branching habit gives rise to the name of 'Spiralis' and the dark-green foliage is arranged in sprays that have a decided fernlike appearance. A fine upright-growing tree that makes its best narrow form when planted in full exposure, well clear of any shade.   Hardiness 5.

473 *Thuja occidentalis* 'Vervaeneana'. Spring. Palmerston North, New Zealand.

Thuja occidentalis 'Umbraculifera'   Umbrella Arborvitae

472 This, yet another globe-shaped arborvitae, is distinguished by its richer bluish-green foliage and neat hemispherical shape extending to ground level—rather too perfectly rounded to represent the umbrella from which it takes its name (and if so the handle must surely be well buried in the ground!). Jokes aside, it is one of the best rounded conifers and makes in ten years a uniform bush of about 1m (3ft) wide and 70cm (28in) high.   Hardiness 4.

Thuja occidentalis 'Vervaeneana'

473 A rather large-growing thuja with a potential height of 10m (33ft) and base width of 5m (16ft), but nevertheless an excellent lawn specimen when young, or background subject for lower-growing plants. Spring and summer sees it at its brightest gold colour, which is not evenly distributed on the leaves but arranged in bands and patches, and as the colder weather approaches it fades, the whole tree often turning brown in extreme winters. I find this cultivar very difficult to distinguish from *Thuja plicata* ·Zebrina', apart from the fact that the latter remains brighter during the winter.   Hardiness 5.

475 *Thuja occidentalis* 'Woodwardii'. Winter. Hastings, New Zealand.

Thuja occidentalis 'Wareana Lutescens'

474 A more compact version of the vigorous and very hardy Siberian Arborvitae 'Wareana', 'Lutescens' has attractive light-yellow-green foliage for most of the year and is at its brightest during spring and summer, taking on a bronzy tone for the winter. It is an unusual colour among the thuja family and may be used to good effect for colour contrast among conifers of other shades. It is a broad pyramidal shrub that can reach 2.5m (8ft) in ten years by 1.5m (5ft) in width, becoming wider with age. Some growers prefer to use the simpler name 'Lutescens' for this cultivar.

Hardiness 4.

474 *Thuja occidentalis* 'Wareana Lutescens'. Winter.
Palmerston North, New Zealand.

476 *Thuja orientalis*. Typical adult foliage and cones.

477 *Thuja orientalis*. Spring. Brisbane, Australia.

Thuja occidentalis 'Woodwardii'

475 'Woodwardii' is distinct among the other globe-shaped arborvitae in that the foliage sprays are held in a predominantly vertical plane, radiating outwards from the centre of the bush to form a ball of foliage of striking uniformity. The foliage is normally a rich green, but changes in winter to a rather potent shade of rich brown once the frosts have done their work. Den Ouden quotes this cultivar as remaining green during winter, while other authors prefer to remain silent on the subject, and it may be that more research is needed before all are in complete agreement about the cultivar. Meanwhile it is a fine, rounded, compact conifer that will make a round ball of 1m (3ft) each way in ten years' growing. Hardiness 4.

Thuja orientalis   Chinese Arborvitae

476, 477 At one time this group was thought to be a distinct genus under the name of *Biota*, and the name is still sometimes met with in descriptions of species and cultivars of *T. orientalis*. Among the adult-leaved forms like this species, identification is easy by noting the way in which the foliage is held in vertical planes radiating from the centre of the plant, and the seed cones are furnished with up to six curious hook-like tips to each scale. A graceful and symmetrical tree, native to Korea and Northern China, and much planted in these regions, *T. orientalis* can reach a height of 15m (50ft) in sixty years. Probably for this reason it is not widely planted as an ornamental outside the Orient, although it is grown for use as a grafting stock, preference being given to the more spectacular coloured and compact forms that have been developed from this conifer. Hardiness 5.

478 *Thuja orientalis* 'Aurea'. Winter. Wanganui, New Zealand.

Thuja orientalis 'Aurea'

478 A golden-foliaged form, selected as a seedling from plants of the preceding *T. orientalis*, 'Aurea' does not have the same ambitions as to height, but is content to make a tidy oval-shaped bush of 2m (6ft) high by 1m (3ft) wide in the space of ten years. The colour is at its brightest yellow during the spring and summer months, from then on fading back to a warm green as shown in the illustration, with a tinge of bronze in the winter. Several similar seedlings of this type have been raised and introduced to the trade and there is some doubt which is the original plant to bear the above name, but all are similar enough to conform to the above description. Full exposure to light is desirable to develop the yellow colouration to its brightest. Hardiness 6.

Thuja orientalis 'Aurea Nana'   Berckmann's Arborvitae

479 A plant that has been under cultivation in the United States for more than 100 years' often better known under its old name of 'Berkmann's Golden Biota'. Ironically, Berkmann cannot be credited with the raising of this cultivar, but rather with the somewhat taller variety 'Conspicua'; yet this is the one that has carried his name for so many years. It has a delightful compact habit, rarely growing higher than 1m (3ft) in a rugged, but generally rounded bush that nedes no trimming to keep it in a tidy and attractive shape. The illustration shows a specimen at its best in spring dress, growing in a fully exposed position in the Gotelli collection in Washington, DC. Plants grown in shade or "forced" in any way tend to be looser and more open in habit and fail to display the brilliant colour of this specimen. Hardiness 6.

479 *Thuja orientalis* 'Aurea Nana'. Spring   Washington, DC, USA.

480 *Thuja orientalis* 'Beverlyensis'. Summer.
New Plymouth, New Zealand.

481 *Thuja orientalis* 'Elegentissima'. Spring.
San Francisco, USA.

482 *Thuja orientalis* 'Filiformis Erecta'. Spring.
Devizes, Wilts, England,

Thuja orientalis 'Beverlyensis'   Beverly Hills Arborvitae

480 As the common name suggests, this popular member of the *T. orientalis* group was named and first distributed in California. 'Beverlyensis' is a fine garden subject and may be expected to reach a height of 2m (6ft) in ten years, by 70cm (28in) wide. Throughout late spring and summer the outer edges of its flattened planes of foliage are aglow with bright golden-yellow. This diminishes towards green as winter approaches, but in colder climates the colour may change to a strong reddish-bronze as the early frosts strike, which is inclined to fool the uninitiated into thinking that the poor plant has died of cold. All ends well in the following spring when brown gives way to green and another seasons' colour cycle has begun.   Hardiness 6.

Thuja orientalis 'Elegantissima'   Golden Tip Arborvitae

481 Growing in the James Noble conifer collection at the Strybing Arboretum in San Francisco, this fine specimen, perhaps somewhat broader than typical, portrays the spring colour of this cultivar at its best. Although too large to occupy anything but a temporary position in a rockery, 'Elegantissima' is ideal for the larger garden layout giving bright colour accent among the more sombre conifer shades of greens and blues. One may expect it to reach 2m (6ft) or more in ten years, but to thicken out with age from then on, up to a maximum of 5m (16ft) for an old specimen. Like the preceding 'Beverlyensis' it follows a similar colour cycle, turning brownish in winter and especially so in colder climates.   Hardiness 6.

Thuja orientalis 'Filiformis Erecta'   Threadleaf Arborvitae

482 An unusual plant among the *T. orientalis* group that does not conform to the usual planar foliage habit but prefers to cover itself in threadlike foliage, consisting of leaves that lie almost flat along the stems. The yellow spring tip growth of the illustration diminishes as autumn comes on and winter finds it in a dress of greenish-brown, in keeping with most other members in this group. The growth is predominantly upward, giving an oval bush with a pointed top which can reach to a height of 1.5m (5ft) for a mature plant.   Hardiness 6.

483 *Thuja orientalis* 'Juniperoides'. Winter. Auckland, New Zealand.

484 *Thuja orientalis* 'Meldensis'. Summer. Palmerston North, New Zealand.

Thuja orientalis 'Juniperoides'

483 This is one of the juvenile foliage forms, and first impressions are likely to be that 'Juniperoides' does not belong in the thuja family at all. The leaves are prickly-looking but soft to the touch and of a soft blue-green colour during the growth season, which in winter turn a rich dark blue—outstanding when viewed in front lighting, i.e., with the sun shining from directly behind the viewer. The heavy bloom on the leaves has a light-returning property similar to that of a glass-bead reflector. In mild climates 'Juniperoides' can reach 2m by 1m (6ft by 3ft) wide in ten years after which it is inclined to become untidy and is better replaced by a new plant. Growth is apparently slower in England as, to quote Mr Hillier, 'In fifteen years it attains 30 in by 20 in'. This slower-growing characteristic produces a neater, more permanent plant. Also widely known under the name of *Thuja decussata*.
Hardiness 6.

Thuja orientalis 'Meldensis'

484 A companion plant to 'Juniperoides' and 'Rosedalis' that differs mainly in colour behaviour, being a soft grey-green at most times of the year, changing to purplish-brown with winter cold. It is a neat-growing rounded, dense little bush that can reach to 1m (3ft) in five years, by 50cm (20in) wide under ideal growth conditions, but less than half this in colder climates. The foliage is finer and crisper than in 'Juniperoides', variable and mostly juvenile in type, 5mm (⅕in) in leaf length, and usually displays the odd piece of adult leaf to confirm its membership in the *T. orientalis* group.
Hardiness 6.

Thuja orientalis 'Rosedalis'

485 Another juvenile-foliaged form that has prickly-looking foliage but is nevertheless quite soft to the touch. Three colour changes through the year are the chief attraction of this excellent dwarf conifer, from the canary-yellow spring colour of the illustration, to green in summer, finishing with a winter dress of glaucous plum-purple—enough spectacular behaviour to merit its inclusion in any conifer planting. A ten-year plant should attain at least 1m (3ft) in height by 50cm (20in) in breadth and requires no trimming to retain the compact, rounded shape of the illustrated plant. It is also met with under the rather cumbersome name of 'Rosedalis Compacta'.
Hardiness 6.

485 *Thuja orientalis* 'Rosedalis'. Spring. Devizes, Wilts, England.

486 *Thuja orientalis* 'Semperaurea'. Spring. Wisley, Surrey, England.

487 *Thuja orientalis* 'Westmont'. Summer. California, USA.

488 *Thuja plicata.* Winter. Christchurch, New Zealand.

Thuja orientalis 'Semperaurea'

486 Virtually a larger edition of the compact variety 'Aurea Nana', and indistinguishable from it when small, 'Semperaurea' can grow to a height of 1.5m (5ft) by 1m (3ft) broad in ten years and double that for an old plant. As the name suggests, the yellow tip colour is present the year round. This is true to some extent only; the brightest period, as shown in the illustration, is spring to early summer with a somewhat diminished brilliance for the rest of the year. Altogether a most attractive garden plant with its informal yet neatly-groomed appearance. Specimen growing in the Nisbet collection of conifers at Wisley.   Hardiness 6.

Thuja orientalis 'Westmont'   Westmont Arborvitae

487 To quote from the catalogue of the Monrovia Nursery Company, Azusa, California, to whom we are indebted for this illustration: 'This ten-year-old plant has just reached 30in in height and 20in in width. It has never been trimmed or cut to maintain its upright, broadly conical shape.' 'Westmont' is a re-selected form of the 'Aurea Nana' type with a closer habit of growth and compacted branch tips which from spring to autumn carry the brilliant lemon-yellow colouration, the interior of the bush remaining green. Winter sees the foliage turn towards a bronze colour which fades to green by the time spring growth re-commences.   Hardiness 6.

Thuja plicata   Western Red Cedar

488 This is a native of coastal north-western America and California. There are still vast natural forests of it in those areas in spite of steady milling for many years, for its highly durable timber is valued for general construction work and in particular for shingles for roofing. As an ornamental or shelter tree it has great virtues, having a symmetrical conical form and rich-green foliage resistant to disease; it makes a fine specimen for a large lawn, or an ideal windbreak with foliage extending to ground level. The leaves are large, smooth and flattened and give off when crushed a distinctive sweet tangy-like odour. While old forest giants are recorded to have reached heights of 60m (200ft), it is not classed among the fastest growers, but may be expected to make 4m (13ft) in ten years.   Hardiness 5

489 *Thuja plicata* 'Cuprea'. Spring. Wisley, Surrey, England.

490 *Thuja plicata* 'Hillieri'. Spring. San Francisco, USA.

Thuja plicata 'Cuprea'

489 A slow-growing dwarf cultivar that seldom grows taller than 1m (3ft), is broadly pyramidal in shape, bronze-green in colour, with the tips golden-yellow when in growth. The leaves, of typical *T. plicata* foliage, are uniformly arranged in small sprays, most of which nod at the tips. An attractive dwarf conifer.   Hardiness 5.

Thuja plicata 'Hillieri'

490 A large irregular ball of bright-green moss studded with numerous vertical, spindly 10cm (4in) leader shoots—this is the apt description of this unusual cultivar. It occurred among a seedling batch of *Thuja plicata* at Hillier's Nursery, England, around the year 1900, and although a dwarf, increasing annually by about 10cm (4in), it has been known to reach a diameter of nearly 3m (10ft) in twenty-five years. Mr Welch reports that on some plants vigorous growth sometimes predominates, and if not cut out one is liable to be left with a plant that is no longer dwarf or compact. The leaf is typical *T. plicata* type, but much more compressed and reduced in length.   Hardiness 5.

491 *Thuja plicata* 'Old Gold'. Winter. Invercargill, New Zealand.

Thuja plicata 'Old Gold'

491 This New Zealand-raised cultivar originated in Messrs Millichamps' nursery at Ashburton and is a popular ornamental in New Zealand, either as a garden specimen or lined out for decorative shelter. With a growth rate a little slower than its parent, it can be expected to reach 3 to 4m (10 to 13ft) in ten years in an erect pyramidal shape, with all outer growths clothed in golden yellow. This colour remains in the current season's growth and well into winter before changing to a rich bronze, in colder areas deeper in colour. It is a tree that adapts well to pruning and I have seen specimens retained to a width of 50cm (20in) at a height of 4m (13ft), densely furnished in foliage from the ground up.   Hardiness 5.

492 *Thuja plicata* 'Rogersii'. Spring. Wisley, Surrey, England.

493 *Thuja plicata* 'Stoneham Gold'. Spring. Wisley, Surrey, England.

Thuja plicata 'Rogersii'

492 Probably the best-known of the dwarf *T. plicata* cultivars, 'Rogersii' carries foliage that is finer and more compact than any other in this species. The bright golden-yellow colour is carried on all outside leaf and takes on a bronzy shade towards the end of the season. The typical shape is a rounded bush with a pointed top, in ten years reaching to 70cm (28in) high by 40cm (15in) wide, but its shape is easily influenced by pruning and I have seen plants of the same height kept to a width of only 12cm (5in), making a beautiful compact spire of rich golden foliage. For many years this cultivar was known as 'Aurea Rogersii'.   Hardiness 6.

494 *Thuja plicata* 'Zebrina'. Winter. Invercargill, New Zealand.

Thuja plicata 'Stoneham Gold'

493 A particularly attractive cultivar with dark-green inner foliage, tipped at all growing points with bright orange-yellow throughout the growing season. The leaf is of normal *T. plicata* type, closely arranged in compact upward-facing sprays, and it is the upper and outer edges of these sprays that carry the colour. An attractive garden conifer that can in time exceed 2m (6ft) in height, but for many years is slow-growing enough to be used as a dwarf.   Hardiness 6.

Thuja plicata 'Zebrina'

494 A lemon-yellow variegated pyramidal conifer that does not, as do so many of the thuja forms, degenerate to a drab brown during midwinter. It is medium in growth rate, can be expected to make 3m by 1.5m (10ft by 5ft) wide in ten years, and is not too large to be used in a shrubbery among other conifers. It carries the typically-flattened *T. plicata*-type foliage, with the colour set in bands across the spray, the effect thus produced giving rise to the name 'Zebrina'. For many years it seems to have been confused with *Thuja occidentalis* 'Vervaeneana', which appears almost identical in all respects, but loses most of its colour during winter to become a dull green or brown, with just a suggestion of colour on some leaves.   Hardiness 6.

495 *Thujopsis dolabrata* var. *hondai*. Spring. Washington, DC, USA.

496 *Thujopsis dolabrata* 'Nana'. Spring. Auckland, New Zealand.

Thujopsis dolabrata 'Nana'

496 This, the most widely-grown ornamental member of the *Thujopsis* family, is compact enough to be classed among the dwarfs and can be expected in ten years to have formed a low, spreading bun 1.5m (5ft) wide by 60cm (24in) high. While the normal colour is a fresh green, it often carries a tinge of bronze (and sometimes even orange where the soil is very poor) but at all times it maintains a clean, healthy leaf, undamaged by the elements or the ravages of insect pests. The leaf is more compact than the typical form, held in upward-pointing sprays and marked on the reverse with the distinctive white panels peculiar to this genus.   Hardiness 6.

Thujopsis dolabrata var. *hondai*
Broad-leaved Arborvitae

495 The genus *Thujopsis* (meaning thuja-like) embraces fourteen forms and cultivars, all natives of Japan, most of which are not well known apart from the two listed here. In leaf type it is most like the coarser adult foliage of *Thuja occidentalis*, but almost double the size in all parts, the thick, overlapping scales looking not unlike the scales of a lizard, which explains why the name 'Lizard Tree' is sometimes applied to members of this genus. The leaf undersides are distinctively marked with a white panel below each scale. Illustrated here is the botanical variety *hondai* found in northern Japan, which differs from the type in having more compact foliage and a denser branching habit, and is probably the better form for ornamental use. In its native state it attains a height of 30m (100ft) in many years, but one need not expect a height of more than 2m (6ft) in ten years of growing.   Hardiness 6.

497 *Thujopsis dolabrata* 'Variegata'. Foliage detail.

Thujopsis dolabrata 'Variegata'

497 A variegated form that seems to vary in markings from tree to tree, some having bold patches of creamy-white well distributed throughout the foliage, while others show little more than the occasional patch of colour here and there. From a distance larger trees present an overall green colour, the variegation being of little effect unless viewed close up, and for this reason younger trees are the more attractive. It grows in a broad pyramidal form clothed in foliage to ground level, and in ten years may be expected to reach a height of 3m (10ft) and be 1.5m (5ft) across at the base.   Hardiness 6.

498 *Torreya nucifera.* Foliage.

499 *Tsuga canadensis.* Spring. Hilversum, Netherlands.

500 *Tsuga canadensis.* Cones.

Torreya nucifera

498 The Torreyas, members of the family Taxaceae, comprise a small genus of six species, native to North America and East Asia. They bear aromatic yew-like leaves radially set on lateral shoots which are twisted to give an apparent pectinate (i.e. opposite) leaf arrangement. *T. nucifera*, a native of Japan, has a recorded maximum height of 24m (80ft), but is more often a slow-growing small tree and is distinguished by its strongly-curved 15–35m ($\frac{1}{2}$–1$\frac{1}{2}$in) leaves and the reddish-brown colour assumed by the branchlets in the second year. Like other Torreyas the large 25mm (1in) seeds are fully enclosed in a green fleshy plum-like aril, are rich in oil and are commonly eaten by the Japanese.

Hardiness 5.

Tsuga canadensis   Eastern Hemlock

499, 500 A pyramidal tree reaching to 30m (100ft) in its native state in eastern USA and Canada, and similar in most respects to *T. heterophylla*. Generally however it is a more untidy grower, often with more than one leader and a ragged top and lacking the erect symmetry of its western counterpart. It has no great claim to inclusion here as an ornamental apart from the great number of cultivars that have developed from it—no fewer than seventy-five are on record in contrast to only four for *T. heterophylla*. The small 2cm ($\frac{3}{4}$in) grey-brown cones are borne in profusion on short stalks on the tips of the branchlets.

Hardiness 4.

501 *Tsuga canadensis* 'Aurea'. Spring. Washington, DC, USA.

502 *Tsuga canadensis* 'Brandley'. Spring.
Washington, DC, USA.

Tsuga canadensis 'Aurea'
                    Everitt's Golden Hemlock

501 Probably the only golden form of Eastern Hemlock in cultivation, the cultivar 'Aurea' (syn. 'Everitt's Golden') is a slow-growing pyramidal form with a height potential for ten years of 2m (6ft). It should be planted in full exposure if the golden foliage is to provide its brightest colour.   Hardiness 4.

Tsuga canadensis 'Brandley'

502 A handsome dwarf conifer densely furnished in dark-green foliage which contrasts well in spring with the new season's growth of light green. It has a somewhat irregular growth habit, generally pyramidal in form but with often more than one leader, and eventually reaches a height of 1m (3ft) or a little more. Of similar habit are the cultivars 'Broughton' and 'Compacta'.   Hardiness 4.

503 *Tsuga canadensis* 'Cole'. Spring. Washington, DC, USA.

Tsuga canadensis 'Cole'
                    Cole's Prostrate Hemlock

503 It must appear a little misleading to describe a plant as completely prostrate when its photo shows it standing all of 70cm (28in) high. The answer is that this particular specimen has been either grafted on to a short standard, or was trained upwards when young and later allowed to take on its naturally weeping habit. It is indeed one of the most prostrate of dwarf conifers (if not trained as above), and one of the best for rockery planting with its ability to flow gracefully over and around rocks, following contours almost as though glued to the ground. In ten years it may be expected to be almost 1m (3ft) in diameter.
                    Hardiness 5.

504 *Tsuga canadensis* 'Jeddeloh'. Spring. West Germany.

Tsuga canadensis 'Jeddeloh'

504 This recent introduction from a nursery in Europe appears likely to become one of the most popular dwarfs, as it is rather like a much-compressed and densely-furnished version of the well-known cultivar 'Pendula', making it suitable for smaller rockeries, or planting in groups. The light-coloured foliage is accentuated when in spring growth and it makes a squat little bush of bright lime-green with often a bird's-nest-like depression in the centre. I should imagine a ten-year old plant to measure 1m (3ft) wide and 50cm (20in) high.   Hardiness 5.

505 *Tsuga canadensis* 'Jervis'. Spring. Washington, DC, USA.

506 *Tsuga canadensis* 'Minima'. Spring. Washington, DC, USA.

Tsuga canadensis 'Jervis'

505 One of the slowest-growing cultivars of Eastern Hemlock, 'Jervis' forms in the course of many years into a much-compacted, irregular little bush of smaller-than-typical leaves, densely set in tight clusters, often with a short length of stem between each cluster. The photograph of a specimen in the Gotelli collection in Washington is of a plant probably twenty-five years old, yet no more than 35cm (14in) in any dimension. A true dwarf in every respect.   Hardiness 5.

Tsuga canadensis 'Minima'

506 A first-class low spreading bush, 'Minima' rarely exceeds 1m (3ft) in height by 3m (10ft) in width, and once having gained these dimensions is reputed to gain little or no further size. It has an inner branch system that ascends at a low angle, giving the bush its height, and these terminate in graceful sprays of slightly-drooping foliage to create a many-tiered and softly-rounded effect. A wonderful plant for lawn or rockery.   Hardiness 5.

507 *Tsuga canadensis* 'Minuta'. Spring. Washington, DC, USA.

508 *Tsuga canadensis* 'Nana'. Spring. Washington, DC, USA.

509 *Tsuga canadensis* 'Pendula'. Spring. Wisley, Surrey, England.

Tsuga canadensis 'Minuta'

507 Very aptly-named is 'Minuta', with its tightly-compressed growths, bunchy globose habit and maximum height of about 45cm (18in). It is virtually a botanical variety as several plants of this type were found growing wild in the state of Vermont, USA, having apparently grown as seedlings from a cone-bearing plant of the same type growing nearby. A variety that will never be plentiful unless a regular supply of seed is discovered, as it does not seem to propagate satisfactorily from cuttings.

Hardiness 5.

Tsuga canadensis 'Nana'

508 This slow-growing form has leaves a little shorter and more crowded than the type, and forms an irregular many-branched, chunky little bush that may reach a height of 80cm (30in) in ten years' growing. It seldom displays any distinct leader, as most tip growths finish in a much-divided cluster of shoots, but in spite of this it steadily builds itself up in height in a picturesquely haphazard manner that is not out of keeping with today's style of gardening.

Hardiness 5.

Tsuga canadensis 'Pendula'　　　　　Weeping Hemlock

509 The name 'Pendula' has been rather loosely applied in the past to many different different forms of weeping hemlock, many of which have since assumed tree-like proportions and have been re-named as separate cultivars, leaving the above name for the one described here. It is a beautiful garden conifer at all times of the year with its wonderful rounded, weeping form, highlighted in spring when displaying its fresh growth of bright lime-green on all tips. It is best planted on a bank or slope to display its full weeping effect, and young plants need to be staked and trained upwards for 1m (3ft) or so unless one desires a plant that is almost prostrate in habit. In ten years it may be expected to cover a circle of about 1.5m (5ft) in diameter.　Hardiness 5.

Tsuga canadensis 'Von Helm's Dwarf'

510 A compact tsuga of ideal pyramidal proportions for general garden or rockery use with an average height of 1m (3ft). The densely-set leaves are a rich dark-green colour, and make fine contrast in spring when the new growth emerges a light lime-green.　Hardiness 5.

510 *Tsuga canadensis* 'Von Helm's Dwarf'. Spring. Washington, DC, USA.

511 *Tsuga canadensis* 'Young's Coning'. Spring. Washington, DC, USA.

512 *Tsuga diversifolia*. Foliage and cones. Autumn.

513 *Tsuga heterophylla*. Winter. Taihape, New Zealand.

514 *Tsuga heterophylla*. Foliage and cones.

Tsuga canadensis 'Young's Coning'

511 In the Gotelli collection of Dwarf and Slow-Growing Conifers, in Washington, DC, this specimen has reached about 1.5m (5ft) in height, and is listed under the name 'Young Cone'. The plant is in fact well furnished in cones, and this feature may well have given rise to either of the above names. The only reference to this cultivar is by Mr Hillier where he refers to it as 'Young's Coning', and describes it briefly as 'branchlets clad in rusty brown pubescence'. It appears to be a promising garden cultivar with the unusual combination of weeping branchlets and an upright growth habit.   Hardiness 5.

Tsuga diversifolia   Northern Japanese Hemlock

512 Very similar to the closely-related Southern Japanese Hemlock, T. sieboldii, but rather smaller, this native of the mountains of central and southern Honshu occurs there in vast untouched forests at an average altitude of 1,600m (5,300ft), where it makes a pyramidal tree to 20m (65ft) in height. The trunk colour is noticeably reddish-brown, leaves a dull dark-green, blunt-ended, to 10mm ($\frac{2}{5}$in) in length, with a yearly crop of attractive 20cm ($\frac{3}{4}$in) cones maturing each autumn. In cultivation it rarely reaches more than 2 to 3m (6 to 10ft) in height.   Hardiness 5.

Tsuga heterophylla   Western Hemlock

513, 514 A tall, stately conical tree that reaches heights of up to 70m (230ft) in its native North America and may be readily distinguished from its eastern counterpart because of its single unforked straight trunk, making it the better of the two for ornamental planting. Needless to say, it is a tree that should be given ample space to develop and be viewed to best advantage, and looks its best on a large lawn. Commercially it is used for timber, and the bark is processed to yield tannin for the tanning industry in North America. Seed is borne freely in light brown 2cm ($\frac{3}{4}$in) oval cones which are carried in profusion on the tips of the branchlets. While it grows well in most soil types it prefers a rich, moist well-drained soil, and in such conditions may be expected to make a height of 6m (20ft) in ten years.   Hardiness 6.

Tsuga mertensiana   Mountain Hemlock

515 A tree native to the highlands of western North America with a range from Alaska in the north down to California where it is found growing in the High Sierras up to altitudes of 3,500m (11,500ft). It is an excellent park or garden ornamental, noteworthy features being its straight well-defined leader, the liberal covering of foliage from closely-spaced horizontal or slightly-ascending branches, and the way it furnishes itself right to ground level, making a tall tapering tree three to five times as high as its base width. Distinguishing details are the greyish or glaucous 2cm ($\frac{3}{4}$in) spirally-arranged leaves and the cylindrical cones, the largest of this genus (up to 8cm) (more than 3in) which begin a violet purple colour and mature to a light brown. It grows slowly when young and may not reach to more than 2m (6ft) in its first ten years—rather a poor start for a tree that can grow to 50m (165ft). It prefers a cool climate and is not tolerant of city air pollution.   Hardiness 5.

Widdringtonia schwarzii   Willowmore Cedar

516 The five known species of Widdringtonias or Cypress Pines, all South African natives, range in size from the shrubby 2 to 3m (6 to 10ft) W. cupressoides to the 45m (150ft) forest and timber tree W. whytei. They have proved highly resistant to hot, dry summer conditions in their native mountain habitat, and should adapt well to similar conditions in other countries. W. schwarzii, while capable of reaching 30m (100ft) in its native state, is well suited to tub growing; can reach 2m (6ft) in three years under favourable conditions, but reduces in growth rate once the roots become restricted. It is said to tolerate such semi-stunting conditions for many years without any apparent effect in foliage injury.   Hardiness 7.

515 *Tsuga mertensiana.* Foliage and cones.

516 *Widdringtonia schwarzii.* Autumn. Palmerston North, New Zealand.

517 Entry planting using prostrate junipers.

518 Tamarix juniper used as a 40 cm (15 in) deep ground cover.

519 A dry bank effectively clothed with Golden Thuja and Tamarix junipers.

520 Exciting entry planting featuring pines, Araucaria, Junipers, Podocarpus and Cypress.

521 The Japanese touch in a Californian garden.

522 Effective bank treatment using pines and prostrate Junipers, interplanted with Arctotis.

523 Deodar Cedars in San Francisco where the warm climate produces a pendulous growth habit.

525 A "Witches Broom" high in the branches of *Pinus radiata*.

524 Golden Pfitzer Juniper leads in from the street.

526 Cypress "knees" of *Taxodium distichum*.

528 Dwarf conifers in the Gotelli collection skilfully incorporated in a rockery setting.

527 The Gotelli collection of conifers in the United States National Arboretum, Washington, DC, USA.

529 An elderly Mugo Pine presides over the rockery at the Brooklyn Botanic Gardens, New York.

530 Dwarf Japanese Juniper as a bonsai specimen.

531 Excellent use of Chamaecyparis and Junipers in an English garden.

532 Dwarf conifers at the Royal Horticultural Society's gardens at Wisley, Surrey, England.

533 The rock garden at Kew, London, featuring dwarf conifers.

534 The Pinetum at Nymans, Sussex, England. An old planting of
beautifully-proportioned trees.

535 Part of the extensive range of conifers in the Pinetum Blijdenstein, Hilversum.

536 Dwarf conifers in the Madurodam Model City, The Hague, Netherlands.

537 An island planting using conifers at Gouda, Netherlands.

539 Oregon pines and rugged mountains harmonise at Queenstown, New Zealand.

538 Dwarf Alberta Spruce feature in a mountain setting in miniature.

540 *Pinus pinaster*, one of the many conifers with attractively-fissured trunks.

541 Conifers decorate a restful corner in the heart of a city.

542 Colour contrasts in Horizontal Junipers.

543 Cedars, Thuja and Taxus in a motel garden planting.

544 Water and dwarf conifers make a pleasing combination.

546 Compact conifers, berries and dwarf evergreens beautify a traffic island.

545 A decapitated Deodar Cedar becomes an attractive
weeping standard.

547 Colourful spring display of *Picea jezoensis* var. *hondoensis*.

548 Thuja and Taxus blend cosily with thatched roofing in the Netherlands.

549 *Cupressus macrocarpa* is trimmed to a remarkably smooth hedge.

550 Skilful use of conifers in an Australian garden.

551 *Thuja orientalis* in a Honolulu garden.

552 *Pinus thunbergii.* Pruning in process at the Japanese Tea Gardens, San Francisco.

553 Golden Monterey Cypress dwarfed through being grown in a pot.

554 Thuja orientalis in the gardens of the Taj Mahal, India.

TAKING THE PHOTOGRAPHS

The photographing of conifers would on first thoughts seem to be a relatively easy task requiring a minimum of technical skill or specialised equipment. In many cases this has proved to be so, where the subject was found to be set in photographically congenial surroundings and the lighting good, so that all that one had to do was to focus and expose correctly. Not too many specimens however were so ideally situated, and in many cases one had to resort to a photo trick in order to obtain correct colour rendition along with sufficient subject contrast for an accurate representation of the plant. Coniferous plants tend to run rather low in contrast, lacking the colour and glamour of flowering shrubs and perennials, yet do not photograph well in bright, often contrasty sunlight. The best effects are usually obtained under an overcast sky. Many slides taken in such dull and cloudy weather, though accurate in colour and detail, were lacking in contrast, and such slides were re-photographed to give the contrast, while also providing an opportunity to correct any colour bias or change in density needed, thus enabling us to give the printer a more consistent type of slide to work on.

Photographically-minded readers will probably notice that a number of the photographs in this book are flash-illuminated. There are both advantages and drawbacks in using flash on a subject such as this. On most conifers flash-on-camera has a peculiar effect which, if overdone can give a completely wrong colour rendition, sometimes turning a green plant a light silvery-grey on the resulting slide. This is because many conifers have a glaucous "bloom" all over their foliage — a substance not unlike that seen on a ripe grape and likewise easily rubbed off with the fingers. The bloom reflects light in much the same way as a glass-beaded reflector by returning it back the way it came, and can with certain species result in a "turned-on" conifer photo. This can be an advantage when seeking to enhance the colour of certain blue-foliaged forms, but the photographer can get caught when forced to use flash on a green or brown conifer. The only solution is to mount the light unit at an angle away from the camera so that the reflection of the bloom does not return back to the camera lens.

In photographing for this book as well as others in this series, Nikon 35mm equipment has been used almost exclusively, comprising Nikon Photomic FTN and Nikkormat FTN bodies, the latter usually loaded with a fast film for use where lighting was poor. To these were available four lenses, the one used most being the 55mm f3.5 Micro-Nikkor macro lens for all general and close-up work. Where a wider angle was needed, a 45mm GN Nikkor was used, and at the other end of the scale a 105mm to give a narrower angle and reduce background detail, and finally a 300mm telephoto provided the extra photographic "reach" to many an otherwise inaccessible plant. All these lenses, being interchangeable with either camera body and fully coupled for TTL exposure metering, made a versatile unit and helped to take a lot of guesswork out of a difficult assignment. Electronic flash illumination was provided by Sunpak and Metz computer compact rechargeable units. The preferred film for most of the photos as well as for slide copying is Kodachrome II with its excellent resolution and colour rendition, switching to High Speed Ektachrome where light was limited, with the occasional shot taken on Ektachrome X and Agfa CT18.

The combination of photography and conifers has been a particularly happy one from the point of view of identification. Because of the confusion over conifer names in the past it has been most gratifying to compare slides of specimens taken in different parts of the world and find that the confusion is not nearly as bad as it seemed. It is a great help to be able to put such slides side by side and compare details using latest books on the subject, and in most cases arrive at a conclusive decision as to name. I am often surprised how easily an impression of any particular conifer can become distorted in one's mind (usually after having studied as many other similar forms) and it is little wonder that Mr Hillier, the late Mr den Ouden and other conifer authorities were so diligent in recording in written form the identifying details as they were freshly before them. The colour camera is now becoming a powerful aid to such research. In many cases, however, a photo alone is not sufficient, particularly with some of the compact *Picea abies* cultivars, and further more detailed research is needed in one or more of the excellent books on the subject. While I have made every attempt to ensure that every photo presented here is correct in name, it must be remembered that it was never the aim of this book to delve deeper into identification than what a photograph can communicate, or by what can be conveyed in average garden language.

WHAT IS A CONIFER?

To answer this question correctly, I am going to have to use some technical botanical terms for which there are no common alternatives; but reference to the Glossary at the end of this book will help in the understanding of some of them.

Current botanical thinking indicates that the title "conifer" embraces all those plants belonging to three of the five orders that make up the class of plants known as the Gymnosperms, and these three orders, the *Gingkoales*, the *Taxales* and the *Coniferales*, are further divided into their respective families and genera as set out at the end of this chapter. These genera are further split into species, varieties and cultivars to give us our garden conifer names as we know them. Most species are erect-growing evergreen trees, which in their varied localities grow into dense forests and provide a large part of the world timber. Their valuable by-products include resin, tar and turpentine, while in some the large seeds are edible. They thrive in a wide range of climatic zones from almost frigid through to temperate and subtropical regions, and specially on mountain areas. Most conifers possess resin passages in all parts, and in all except the subtropical araucarias and podocarps, the leaves are very narrow, needle or scale-like. The flowers are always unisexual, the staminate in cones or on catkins on the main axis, and female in cones with naked ovules.

Except for a few very hardy high alpines, most species of conifers grow into large specimens, generally too large for the average modern garden. But as will be observed by a quick glance through these illustrated pages, the greater part of the vast range of ornamental garden cultivars are smaller-growing forms of the more common wild species. Most forms or "sports" of such species which have developed bluish, golden or variegated foliage, are naturally much slower in growth than the plain green-foliaged type, and are therefore more suited for average garden culture.

Although nearly all conifers are evergreen, yet for autumn-foliage effect in suitable areas with colder winters, there are also a few most attractive deciduous species. The foliage of the well-known larch timber tree *Larix decidua* changes to a rich gold and brown in late autumn, retaining its beauty for quite a lengthy period if sheltered from persistent winds. The lovely fresh larch-green spring foliage is also impressive, and provides a distinct colour among the numerous greens not furnished by any other tree. Then we have the Bald Cypress, *Taxodium distichum*, likewise most impressive in the autumn, with its graceful deep golden-brown foliage. It is a large-growing conifer that will thrive in swampy ground, even in water up to 1m (3ft) deep, the quaint knee-like roots of old trees protruding above the surface.

Another well-known deciduous conifer is the Maidenhair Tree, *Gingko biloba*. Few people recognise this lovely specimen tree as a conifer and in fact it resides in a separate family of its own, the *Gingkoaceae*. Its description is covered alongside the illustration.

It is beyond the scope or the ability of the writers to cover the conifer field in its full extent, as it involves some 300 species and several thousand forms or cultivars, and the number is added to yearly. However, it is thought that a list of the genera included in the conifer world should be furnished, and those distinguished by an asterisk (*) are those referred to in this book, either in general description or illustrated.

Set out below is a chart showing the botanical classifications under which the various conifer genera are currently placed. The word "currently" is unfortunately a necessary one for the reason that there have been many changes in the past as botanical findings came to light and it is just as likely that further research will result in yet more changes in the future.

THE LIVING GYMNOSPERMS——
ORDER GINGKOALES
  FAMILY GINGKOACEAE
    Genus; *Gingko.
ORDER TAXALES
  FAMILY TAXACEAE (Yew family)
    Genera; Amenotaxus, Austrotaxus, Pseudotaxus, *Taxus, *Torreya.
ORDER CONIFERALES
  FAMILY CEPHALOTAXACEAE (Plum-Yew family)
    Genus; *Cephalotaxus
  FAMILY PODOCARPACEAE (Podocarpus family)
    Genera; *Acmopyle, *Dacrydium, *Microcachrys, *Microstrobus, *Phyllocladus, *Podocarpus, *Saxegothaea.
  FAMILY ARAUCARIACEAE (Monkey-Puzzle family)
    Genera; *Agathis, *Araucaria.

FAMILY CUPRESSACEAE (Cypress family)
  Genera; *Actinostrobos, *Austrocedrus, *Callitris, *Calocedrus, *Chamaecyparis, *Cupressocyparis, * Cupressus, *Diselma, *Fitzroya, * Fokienia, *Juniperus, *Libocedrus, *Neocallitropsis, * Papuacedrus, Pilgerodendron, *Tetraclinis, *Thuja. *Thujopsis, *Widdringtonia.
FAMILY TAXODIACEAE (Deciduous Cypress family)
  Genera; *Athrotaxis, *Cryptomeria, *Cunninghamia, *Glyptostrobus, *Metasequoia, *Sciadopitys, *Sequoia, *Sequoiadendron, *Taiwania, *Taxodium.
FAMILY PINACEAE (Pine family)
  Genera; *Abies, Cathaya, *Cedrus, *Keteleeria, *Larix, *Picea, *Pinus, *Pseudolarix, *Pseudotsuga, * Tsuga.

To relate all these complicated names to a well-known garden conifer such as, for example, Koster's Blue Spruce, we can construct its place in the plant kingdom as follows:

CLASS — GYMNOSPERMAE
 ORDER — CONIFERALES
  FAMILY — PINACEAE
   GENUS — *Picea*
    SPECIES — *Picea pungens*
     CULTIVAR — 'Koster'

= *Picea pungens* 'Koster', commonly known as Koster's Blue Spruce.

It will be noticed that in naming conifers only the last three levels are necessary, and where our plant is a species only and not a cultivar, only genus and species are needed. Thus the Colorado Spruce as known in its native habitat is simply *Picea pungens*, and this name holds good for all Colorado Spruce regardless of habit or colour variations.

VARIETIES, CULTIVARS AND CULTIVARIANTS

The difference between these complicated-sounding titles is often a puzzle to many, but when one understands their meaning it is not as difficult as one may think. As a working example we shall use the popular prostrate juniper, *J. taxifolia* var. *lutchuensis*. In its native Japan *J. taxifolia* is normally a tree of up to 15m (50ft) tall that gives no hint of prostrate habit. Over many years however, offspring have occurred with a prostrate habit and have become established almost like a separate species in itself, yet inseparable botanically from *J. taxifolia* because of affinities in fruit, seed, leaf and stem types. This prostrate form then must retain the species name of *taxifolia* and have added to it var. *lutchuensis*, and to be in conformity with botanical practice should be written as shown, in italics with no capitals or quotation marks. Most botanical varieties are genetically stable and reproduce from seed a similar plant to the variety, give or take the odd colour variant or slight change in habit which usually happens in any seed-grown crop.

This leads us to our second type, the cultivar. Supposing that from a batch of seed or a bud mutation of the above variety a noticeably blue-foliaged specimen appeared which was then propagated asexually (i.e. by cutting or graft) and given the name (say) 'Blue Pacific' with a view to its introduction and sale. It is then a cultivar, and to be true to the cultivarietal name must always be grown by asexual means from the original plant or descendants of it. Such a plant would then correctly be named *Juniperus taxifolia* var. *lutchuensis* 'Blue Pacific'. Or should the mutation or seed have come direct from the species *J. taxifolia* it should carry the name *Juniperus taxifolia* 'Blue Pacific'.

Finally, we have cultivariants. These are plants that appear different in habit or foliage to their vegetative parents as a result of propagating from other than typical type foliage. This can be illustrated with certain types of *Abies*. If one studies the foliage on these firs it can be noted that the tree carries two types of foliage — leading shoots with completely radially-arranged needles, and horizontal side-branches that carry pectinately-arranged needles (Plate 22). If one propagates from the former leading shoots the resultant tree will be erect like its parent, given normal growing treatment, while a grafted side-branch will lack any tendency to grow erect and may spread for several metres without making height of any consequence; a plant of this type is then known as a cultivariant. One cannot however assume that such a plant is not irrevocably committed to this spreading habit, and in fact it often happens that an erect leader does emerge after many years and (if not removed promptly) completely changes the habit of the plant. Such emergence of an embryonic leader is usually triggered off by any kind of breakage at the growing tip or along the main stem, and for this reason cultivariants cannot be considered as likely to be permanently of any specified foliage type or growth habit, and are liable to revert at any time. It is likely that some of our best spreading so-called cultivars of *Abies* and *Picea* are merely cultivariants of upright forms, but because they are well-known under their given names and have remained stable over the years, they are left alone in the hope that they will continue to behave themselves as well as they have done in the past.

HOW DOES A CULTIVAR ORIGINATE?

Practically all of our present great range of conifer cultivars have arisen either by way of seedling variations or through vegetative "sports", sometimes called bud mutations (Plate 197), and no doubt a lot more of these occur both in nurseries and in the wild state than are actually detected and used for propagation of a (hopefully) new cultivar. It is not unusual for a batch of seed-raised plants to show one or two individuals a little different to the rest, and that the larger the batch the greater the chance of finding a few oddities. So it is that many unusual cultivars have arisen to be tested and finally given cultivar names, some of them worthy garden subjects while others not so good and losing favour to superior forms after a few years. Once such a plant is selected it stands to reason that all propagation, in order to be identical to its parent, must be done vegetatively, either from the actual parent or from vegetative descendants of the parent, or it is not eligible to carry the same cultivar name. It has happened more than once where two cultivars of completely different origins and raised in different areas turn out to be almost identical to each other; and when they are eventually brought together much argument usually follows between the promoters of each as to whose plant is the better and which one should be discontinued, or as is often the case the two continue on in the trade and eventually become confused so that the names still exist but nobody knows which cultivar is which. There are many such conundrums in the conifer world but thankfully botanical research is tracking some of these down to their origins and giving us a clearer picture as to names.

A "sport" (see Plate 197) or bud mutation is the occurrence of a different type, colour or shape of foliage on a species or cultivar, and plants grown from such foliage pieces normally retain the characteristics of the sport. Sometimes the change is very marked, producing a new plant of a completely different habit to its parent, and in other cases the change is not so marked but regarded rather as a refinement on the original. Typical examples of such behaviour is the *Chamaecyparis lawsoniana* 'Fletcheri', which has produced through sports such cultivars as 'Ellwoodii' (same colour but more compact), 'Ellwoods Pigmy' (very compact and squat), 'Ellwoods Gold' (golden foliage), 'Gold Splash' (gold splashes on foliage), and 'Fleckellwood' (a creamy-flecked 'Ellwoodii'), to name those illustrated in this book alone. Obviously 'Fletcheri' is very prone to this type of behaviour, and such a host of diverse cultivars originating from one plant carries with it a proneness to reversion, either back to the original or yet further astray.

A further type of mutation sometimes found on *Larix*, *Picea* and *Pinus* and a few other genera is a condition known as witches broom (Plate 525) where the

195

foliage grows in a densely congested mass, often to 1m (3ft) or more in diameter. Plants propagated from such parts usually make excellent dwarf or bun-shaped specimens and many of the dwarf *Picea* and *Pinus* cultivars have originated as witches brooms. These growths occur as natural cell mutations (sports) and as a result of attacks by insects and mites. Possibly certain viruses may also induce condensed or dwarf growth. Whatever the cause, plants from witches brooms are always likely to revert by producing normal sized shoots. These must immediately be removed or they will over grow and swamp the dwarf.

Dwarf conifers can be grouped into several classes. Firstly there are numerous forms which hug the ground or rocks, these being usually sports or mutations of the taller-growing species. Some also are alpine or mountain forms or species, which have evolved a compact or prostrate habit which enables them to survive the cold windy mountain conditions. Secondly, we have true erect-growing but compact alpine forms of the taller-growing lowland species. But perhaps by far the greater number of real dwarfs have occurred in cultivation in what is called seedling mutations, juvenile mutations or bud mutations, these latter forms developing on the original plant. It does not mean that such mutations or sports do not occur in nature as well, but usually such freaks soon become swamped or crowded out by the normal growth of fresh and more vigorous seedlings. For instance, what chance of survival would a real miniature or a slow-growing variegated-foliaged seedling mutation possess in a forest of young pines? Furthermore such natural "sports" are often unable to reproduce from seed — as has been said, "Nature preserves her species by making her freaks sterile", so that few in nature ever survive. But in the numerous nurseries where many thousands of plants of the various species are raised, occasionally some of these freaks will also appear, and instead of being eliminated eventually as in nature, man preserves such if they possess features of ornamental quality. Lastly, dwarfs can be produced artificially, as in the Japanese art of producing bonsai plants, where specimens are dwarfed by the constant trimming back of the roots along with the "nibbling off" of the top growths. Plants also can be dwarfed by growing them as specimens in containers, such as large pots, old cans and the like (Plate 553).

CONIFERS

ABIES — SILVER FIRS

This is an important genus comprising about forty species, although admittedly the difference between some is very slight, while there is still some confusion over other genera, such as *Tsuga*. They are called the Silver Firs, and are distinguished from the *Picea* by the conspicuous fact that the leaves are swollen at the base, leaving, when they fall, a disc-like scar. The leaves of *Picea*, when they fall, leave a peg-like base on the branch which gives the bark a roughened surface. Cones are erect in the *Abies*, and they fall apart as soon as the seeds are ripe, leaving an upright stick-like spike on the branch. In the *Picea* the cones are pendulous, not breaking up when the seeds are ripe.

The *Abies* are distributed widely in the mountain regions of Central and South Europe, Asia, Japan and North America, while man-made forests for timber have been developed in many countries that are suitable for their culture. Unfortunately, the various species have given rise to very few really dwarf forms, although a number are reported as being cultivated in Europe. The species which have provided some interesting variations are here briefly described.

Abies alba. This is the common Silver Fir, of which two compact-growing forms are cultivated; one named 'Brevifolia' is distinct in that the leaves are broad and short, while a still more compact form is called 'Compacta'. The other is known as 'Pendula', in which the outer branches gracefully weep, the main central trunk reaching some height in time.

A. balsamea. The North American 'Balsam Fir', also called Balm of Gilead, hails from the White Mountains of New Hampshire, and its habitat extends to the highest region of alpine plant life and also into the Arctic Circle. It is, therefore, to be expected that some of these naturally dwarf, alpine, or prostrate forms should be found in cultivation. So we have one called 'Hudsonia' which is a dense growing plant of spreading habit, seldom exceeding 60cm (24in) in height. Another English-raised form called 'Nana' develops into a globose bush, the characteristic rich glossy green leaves in this form being yellowish on the tips.

A. concolor. This is the Colorado White Fir which grows into a noble tree up to 50m (165ft) tall, the glabrous, soft, olive-green spring growths changing later to grey-green. The low-growing forms that have developed in cultivation are 'Compacta', a rare plant of dwarf compact habit, but irregular growth, and short, very stiff deeply glaucous foliage. There are several forms called 'Pendula', which appear to be semi-prostrate growing types developed by taking grafts or cuttings from lower side branches. A similar type of plant can usually be secured from most firs by propagating from low side branches, as such wood will seldom if ever produce a main stem lead. Mr Welch in his splendid work, *Dwarf Conifers*, coins the word 'cultivariant' for this type. The other really worthwhile dwarf-growing form is known as 'Wattezii Prostrate', being a form of the taller-growing cultivar of the silvery-leafed 'Wattezii', and retaining the attractive creamy-tipped foliage which changes later to white. Because of this foliage feature, the plant is much less vigorous than most other prostrate-growing firs, and therefore of great interest to those with limited space.

A. koreana. This Korean Fir, although too large for the average garden, reaching 20m (65ft) in nature, is worthy of consideration because of its neat habit and attractive foliage, together with the fact that the tree, even at the young stage, bears freely a crop of long violet-purple cones, the bracts being also attractively tipped white. The only recorded dwarf-growing form is called 'Compact Dwarf', a selected slow-growing form without a leader, leaves somewhat shorter and the plant never bearing cones. A form sold in the trade as 'Nana', which is just a slower-growing form of the type, does cone freely on small plants.

CEDRUS — THE CEDARS

Botanically there are only four or possibly five recognised species of this genus, though, some people still hold that they are but geographical forms of the one species. However, they are all majestic evergreens with large spreading branches, carrying with them the impression of stability and dignity. Unfortunately all species are too robust for planting in anything except large gardens and parks, but the various forms that have developed over many years provide us with some excellent garden foliage plants. A good free open subsoil is necessary for success, and as they are mountain plants good drainage is likewise important, so that stagnant soil cannot be tolerated. The species and their forms are however amongst the most drought-resisting of all conifers, and thus come close behind the *Juniperus* in this respect.

Cedrus atlantica. The Atlantic Cedar grows to 40m (130ft) with a broad trunk and closely resembles *C. libani*, but is more pyramidal in growth particularly in its earlier stages. There are a number of most attractive foliage forms grown, and these are usually planted as specimens on lawns; a wise decision as the beautiful symmetrical outline of many conifers is often spoilt by being planted too close, so that they are in competition with other robust-growing trees. The most popular form is the distinctive glaucous-blue foliaged *C. altantica* 'Glauca'.

Other forms of *Cedrus atlantica* in general cultivation include 'Aurea' in which the foliage, particularly where well exposed to the elements, is a golden-yellow. There are several reported dwarf forms which may come under the epithet 'Compacta' and likewise prostrate or weeping forms under the name of 'Pendula', but these do not seem to be in general cultivation.

Cedrus deodara. The Indian Cedar or Deodar, native to the Western Himalayas, grows into a handsome majestic tree, reaching in nature the height of up to 60m (200ft). The wood, like that of the other cedars, is long-lasting, yields a pleasing fragrance when used for furniture, and important oils are distilled from them. As with *C. atlantica*, there is a golden-foliaged form called 'Aurea', a fastigiate form called 'Erecta', and the erect-growing, silvery-glaucous foliaged form is known as *C. deodara* 'Verticillata Glauca'.

Several lower-growing forms are cultivated which grow into dense, compact bushes. Some recorded names are 'Hesse' and 'Nana', while one under the name of 'Pygmy' is extremely dwarf and glaucous in the foliage. There are also several prostrate-growing forms which are usually arranged under the obliging name of 'Pendula'. When trained up to a height with a main leader and the other branches strictly cascading, a good specimen is quite effective. If allowed to sprawl over the ground, such plants can in time cover quite an extensive area.

C. brevifolia. Known as the Cypress Cedar, this species is often grown in containers, also in gardens, under the impression that it is a low-growing species, but actually it is really just a plant of slow growth. As a patio plant it is very suitable because grown in this way it remains dwarf, while the foliage is small and neat. There does not seem to be any recorded miniature forms cultivated.

C. libani. This is the true Cedar of Lebanon, and often cultivated because of its Biblical associations. It grows up to 35m (115ft) with a large horizontal topped head, the branches set in horizontal planes. There are a number of recorded dwarf, compact-growing forms most of which seem to be included under the name of 'Nana', so that some slight variation exists in the different clones offered and cultivated in different areas.

All forms of cedars require to be grafted, as they do not readily root from cuttings as do most other conifers. The stronger-growing *C. deodara* seems quite compatible with other species, and seedlings reach grafting size much quicker. It has been found that a higher percentage of "takes" is secured by using strong one-year-old seedling stocks, and side-grafting where the cambium layer is thickest. Care should be exercised that none of the species or their golden or glaucous foliaged forms should have their main trunk or leader damaged or removed, otherwise the beauty of the specimen would be entirely lost, the damaged specimen then growing into a dense, shapeless mass of branches. A central leader of the stronger-growing weepers should also be selected and tied to a firm stake, lifting up this support and staking the leader to it each year as growth proceeds. This will result in a beautiful effect of outer cascading branches from a central main trunk. Other weeping trees such as the betulas and fagus should be trained in the same way. Some of the prostrate-growing forms are also more attractive if a leader is selected and staked, so that several tiers of growths can develop, instead of the plant just sprawling over the ground.

CHAMAECYPARIS

The name is derived from *chamai*, meaning on the ground, that is dwarf, in contrast to the other taller-growing cypress species. The name also supports the common name of Bastard or False Cypress. It is well within the memory of most gardeners when *Chamaecyparis lawsoniana* and its forms were offered in nursery catalogues under the old name of *Cupressus lawsoniana*, while the forms of *C. pisifera* were listed under the then generic name given of *Retinospora*. From the viewpoint of the average gardener who finds the changing of names rather confusing, and particularly when the newer ones are more difficult to pronounce or remember, it is a pity that this fresh genus of *Chamaecyparis* needed to be selected from that of *Cupressus*. However, our botanists fully justify the change and the distinction that warrants this separation. One of the main distinguishing features is that the larger, rounded seed cones of the *Cupressus* usually take eighteen months or more to mature, and furthermore, remain closed for many years, whereas the smaller cones of the *Chamaecyparis*, usually produced in flattened clusters on the frondose branches, develop, ripen and shed their seeds within the growing period of the year.

The *Chamaecyparis* produce only from one to five seeds in each of the woody scales that compose the cone, while in the *Cupressus* there are up to twenty seeds in each of the six to ten fertile scale departments. In their seedling stage the former produces but two cotyledons, whereas with the latter these can be up to five.

The various species of *Chamaecyparis* are natives of North America, Japan and Formosa and belong to the family *Pinaceae*. The species *C. lawsoniana* and *C. nootkatensis* are planted under forest conditions in some countries, and provide timber of commercial importance. To be successful with such plantings, the soil must be free and open, with adequate rainfall and freedom from excessive prevailing winds.

Chamaecyparis lawsoniana. Commonly called the Lawson Cypress, this species will grow to a pyramidal tree 40 to 60m (130–200ft) tall. The bark of old trees is thick, soft, and reddish-brown. This variable species has given rise to more garden or ornamental forms than possibly any other species of conifer. No less than over 200 named cultivars have been recorded over a number of years, although less than a fifth are in general cultivation. New sports and forms are however, constantly being discovered in different parts of the world, particularly from the northern temperate zone where most of the coniferous forests grow.

It would be quite a study to discover why some species of trees and shrubs develop various sports on mature trees and also seedling mutations, while others seem to be "fixed" in their ability to vary. Why is it that among the many millions of *Pinus radiata* which have been planted for forestry purposes and for shelter, that only one seedling mutation has so far been recorded, the lovely golden-foliaged form called 'Aurea'? *Chamaecyparis lawsoniana* produces its hundreds of mutations, so why does not *Pinus radiata* do the same?

Some of the best ornamental foliage forms are illustrated and described in this book, giving a good idea of the range available but limited here because of the necessity to include cultivars of other genera. This species and its forms, while hardy and easily grown, will not tolerate drought conditions. The browning or apparent burning of golden-foliaged forms during summer is usually traceable to a spell of dry weather experienced earlier, and not sun-scald as often considered to be the case. That serious disease called cypress canker is known to have ruined many fine plantations on farms and forests, there being so far no known practical cure. Fortunately it seldom attacks isolated trees in the garden, the infection being passed on from tree to tree by air movement, making entry at any damaged or cut parts. If any such infection should appear, the branch should immediately be removed and burned, and the stump and remaining plant treated by a copper fungicide spray.

C. obtusa. This is the Hinoki conifer of Japan which in nature develops into a specimen up to 35m (115ft) tall, with reddish-brown bark that sheds in long narrow strips. The branches are flattened or fan-like, leaves scale-like pressed close to the shoot, and in whorls of four. Although this species does not grow into a large specimen in this or most other countries, in Japan it is one of the most important timber trees, the fragrant and long-lasting wood being used for carpentry and joinery. However, the numerous garden forms, of which some named cultivars have been recorded, provide us with attractive-foliage small trees in a great variety of types, shades of green, gold, glaucous and brown.

C. pisifera. In many of the ornamental garden types of this species often a juvenile foliage form persists for some time. This distinguishing feature gave botanists the opportunity to separate such plants under a fresh genera, namely *Retinospora,* but later to be found an unnecessary name. Again we have here a great number of recorded sports or bud mutations that have given rise to numerous highly ornamental garden forms, some of which are illustrated in this book. There are quite a number of the plumose-foliaged forms, and further mutations are constantly appearing.

C. thyoides. From this species, a native of North America, have come a number of smaller-growing forms, which like the parent, are tolerant of quite wet conditions. The true *C. thyoides* 'Andelyensis' is a slow-growing, upright branching, more open foliage plant, assuming its adult foliage quickly, and noted for its crop of small cones which appear at an early age. A more compact-growing form still with erect branches and more foliage of juvenile type, more broad than high, is called *C. andelyensis* 'Nana'. It occasionally reverts to the common type, but as with such reversions in any other miniatures, the offending branch can be simply cut out as it appears.

A form that has been very popular for many years is known as *C. thyoides* 'Ericoides'. It forms a neat close-growing pyramidal bush seldom exceeding 2m (6ft) in height. The juvenile type foliage, said to be fixed, is a deep greyish-green in summer, changing in winter to a rusty-red, and eventually deep purplish-brown. It is therefore a most useful dwarf for associating in contrast with other foliaged conifers in the golds and glaucous types. Another interesting variegated form in which the foliage is splashed with lemon-yellow is called *C. thyoides* 'Variegata'. It is more open and loose-growing in habit, eventually reaching 4m (13ft). It has for some years been distributed under the name of 'Barkeri'.

CUPRESSUS — THE CYPRESS

This genus at one time included the *Chamaecyparis,* but now it embraces but a dozen species, all hailing from the temperate parts of the northern hemisphere. None is quite hardy in the colder parts of Europe and America, but some species, particularly *Cupressus macrocarpa* and *C. sempervirens* and their forms, are popular in Australia, New Zealand and South Africa. For some years in New Zealand *C. macrocarpa* was much employed for farm shelter (termed in Europe "storm trees") to protect animals from prevailing winds. In the warmer parts of Australia it was found that many seedling-raised plants of this species were not long lived, and just as the shelter line matured and became really useful, odd trees here and there collapsed and died. A long-lived and more horizontally branched form was selected, and for many years this was propagated from cuttings. As an attempt to distinguish this special clone from the ordinary seedling-raised stock, it was called *C. lambertiana,* while a spreading horizontal branched golden foliaged form was named *C. lambertiana* 'Aurea'. Although these distinct clones were

weather. The wood of this species, as with *Calocedrus decurrens*, is much employed for the manufacture of lead pencil casings. The berry-like fruits, usually round and covered with glaucous bloom, enclosing one or more seeds, are normally black or bluish-black, in contrast to the fruits, or more correctly arils, of the *Taxus* (yews), which are bright coloured, usually cherry-red.

One of the most interesting features of the junipers, and one that has considerable additional charm for the plant lover, is that most species (and many other genera of conifers), pass through a juvenile stage of foliage in eventually reaching that of the adult form. This means that young plants present a different foliage formation to that of mature plants, almost suggesting at times two different species. In some plants the change is often gradual, so that at one stage both forms of foliage may appear on the same plant, while with a few species the foliage does not even change when reaching maturity. This feature must no doubt have caused complications for botanists until they got everything sorted out. Usually the name of a particular species of plant is identified from dried specimens of foliage held in a herbarium, and not from live growing plants. Thus a specimen sent in for identification could be either from a juvenile or mature plant, and unless the botanist has access to dried specimens of both forms, an incorrect finding could be returned. We are thankfully not dealing with the problems of the botanist, although duly thankful for him and his work.

As one turns over the pages of the various botanical works on conifers and studies the carefully recorded descriptions of the hundreds of species and thousands of cultivars, one feels that any attempt to provide further information, apart from the brief notes that attend the colour pictures, would fall miserably short. So with the junipers and the 250 or more carefully recorded forms and cultivars, no attempt is made beyond these brief general notes of the most important genera. Once again, we affirm that this is primarily a picture-book to assist in the selection of conifers, and those desiring to study these plants in a fuller way should acquire copies of the recommended books.

Juniperus chinensis. Originally certain plants that have since been classified as distinct species were included in this Chinese genus. Likewise, a complex group of hybrids, mainly between *J. chinensis* and *J. sabina*, were also included under this specific heading. This most interesting group of hybrids has now been re-classified under the name of *J.* x *media*, and the separation is becoming accepted by growers. Of the remaining forms and cultivars of *J. chinensis*, no less than seventy have been recorded, but less than half of these have any great value as ornamentals.

J. communis. The common juniper, in nature widely distributed throughout Europe and Northern America, is most variable in habit, with geographical forms which have developed through regional variations of conditions. Because of these wide variations a number of forms were originally classified as separate species. In a number of cases the forms reverted to the common species when grown in a different environment. H. J. Welch in *Dwarf Conifers* helpfully divided the various forms and cultivars into three main groups — a few other cultivars not conforming:

The *Hibernica Group* includes the columnar forms, either tall or dwarf-growing, examples of which are 'Compressa', 'Hibernica' and 'Suecica'.

The *Canadensis Group* embraces the prostrate or spreading forms with thick stems, and coarse wide leaves, all turned toward the ground. Examples are the 'Depressa' and 'Vase' cultivars.

The *Saxatilis Group* is likewise a prostrate and spreading form with thin stems and densely set leaves showing the white upper side to a noticeable extent. The cultivars 'Repanda' and 'Silver Lining' come in here.

J. horizontalis. This more or less prostrate-growing species from North America has given rise to about twenty recorded forms, most of which are robust-growing, covering quite an area of ground in a few years. The main branches are long with numerous supporting branchlets, foliage dense, soon forming a solid mat. In America the various cultivated forms are much employed as ground covers, and being drought-resistant are often established on dry banks where few other plants could survive. No attempt is made here to describe all the cultivars grown, but there are several attractive foliage forms in shades of greens, glaucous and bluish-grey, and some of the best are illustrated in this book.

J. x media. As mentioned previously under the description of the species *J. chinensis*, this represents an interesting group of natural hybrids of considerable garden appeal. The hybrids naturally fall into two distinct classes, firstly the 'Plumosa' group in which the bushes almost exclusively display the smooth adult foliage which appears in a plumose effect in dense tufts. The various forms of 'Plumosa', including the golden and variegated types, belong here as also the 'Globosa' types. The other class is called the 'Pfitzeriana' group in which the foliage is coarser and often raspy, the main branches ascending slightly and grace-fully arching at the tips. The plants carry both juvenile and adult form foliage, but often semi-juvenile. The various foliage forms of 'Pfitzeriana' of course are included here and several others such as 'Hetzii' and 'Blue Cloud'.

J. sabina. The wild species, seldom cultivated, is a native of the high mountains of Europe and Asia. All the garden forms carry the characteristic disagreeable pungent odour of the foliage when crushed, and it is bitter to the taste. Both the juvenile or awl-shaped, and adult or scale-like, leaves are usually found on all forms. The desirable hybrids of this species, mostly crossed with *J. chinensis*, are often identified by this smell and taste of the foliage. Most of the various cultivars or botanical varieties are of low-spreading habit, some more erectly so than others, while one known as 'Fastigiata' is strictly erect and narrow, more so than the Irish Yew. Some twenty or more garden forms are recorded.

J. scopulorum. This is the Western Red Cedar or Rocky Mountain Juniper, which in nature grows to 15m (50ft). It is closely related to *J. virginiana* which it resembles, except that its branchlets are shorter and the foliage set more closely. Although some forty different forms have been recorded, about a dozen "here-to-stay" dwarf or semi-dwarf forms are being cultivated and distributed. They exist in prostrate, pyramidal and globose types.

J, squamata. This is a most variable species hailing from Central Asia, usually forming a low semi-prostrate shrub. It is very close to and difficult to distinguish from the related species of *J. procumbens* and *J. recurva*, one reliable feature being that the growing tips of *J. squamata* turn downward. The more widely-grown form, with dense foliage of bluish-grey and characteristic dominant protruding branches, is the one most widely cultivated. There are six recorded cultivars including some of neat pyramidal habit.

J. virginiana. This is the Western American species, having its counterpart in the eastern mountain states in the closely related *J. scopulorum*. In nature it grows erectly when young, developing a spreading top with age, reaching a height of 35m (115ft). Although such a large tree, producing valuable timber, it has furnished us with quite a number of fine foliage forms, both tall and low-growing, globose, fastigiate and prostrate, some with distinctly glaucous foliage, others changing to a purplish colour in the winter. Some sixty-five named forms have been recorded, and as with all garden forms, the number is being constantly added to as fresh worthwhile sports appear in different parts of the world. Many soon drop out of favour so that, as can be expected, only a dozen or so of the best and most distinct forms are generally cultivated.

PICEA

The name is said to be derived from *pix*, meaning *pitch* — no doubt a reference to the resinous character of these plants. Some thirty of these hardy evergreen trees are recorded. They are widely distributed over the higher mountainous areas or colder parts of the northern hemisphere. Identification is difficult in some species, as they closely resemble the *abies* (the conspicuous differences are discussed under this genus).

Most species are too large in habit and growth for any but large grounds or parks, but the genus provides us with a considerable number of attractive dwarf-growing forms, in all shapes and sizes, greens and glaucous-blues.

Picea abies (syn. *P. excelsa*). This is the Norway Spruce, which in nature grows into a large tree up to 60m (200ft). As there are no less than 150 recorded forms of this very variable species, no attempt can be made to cover the ground fully. Some of the forms are very similar in appearance, and almost impossible to identify accurately while in growth. However, from this confusing range that has been selected a number of popular forms, each quite distinct in habit and foliage. The cultivars may be briefly divided into five groups, that is prostrate or spreading, small bun-shaped or globose, squat forms, conical and upright, and pendulous or weeping. Someone could plan a rock garden alone with the widely diversified forms of *Picea abies*.

P. glauca. This is the White Spruce, a tree of moderate size, and one of the most important North American sources for wood pulp. It has given us a limited number of dwarf forms, few of which are in general cultivation. It is worthy of mention here that the well-known and deservedly popular *P. albertiana* 'Conica', one of the finest dwarf conifers, is considered to be but a geographical form of *P. glauca* and not a distinct species. A coloured illustration, with description, appears in this book, so no more need be added.

P. pungens. This handsome pyramidal tree of noble outline, commonly known as the Colorado Spruce, grows slowly into a specimen 35m (115ft) high or more. The richly glaucous foliaged form known as *P. pungens* 'Glauca' is much appreciated and grown as a lawn specimen in larger gardens. Seed collected from stands of mature trees where in nature this bluish form is dominant yield a high percentage true to type. However, the particular rich bluish-foliaged form 'Koster' and the softer blue of 'Moerheimi' are the types to be preferred, although more expensive to purchase, as plants are raised by grafting.

A number of bun-shaped and prostrate-growing forms are cultivated, some with glaucous-blue foliage in varying shades, others dark green.

PINUS—THE PINES

This is a most important family, embracing about 300 different species, varieties or cultivars This large order contains many trees of great economic importance, as the forest pines of the world furnish most of man's requirements in softwood timber and wood pulp besides various oils. The original species in most genera assume large proportions and are therefore, in the main, too large or robust-growing for the average garden of today. Employed as specimen trees in parks and large areas, or suitably set as a background or shelter belt to the larger home gardens, they are of course indispensable. Fortunately, in some of the various species low-growing sports or mutations have arisen over the period of commercial plantings or in nature, and these have proved much more suitable for the average garden ornamentation. Brief reference is made here to some of the more important genera that have yielded their quota of garden forms. Descriptions of the various cultivars illustrated are furnished on the respective pages elsewhere.

The flowers of *Pinus* are usually monoecious, and are produced independently of the cones, which are either massed together in spikes or heads, or encircle the stem. The ovules are concealed between the scales of the cone, these cone-scales being woody, leathery or parchment-like. Some of the cones are highly ornamental in their varied stages of development, as also when mature. Besides their great variety of shapes and sizes, some are coloured gold, brown or reddish, as well as many shades of green, while the great size of others, as in *Pinus coulteri*, is always impressive. Very few natural hybrids have occurred throughout this family, but nature in its various mutations has provided us with many desirable, more accommodating garden plants.

Pinus mugo. Commonly called the Mountain Pine, *mugo* being a local name, this variable alpine species is a native of the high mountains from the Pyrenees to the Balkans. The botanists divide this species into three geographical forms, namely, var. *pumilio*, var. *rostrata* and var. *rotundata*, and when raised from seed these types reproduce fairly true to form. The ordinary type will grow to 5m

(16ft), but seedlings raised from the alpine form *pumilio* produce low compact plants, seldom exceeding 1m (3ft) high and across. There are recorded some twenty or more selected named garden forms of this species, stocks being increased vegetatively from cuttings or grafts. A group of dense globose-growing plants with slender deep-green foliage is embraced in the name 'Compacta', and further selected desirable forms are known as 'Gnom', 'Hessie', 'Kobold' and 'Mops'.

P. sylvestris. This is the Scotch Fir or Pine, an important timber tree growing to 35m (115ft). It posseses ornamental and picturesque value in that the mature branches of the higher parts of the tree are orange and reddish colour, the bark peeling off in thin layers. Apart from being the most widely used pine in Britain, it is a tree which will thrive under the most diverse climatic conditions, resulting in several distinct local types. This species has also given rise to a considerable number of forms, most of which have been bud mutations of the type commonly known as 'witches broom''. Some fifty or more forms are recorded by Mr den Ouden in the *Manual of Cultivated Conifers*, of which barely a dozen are extensively cultivated. These include dwarf plants with silvery-grey foliage, golden-yellow, rich and soft green, while many forms are compact-growing, others erect or fastigiate; but there does not seem to be any that are really prostrate.

Brief mention should be made of other species that have yielded their more limited quota of lower-growing ornamental garden forms. *P. cembra*, known as the Stone Pine, is a rigid erect-growing species with orange-coloured down on its young shoots. Several dwarf forms are cultivated under the names 'Globe', 'Nana', and 'Pygmaea'.

P. densiflora is the Japanese Red Pine with reddish bark like the Scotch Pine, and growing in nature to 40m (130ft). The species itself is worthy of cultivation, and a few foliage and dwarf forms are recorded. *P. parviflora*, the Japanese White Pine, is an interesting species producing flattened heads of branches, its habit of growth lending itself to the culture of dwarfed Bonsai specimens. The young shoots are covered with greyish-white down. The plant is always well-furnished, retaining its bluish to grass-green leaves for up to four years. Several dwarf or pyramidal-growing forms have been recorded and are cultivated. *Pinus pumila*, the dwarf Siberian Pine, is worth growing as a species, being closely related to *P. cembra*. It has yielded some fine dwarf forms, both erect-growing and prostrate. *P. strobus*, the Weymouth Pine, grows into a tree 35m (115ft) or more, and although attractive with its long-leaved glaucous-green foliage, the dwarf forms are the only cultivars that the average garden would have room to accommodate. Several such forms are in cultivation under the names of 'Minima', 'Prostrata', 'Pumilo' and 'Nana'.

Some reference should be made to a few other highly ornamental species even though they are rather strong-growing for the average garden, and the fact that they have not so far provided us with miniature forms. Some are not fully hardy, and therefore referred to but briefly in books written for colder climates. For instance, *P. canariensis*, the Canary Island Pine, has distinctive long, grey-green needles and graceful spreading branches. In the same class is *P. patula*, likewise with long, slender drooping needles of bright green, this species being slightly hardier than the preceding one. Both species provide handsome and impressive lawn specimens. In the hardier species those much grown in gardens in some countries include *P. halepensis*, the Aleppo Pine, noted for its rich grey-green needles, being an excellent subject for coastal planting in dry areas. *P. thunbergii*, the Japanese Black Pine, is specially appreciated for bonsai work and for its informal pattern of irregular growth, blackish-grey bark, and sharp, dark green needles. We should not neglect the Big Cone Pine, *P. coulteri*, in which the giant woody-scaled cones, horn-clawed at the tips, are 15cm (6in) wide and 25 to 35cm (10 to 14in) long, and weigh 1.4 to 1.8 kg (3 to 4lb) each. When polished or varnished these cones are highly decorative.

PODOCARPUS

The name is derived from *pous* or *podos*, meaning a foot, and *carpus*, fruit, having reference to the fleshy foot-stalk of some specimens. This genus, now reclassified in its own family *Podocarpaceae*, embraces some sixty-five species many of which are subtropical and therefore not very hardy, but a number hail from temperate regions in both hemispheres. Several species and their forms have come rapidly into favour, particularly in California and the milder countries, while several of the long-neglected New Zealand species are again receiving the attention they deserve. Most are grown for their neat habit and narrow evergreen foliage, but the bright red yew-like fruits are also attractive.

There is a useful rock plant in the low-growing species *Podocarpus alpinus* with its long intertwined branches and dense, small yew-like foliage of deep blue-green, being the Tasmanian counterpart of the New Zealand alpine totara called *P. nivalis*. Both are hardy in the milder parts of Europe and North America, but so far have not become popular. The New Zealand species is rather variable according to localities, and an attractive deep bronzy-green foliaged form is also cultivated.

In the taller-growing species, perhaps the most popular is the variable, but usually erect-growing Chinese species, *P. macrophyllus*, which forms a neat yew-like tree with leathery deep-green foliage. A slower-growing more erect form is called 'Maki'. Both are very popular in California as garden ornamentals, and in colder climates make a fine tub specimen for use either indoor or outdoors. The New Zealand *P. totara* is one of the most important forest timber trees, the finely-grained reddish wood being very long-lasting, and because it does not twist or warp with exposure is much used for window sashes, rafters for glasshouses and the like, as well as for general building when available. The species itself is not cultivated much in New Zealand as it eventually grows to 30m (100ft) tall with wide, large densely-foliaged head and heavy trunk, but it is more used, being much slower-growing, in colder climates. It permits trimming and forms a very fine, light brownish-green hedge or shelter-belt, and in this respect can rival the

English yew. The slower-growing, golden-foliaged form called 'Aurea' is much cultivated in New Zealand, the densely set small and narrow leathery leaves changing to golden-brown in winter. A larger leafed more open-growing species, hardier than *P. totara* and at one time considered to be but a geographical form of this species, is called *P. hallii*, and is grown in parts of Britain and the USA.

P. andinus, known as the Plum-fruited Yew, hailing from the Andes in South Chile, is the hardiest species of the genus, and is much employed in replacing the more sombre-leafed common yew, the foliage being a rich blue-green. It much resembles the yew, and likewise grows to a bush-like tree 8 to 15m (25 to 50ft) tall. Like most of the species it will lend itself to constant clipping, so can be trained into desired shapes.

TAXUS—THE YEW

This is the old name for the common yew, used by Virgil and others, and much akin to the Greek *Taxos* of Dioscorides. Botanists divide this genus into about seven species, but the flower and fruiting characteristics by which most plants are identified are all the same, the foliage and other features alone deciding the differences. Some day we may be advised that all these species are but geographical forms of the common *T. baccata*. This species has given us a wide range of foliage forms and types which are deservedly popular in Europe and in the southern hemisphere. They, like the *Chamaecyparis lawsoniana* forms, are not particularly happy in California or other more arid parts of America, where the various forms of the more drought-resisting junipers, along with the cedars, pines and thujas, are more at home. The yews, although insisting on good drainage, prefer a moist climate with a higher atmospheric humidity than provided by the areas mentioned.

Although extending through Europe, Asia and the Himalayas northward, the yew tree has become deeply woven into the folklore of Britain. The ancient Britons no doubt held the tree sacred, and the Druids perpetuated the religious association by erecting their temples near them or on the same sites. It was also the most valued wood for the manufacture of bows, for so long the national weapon of defence. Some old trees, with a base trunk width of 6m (20ft) are known to be over 1,000 years old, while other famous yearly-clipped hedges known to be over 400 years old are so dense in the foliage that one wonders if even a mouse could crawl through.

The common species, which takes so kindly to a yearly trimming or pruning, has been much employed in the formation of the famous English formal gardens, as well as in topiary, in which the plants are trimmed to resemble birds, animals, pagodas, or almost anything that fires the imagination of the artist-gardener.

However, it is not intended to submit a descriptive list of the numerous ornamental cultivars of which there are at least fifty recorded by Dallimore and Jackson, with additional forms still appearing. Some are prostrate-growing, others tight bun-shaped forms, there being also golden and variegated foliage types. The very erect-growing deep-green Irish Yew, *Taxus baccata* 'Fastigiata', has also given us a much slower-growing golden-foliage form called 'Aurea', and also a golden-variegated one often confused with the preceding type and called 'Aureomarginata'.

The Japanese Yew, *T. cuspidata*, is an erect-growing species, more resembling the Irish Yew 'Fastigiata', but the foliage is larger, yellowish-tinged beneath, not so dense in habit, and the thicker stems are covered with a greyish-brown bark. It is generally considered to be less attractive, but as it thrives in the drier parts of America where the forms of *T. baccata* are not so happy, several of the numerous ornamental types are cultivated, and are popular in these and other drier countries.

Several interesting hybrids between the species *T. baccata* and *T. cuspidata* have appeared and been named in America, where they are proving most adaptable and popular. The hybrids, which are stronger-growing than most of the forms of *T. baccata*, are now classified under the group name of *T.* x *media*, in the same way that the various hybrids of *Juniperus chinensis* are now called *Juniperus* x *media*.

THUJA

This is a genus of about six species, native to North America, China and Japan. The genus is closely related to the *Chamaecyparis*, likewise preferring similar cool growing conditions. The name comes from *Thuia*, an old Greek name used by Theophrastus. They are dense-growing trees of pyramidal habit when young, and have slender, flattened branchlets.

The *Thujas* differ from their relatives, mainly in the shape of their cones, which are egg-shaped or rounded, with flat, oblong thin scales, whereas in the *Chamaecyparis* they are globular in shape. Practically all the lower-growing ornamental garden forms have developed from the three species now briefly described.

Thuja occidentalis. This species, native to the Northeast mountain area of America, is known as American Arbor-vitae or Northern White Cedar. It grows into a tree 20m (65ft) tall with a strongly buttressed trunk and thrives where atmospheric moisture is high. With its varieties it has, from earliest colonial days been a popular garden subject in the mountain areas of America.

There are about 140 various recorded named forms, and some of the most popular are illustrated in this book; but many are very similar in appearance, while the same plant may be found in different countries under different names. Furthermore, dwarf forms are constantly appearing among seedling-raised stock, and these closely resemble forms already named. Mr H. J. Welch in *Dwarf Conifer* divides the named dwarf-growing garden forms of this species into no less than eight different groups, such as globose, bun-shaped, conical, miniature and coloured foliage forms. He has also attempted to eliminate the various synonyms that occur.

T. orientalis. This is the Chinese Arbor-vitae, a bushy many-branched tree in nature up to 15m (50ft), two forms being recognised, that is those of pyramidal or columnar habit, and the other more globular. All forms are readily distinguished from the other species and the cypresses by the fact that the branches are held erectly, carrying the leaf sprays in a vertical plane, being more or less book-leaved in formation. This distinctive feature at one time influenced the botanists to separate this species into a different genus, namely *Biota*. Several golden-foliaged forms will be found described in some older nursery catalogues under this name.

As can be supposed, this variable species has given rise to quite a number of attractive garden forms, of which a dozen or more of the most popular are in general cultivation. Some are erect-growing, others conical in habit, while the various golden-foliaged forms are among some of our most popular garden conifers.

T. plicata. The Western Arbor-vitae or Western Red Cedar grows to a large widely buttressed tree up to 60m (200ft). It needs a moisture retentive soil. It is the only other species which has provided us with a much more limited number of garden forms. The named cultivars grown are usually golden or bronzy-gold tipped in the foliage, bun-shaped or semi-erect in habit.

WHERE TO PLANT

This is a big question, and really the only answer is (as with many other gardening questions) that it is largely a matter of taste or opinion. Nevertheless, there are a few simple rules that must be followed by all.

Firstly, all conifers prefer an open position in full sun, even though many in their juvenile stages must of necessity in nature tolerate the shade of taller mature trees. But eventually all such plants must either break through to full sunlight or expire. Some plants such as the New Zealand native rimu, *Dacrydium cupressinum*, and the Norfolk Island Pine, *Araucaria heterophylla*, provide us with lovely indoor pot plants, in a rich deep-green, much more attractive than when grown in full sun. But these and others outgrow their juvenile beauty and usefulness, and must eventually find a place in the garden.

The modern trend is for more and more houses to be packed into less and less land. As a result gardens get smaller. This has given impetus to the culture of the smaller garden conifers. It would be a very small holding indeed that could not provide a place for a few of these delightful miniatures, with perhaps their surroundings covered with harmonising metal chips or other forms of scree. Even window boxes, sunken container gardens and cavity-block walls can sustain a few such plants.

But it will be freely admitted that the rockery, whether large or small, offers the greatest scope for the display of this wide range of diversified foliage plants. Many attractive British books, gloriously presented with supporting illustrations, certainly succeed in firing one's imagination. It must be admitted that the British landscape architect, long skilled in the handling of stones and placing them to represent nature as near as possible, is a master at this work. Perhaps that is true also of experts in other parts of Europe and also the United States, but my judgment in this is limited, as I have been but privileged to visit British gardens in the main. I well remember a visit from an English landscape expert who summed up his inspection of the Harrison nurseries in all departments. He said: "I will give you top marks for your nursery and the up-to-date propagating department, but your so-called rockery is but a heap of stones." That may be more or less true of many of attempts to layout rockeries, but we are all able to learn. Obviously it is not for me to try to tell you how to plan a rockery, unless I quote from text-books, a procedure which I have always tried to avoid.

It is assumed that your prepared rockery is arranged with hills or outcrops and valleys below, resembling as it should an alpine scene in miniature. It is therefore important that the type of plant set in each position should be related to the envisaged "hard" conditions expected for survival. It would not be suitable to plant a neat symmetrical conifer on the top of a "peak" which would normally be "windswept". What would be more suitable would be a dwarf pine, the trunk planted on an angle as under stress, with trunk and top of the roots eventually exposed and gnarled. Some careful pruning and training with wires until the right natural shape is secured may be advisable. In the sheltered valleys you would expect to find some erect-growing forest trees, so these should be planted in groups of threes or fives, as odd numbers are better than even. For this purpose the miniature *Juniper communis* 'Compressa' or 'Suecica Nana' are excellent. Prostrate-growing forms are seen at their best cascading between large rocks or at the foot of the bluff. The pleasing effect of an attempted miniature alpine garden is lost if plants are set out in a cosy fashion or just scattered about. Conifers planted in a rockery should yield the impression of existing happily under "hard" conditions. Rounded or bun-shaped plants should therefore be sparingly used, unless they are real miniatures. Furthermore, the site should be well away from any large trees, otherwise these miniatures will appear ridiculous. Nevertheless, a distant background of tall trees provides a delightful setting.

Foundation plants, as they are called, are much employed in the United States and elsewhere, and these include conifers. They are planted close to the brick or concrete foundations of the dwelling in order to break up the hard symmetrical outline. Other evergreen plants may be and are also employed, including hebes, which offer a most interesting range of species. Dwarf conifers however, are particularly suitable, being hardy, evergreen, as well as providing a great range of shapes, colours and types of foliage. The bun-shaped types are often employed, with fastigiate or erect pencil-like types between windows or on the corners. The doorways may also be emphasised or framed with erect-growing conifers such as *Cupressus sempervirens* either green or gold, and *Taxus baccata* 'Fastigiata', likewise in the various green or golden-foliaged forms. Green forms should be used against reddish stone or brick, and the gold against grey or dull buildings.

Likewise in the United States, as also in Europe, a number of prostrate-growing conifers are employed as ground covers, particularly for sloping banks or massed in large beds. Some of the ground-hugging junipers are much used thus, particularly as they tolerate dry conditions. When the surface of the ground is entirely covered, such plants form a solid mass of fine twigs and foliage 15cm (6in) or thicker, thus preventing weed or foreign growths. Such prostrate conifers are likewise very suitably and effectively placed to cascade between large rocks, while some forms will naturally grow downwards. There is now a wide range of most attractive prostrate-growing conifers with foliage in various shades of green, bluish, gold, brown and variegated. Many of these dwarf conifers change their foliage colour several times in a year, beginning with the soft spring growths, and eventually changing to reddish brown or purple with the winter cold.

For growing in large containers such as patio plants, many of the conifers are very suitable, long-lived and colourful. Usually the only cause of failure is the human element in neglecting regular waterings. Unlike many other evergreen or deciduous shrubs, conifers usually display their distress signals too late for recovery, and permanent damage has already been done when wilting or browning of the foliage appears. Recovery is sometimes possible if plants are immediately removed to a shady position and the foliage sprayed with a hose several times a day. It is well to state again that the junipers will withstand more dryness than any other conifers, while at the other end of the scale, the numerous forms of *Chamaecyparis lawsoniana* resent conditions of drought more than most others.

CONTAINER GROWING

Conifers lend themselves to tub culture as patio plants, and provided they are fed a little each year, plants may be retained in good health and appearance for many years, even though apparently so-called root-bound. I have observed strong-growing conifers such as the golden-foliaged forms of *Cupressus macrocarpa* which usually grow to 10m (33ft) or more, thus dwarfed in containers and only 1m (3ft) high. A further advantage of growing specimens in larger containers is that they may be used at will for any form of seasonal ornamentation such as shows, garden displays, weddings or even stage decorations. Although conifers thus grown are very long suffering, and generally tolerate a certain amount of dry conditions, yet when fatigue in some way displays itself through prolonged neglect, such plants — in contrast to some other evergreens — have reached the point of no return, and can rarely be recovered.

Gardeners who treasure their dwarfs and wish to keep their specimens small should seriously consider the advantages of growing their conifers in containers. Apart from the fact that the restriction of root action slows down growth, there is the added advantage that any such plants can without risk and at any time of the year be shifted about from one position to another as desired. Different kinds of metal chips, pebbles, shells or mountain scoria are now much employed as a surface covering to the soil, so that a fresh layer around the transplants will immediately restore the "at home" effect and hide the tell-tale rim of the container.

PRUNING

Happily, conifers take kindly to pruning. With some exceptions the harder one prunes a conifer the cleaner and more decorative the foliage will be. But the observance of several points can make all the difference between an attractive plant and an eyesore. Firstly, prune *regularly*, at least once a year. The time of year is not important but winter or early spring before growth begins is probably when most gardeners will want to do it, and then pruning can be used as an influence to change the growth habit of the plant, if so desired. Some conifers, in particular the *Chamaecyparis lawsoniana* cultivars, will not "break" from old wood. On such species the pruning should not go further in than the current season's growth, otherwise a gap is likely to be left at that place in the plant which may take some years to be covered in from surrounding growth. It is also advisable to cover *Cupressus* and *Chamaecyparis* with a copper fungicide spray after pruning, to prevent the entry of cypress canker, as this fungus disease often gains entry after pruning and can quickly ruin the appearance of the plant.

Pruning at frequent intervals is advisable for a further reason. If only done say every three years to keep a plant to a restricted size, one has to make drastic cuts into rather heavy wood, leaving an unsightly stump along with a gaping hole and probably with dead inner foliage exposed until fresh growth covers it over. If it ever does. An annual or bi-annual pruning overcomes this problem, and if skilfully done the plant should not show cuts at all.

It should be understood that pruning and shearing are not the same thing. For the pruning of conifers the hedging shears or electric clippers are out, unless one desires a hedge like that shown on Plate 549. All pruning should be carried out with sharp secateurs, which is all one will need unless the job has been long neglected and requires the use of a saw. The foliage should be studied and a decision made on how you wish to influence the shape of your plant. In most cases the extent of your pruning will be mainly to correct lopsided or irregular tendencies or to keep the size to what you consider as big enough for your garden.

I do not wish to give the impression that I am advocating perfect symmetry for all conifers. Some of our most charming specimens are delightfully irregular in growth habit and pruning of such should be done with this in mind. On the other hand, with regular pruning it is possible to keep a specimen that normally grows to 3m (10ft) each way back to a 1m (3ft) maximum for many years and it will still look normal in habit. Many an excellent conifer is rejected on the basis that it eventually grows too large, when in fact it would be an admirable subject provided it is pruned annually — an operation that I personally find both interesting and rewarding.

A last word on pruning, and one that can make or break the final effect — always make the cut where it will not be seen. This is not as difficult as it may sound, if you bear in mind that all cuts made below eye-level should be slanted toward the ground, while those made above eye-level should face the sky. Always cut a branch so that there is already a suitable piece of strong-growing branchlet (which will probably become the new leading shoot) projecting past the proposed site of the cut, and this in itself will help to hide the cut and prevent that "lopped-off" appearance.

Follow these few simple rules and you will find that the pruning of conifers is both interesting and rewarding and, (in the case of many species) highly desirable to maintain the plant in an attractive and healthy-looking growing condition.

DISEASES

Much of the popularity of conifers lies in their year-round consistency of appeal and comparative freedom from disease. The spring and summer months are often times of infestation, however, when various insect pests find the fresh growth to their liking and can very quickly make a bush look dull and off-colour. Obviously any such plants should be treated as soon as possible. Aphids can be a problem, particularly on some junipers, but are relatively easily dealt with, using one of the modern systemic insecticides which act on the sap-stream of the plant and poison the pest at its point of attack. In all cases a follow-up spray is advisable some ten days later to catch any new pests that may have emerged from eggs already laid. A number of scale insects attack a wide range of conifers and Taxus in particular, and these can be dealt with in the same way. These pests often result in a sooty deposit on the foliage, making it look darker than usual, and the effect takes many months to disappear, even though the cause may have been removed by spraying.

Leaf-roller catepillars cause damage by chewing the foliage, then gathering it into clumps to form a protective cover in which to pupate, and once they have reached this stage they are almost impossible to poison as they are no longer at the feeding stage.

As with all pests, prevention is always better than cure. Mites are particularly fond of *Picea* species in warmer climates and can easily ruin the appearance of a tree in one season, and even if eliminated promptly their damage will remain for up to two seasons thereafter. Although they are microscopic, spider-like creatures hardly visible to the naked eye, their effect can easily be detected in a plant, with symptoms such as needle drop, dull foliage, along with a dusting of a whitish substance on the infected parts. Once again regular spraying is the answer, this time with a miticide, of which there are several on the market with new products becoming available from time to time.

My recommendation is to prevent rather than cure, and to include the conifers along with other garden spraying three or four times in the growth season, and healthy and unimpeded growth should be the result. I have found Thiodan particularly effective in such spraying, being both a miticide and a systemic insecticide, and thus covering the field in one spray. I do not recommend the use of oil sprays as they submerge the foliage bloom, making some conifers look unusually dark and unattractive; but apart from this effect they do no harm and are a reasonable method of eliminating scale diseases.

Canker is one of the few fungus diseases that attack conifers, but it is one that is causing some susceptible cultivars to be discontinued in the nursery trade. It seems to attack only some *Chamaecyparis* and *Cupressus* species, and entry of the disease is aided by an untreated open cut or wound. It usually appears as a discoloured portion on a bush or tree that soon browns right off and dies, and if traced back to its origin on the main stem one will usually find an open, often bleeding, wound. Removal of this diseased wood at its source, and treatment of the cut and the whole plant with a copper spray solution, is sometimes an effective cure, but in many cases the plant dies piece by piece over a period of some years. Occasionally, devastating outbreaks sweep through the Rocky Mountains pine forests. This disease is primarily a warm climate one and is not much of a problem in Zones 7 or colder, and in some countries it is unheard-of. In the eastern parts of America cedar borer is a constant problem.

KEY TO PRONUNCIATION

(With acknowledgment to *The Friendly Evergreens*, by L. L. Kumlien, 1946)
ALMOST all of the following names will be found in a standard dictionary, but for convenience we have listed the names of the important genera of Evergreens, and also some of the common names and other terms. The authority quoted is *Webster's New International Dictionary*.

KEY TO PRONUNCIATION

ā as in ale	ĭ as in ill
ā as in senate	
â as in care	ō as in old
ă as in am	ŏ as in obey
ă as in account	ô as in orb
ä as in arm	o͞o as in too
a̍ as in ask	ŏ as in odd
a as in sofa	ô as in soft
	ŏ as in connect
ē as in eve	
ê as in event	ū as in use
ĕ as in end	û as in unite
ĕ as in recent	û as in urn
ē as in maker	ŭ as in up
	ŭ as in circus
ī as in ice	ü as in menu

EVERGREEN TERMS

Abies (ā′bĭ-ēz)	Libocedrus (lī′bo̍-sē′drŭs)
Araucaria (ăr′ô-kā′rĭ-a̍)	Picea (pĭs′ē-a̍)
Arborvitae (är′bȯr-vī′tē)	Pinus (pī′nŭs)
Cedrus (sē′drŭs)	Podocarpus (pŏd′ô-kär′pŭs)
Cephalotaxus (sĕf′a̍-lô-tăk′sŭs)	Pseudotsuga (sū′dô-tsū′ga̍)
Chamaecyparis (kăm′ê-sĭp′a̍-rĭs)	Retinospora (rĕt′ĭ-nĭs′pô-ra̍)]
conifer (kō′nĭ-fēr)	Sciadopitys (sī′a̍-dŏp′ĭ-tĭs)
Cryptomeria (krĭp′tô-mē′rĭ-a̍)	Sequoia (sê-kwoi′a̍)
Cunninghamia (kŭn′ĭngham′ĭ-a̍)	species (spē′shēz)
Cupressus (kṷ-prĕs′ŭs)	Spruce (spro͞os)
Cypress (sī′prĕs)	Taxodium (tăk-sō′dĭ-ŭm)
Fir (fûr)	Taxus (tăk′sŭs)
genus (jē′nŭs) (Singular)	Thuja (thū′ya̍)
genera (jĕn′ê-ra̍) (Plural)	Thujopsis (thṷ-yŏp′sĭs)
Juniper (jo͞o′nĭ-pēr)	Torreya (tŏr′ĭ-a̍)
Juniperus (jo͞o-nĭp′ēr-ŭs)	Tsuga (tsū′ga̍)
Larix (lār′ĭks)	Yew (yo͞o)

GLOSSARY
OF BOTANICAL TERMS COMMONLY USED WITH CONIFERS

ACICULAR — Needle-shaped, slender and sharp-pointed.

ACUMINATE — Having a long, tapering point.

ACUTE — Sharp-pointed.

ADNATE — Growing close to the stem.

ADPRESSED, APPRESSED — Pressed into close contact without adhering.

ALBA, ALBUS — Latin, "white"

ALTERNATE — A term applied to leaves or branches which do not grow out opposite one another.

AMORPHOUS — Having no definite form.

APEX — Top terminating point of a leaf or tree.

ARGENTEA — of silvery appearance.

ARIL — A glutinous covering that envelopes certain seeds, like the yew berry.

ASCENDING — Directed or rising upwards.

ATROVIRIDIS — Deep, dark-green colour.

AUREA, AUREUS — Latin for "golden".

AWL — Pointed instrument for boring holes. Applied botanically to leaves similarly shaped.

AXIS — The main stem around which branchlets and leaflets grow.

BACCA (noun). A berry, a succulent seed vessel, filled with pulp, in which the seed is encased.

BACCATUS — Having a pulpy texture.

BASAL — Growing at the base of anything.

BASAL SHEATH — The covering that encircles the base of pine leaves. Also referred to as fascicle or bundle.

BIFID — Split sharply into two points.

BINAE — Used to describe pine trees whose leaves grow in twos in the same basal sheath.

BIPINNATE — When both the primary and secondary divisions of a branchlet or leaflet grow out like a feather.

BLISTERS — Or resin pockets, formed just beneath the smooth surface of the trunk before it becomes furrowed. Often 2.5cm (1in) or more long, and numerous.

BUD — Young folded-up branch or flower.

BUD SCALES — The covering of winter buds.

CAESIA, CAESIUS — Latin, "lavender-coloured," or blue-grey.

CAMBIUM — The layer of cells between bark and wood where new wood is formed.

CLADODE — A flattened leaf-like stem that is capable of photosynthesis.

CLONE — The entire vegetatively-produced descendants from a single original seedling.

COLUMNAR — Shaped like a column.

CONE — The fruit of conifers, made up of overlapping scales. *Synonym*; Strobile.

CONICAL — Shaped like a cone, that is, with vertical section triangular and pointed, and horizontal section and base circular, or of a form gradually tapering down at one end.

COTYLEDON — The temporary "first leaf" of an emerging seedling.

DECIDUOUS — Applied to a tree that sheds its leaves annually.

DECUMBENT — Lying down.

DEHISCENT — Applied to a cone that opens and discharges its seed at maturity.

DENTATE — See MARGIN.

DIOECIOUS — Plants that have the male flower on one plant and the female on another.

DISC — Applied to the round scar left after pulling leaves off the fir.

DIVARICATE — Applied to branches that diverge.

DORSAL — the back.

DOWNY — Covered with soft hairs.

ENTIRE — See MARGIN.

EROSE — See MARGIN.

EXOGENOUS — Applied to trees growing by successive additions to the outside.

FACIAL — See LATERAL.

FASCICLE — Proceeding from a common point like the leaves of a larch.

FASTIGIATE — Of close, erect growth, and branches pointing upwards.

FURROWED — Description of a surface channelled or fissured longitudinally.

GLABROUS — Without hairs. The opposite of pubescent or downy.

GLAUCOUS (bloom) — The blue-white waxy bloom that covers the leaves and fruit of some conifers.

GLAUCOUS (colour) — Used to describe blue, blue-grey or grey-green tints.

GLOBOSE — Nearly spherical in form.

GRACILIS — Latin, "slender".

GYMNOSPERM — meaning "naked seeded". A class of plants in which the seeds are not enclosed in an ovary.

HABITAT — The natural dwelling-place of any plant.

IMBRICATED — Applied to leaves overlapping like tiles on a roof.

LACINIATE — Applied to leaves cut into narrow lobes.

LANCEOLATE — Having the form of a lance, tapering at both ends.

LATERAL — Applied to leaves that grow on the side of the branchlets. Those that grow on the upper and lower sides are called respectively dorsal and facial.

LEAF BUD — A bud producing a stem with leaves only.

LINEAR — Narrow, with the two sides nearly parallel, like the leaf of a yew.

LITORALIS — Growing on the seashore.

LUTEA, LUTEUS — Latin, "a good yellow colour".

LUTESCENS — Yellowish.

MACRO — Long or large.

MACROPHYLLA — Large-leaved.

MARGIN — Edge or border. The edge of a leaf is called its margin. Types are: *Entire* (even and smooth); *Serrate* (sharp teeth like a saw pointing forwards); *Dentate* (sharp teeth pointing outwards); *Erose* (irregularly toothed).

MICROPHYLLA — small-leaved.

MONOECIOUS — With both male and female flowers on the same plant.

MUCRONATE — Abruptly tipped with a hard, short, point.

NANA — Latin, meaning "dwarf".

NEEDLE-SHAPED — Linear, rigid, tapering to a fine point from a narrow base, as Juniper leaves. *Synonym:* Acicular.

NIGRICANS — Blackish.

NODE — Joint of a branch, or the point of a stem where the bud or leaf is given off.

OBLIQUE — Unequal-sided. Deviating irregularly from a direct line.

OBTUSE — Blunt or rounded at the point.

OPPOSITE — Applied to leaves and branches placed in pairs on opposite side of stems.

OVATE — Egg-shaped, broader at base.

PECTINATE — Leaves arranged like the teeth of a comb.

PERSISTENT — Applied to the length of time leaves and cones of evergreens remain on the tree.

PHOTOSYNTHESIS — The name of the process whereby plants use the energy of light as an aid to making growth.

PHYLLOCLADE — Cladode.

PINNATE — Shaped like a feather. Applied to leaves arranged regularly on each side of a common stem.

PLICATE — Folded like a fan.

POLITUS — Of shiny and polished appearance.

PSEUDO — Prefix signfying false and not true to type.

PUBESCENT — Hairy.

PUMILA — Latin, "low, small".

PUNGENS — Implying a strong, disagreeable smell.

QUINATE — Applied to pines whose needle-like leaves grow in bundles of five.

RADIAL (leaf arrangement)-Radiating outwards from the stem.

REPAND, REPANDA — Having a slightly wavy edge.

REPENS — Applied to creeping plants.

SCALES — Applied botanically to the encrusted covering of leaf buds and cones.

SCAR — Applied to the mark on the stem left when a leaf has been pulled off, as in the case of the firs.

SCATTERED — Applied in contradistinction to such terms as whorled, opposite.

SERRATE — See MARGIN.

SESSILE — Growing close to, and indirectly upon, the stem without a stalk.

STOMA, STOMATA — Minute breathing-pores. On conifers, often in lines on the leaf and whitish or pale blue.

STRICTA — Very upright or straight.

STROBILE (*Plural:* STROBILII) — Cone.

SYLVESTRIS — That which grows in a forest.

TABULIFORM — Flat-topped or table-like.

TERNATE — Growing in threes or whorls of three. Applied to the pines that have three leaves in a bundle.

TOPIARY — Training of shrubs and trees into ornamental shapes.

TORULOSE — Cylindrical, with slight contractions.

TRIQUETRAL — Three-sided or three-angled.

UNDULATE — Waved on the surface.

VIRIDIS — Green.

WHORLS — Where there are more than two growths of branchlets, flowers or leaves, borne in a circle from the same node.

BOOKS ON CONIFERS

For those who wish to delve further into the subject of conifers, the books listed below are the most recent works on the subject and will prove of interest:

MANUAL OF CULTIVATED CONIFERS by den Ouden and Boom (1965). MARTINUS NIJHOFF, THE HAGUE.

DWARF CONIFERS by H. J. Welch (1968). FABER & FABER, LONDON.

A HANDBOOK OF CONIFERAE AND GINGKOACEAE by Dallimore and Jackson, fourth edition revised by S. G. Harrison (1966). ARNOLD, LONDON

HILLIER'S MANUAL OF TREES AND SHRUBS by H. G. Hillier (1968). HILLIER and SONS, WINCHESTER.

HILLIER'S MANUAL OF TREES AND SHRUBS by H. G. Hillier (Rev. Ed. 1975) DAVID & CHARLES LTD. NEWTON ABBOTT, DEVON.

HANDBOOK ON CONIFERS by the Brooklyn Botanic Garden, NEW YORK.
  Earlier works, some no longer in publication, that will be of interest are as follows:
THE FRIENDLY EVERGREENS by L. L. Kumlien (1946). HILL, DUNDEE, ILLINOIS, USA.

THE CULTIVATED CONIFERS IN NORTH AMERICA by L. H. Bailey (1933).

HANDBUCH DER NADELHOLZKUNDE by Beissner (1909).

DWARF AND SLOW-GROWING CONIFERS by M. Hornibrook (1938).

DIE NADELGEHÖLZE by G. Krussman (1960).

THE GENUS PINUS by G. R. Shaw (1914).

INDEX

Bold figures give the page number on which a colour plate will be found.